Dickens and Imagination

Dickens and Imagination

Robert Higbie

University Press of Florida
Gainesville / Tallahassee / Tampa / Boca Raton
Pensacola / Orlando / Miami / Jacksonville

Copyright 1998 by the Board of Regents of the State of Florida
Printed in the United States of America on acid-free paper
All rights reserved

03 02 01 00 99 98   6 5 4 3 2 1

Library of Congress Cataloging-in-Publication Data

Higbie, Robert.
Dickens and imagination / Robert Higbie.
p. cm.
Includes bibliographical references and index.
ISBN 0-8130-1593-6 (cloth: alk. paper)
1. Dickens, Charles (1812–1870)—Criticism and interpretation.
2. Belief and doubt in literature. 3. Romanticism—Great Britain.
4. Imagination. I. Title.
PR4588.H48 1998
823'.8—dc21   98-10525

An earlier version of a portion of chapter 7 was previously pub-
lished as "*Hard Times* and Dickens' Concept of the Imagination,"
Dickens Studies Annual 17 (1989): 91–110 (copyright 1990). It is
reprinted in this volume courtesy of AMS Press, Inc.

The University Press of Florida is the scholarly publishing
agency for the State University System of Florida, comprising
Florida A & M University, Florida Atlantic University, Florida
International University, Florida State University, University of
Central Florida, University of Florida, University of North Flor-
ida, University of South Florida, and University of West Florida.

University Press of Florida
15 Northwest 15th Street
Gainesville, FL 32611
http://nersp.nerdc.ufl.edu/~upf

Contents

Introduction

This study is an attempt to understand the use of imagination in Dickens's fiction by seeing Dickens in terms of his relationship to Victorian idealism and to the concept of imagination that idealist writers adopted and adapted from the Romantics. A study of this kind can not only help us comprehend more about Dickens but can also throw considerable light on some of the main tendencies in nineteenth-century thought and even on the nature of imagination in general.

I hope the following chapters will make clear the ideas on which my discussion is based, but perhaps I should briefly mention them here. My research began with the observation that many nineteenth-century writers frequently referred to imagination in similar ways. I gradually realized that certain strands of thought related to imagination ran through nineteenth-century culture and that an understanding of these concepts would cast light on the literature of the period. In order to comprehend those concepts, I needed to develop an idea of what imagination was and how it worked in literature, an idea that fitted what nineteenth-century writers said. For the sake of clarity, I want to begin by explaining that idea, even though it is the result, not the starting point, of my research. To put it in the most general and widely applicable terms, I have found it useful to see works of literature as attempts to imagine some desired object but also as efforts to deal with the difficulties created by such attempts—for example, by trying to find ways of compensating for literature's inability to make the imaginary seem completely real or to accommodate impulses in the imagination that work against desire.

This way of thinking about literature has two advantages. Because it focuses on the way desire acts (through imagination) upon the work's content, it can get at much that is most basic in the work, since desire is so basic. Thus it can apply to a wide range of works—particularly to works in the nineteenth century, where imagination is particularly important. In addition, this approach enables one to discuss not only the ideas of each work as a whole but also much of its specific detail.

I do not understand what it means to say a work has a "theme" or "meaning," but I think it makes sense to ask what a work seems to be trying to make us desire and believe in. Virtually all the literature I know offers some object or state that it presents as desirable, if only by implication through the presentation of the absence or opposite of what is desired. And most works try to make us believe something about the goal they present—that it is attainable under certain conditions, for example, or that it is wrong to desire it and one should accept its absence. Insofar as a work of literature states some "idea," I think it is most useful to see that idea as the belief or attitude the work implies we should take about the desire that the work evokes. The work induces a process in us, a way of dealing with the desires and resultant tensions it causes.

If we see a work's "thematic" concerns in these terms, we can relate them to the particular details of which the work is composed, since it is through those details that the work arouses our desire, making us believe an object is desirable, and gives expression to those impulses that seek to deal with that desire. This approach is useful for a study of imagination since (as I argue in chapter 1) we can see imagination as the agent through which desire is translated into an object (or rather the image of an object). And as Dickens's example shows, imagination also has an especially important relationship to the "thematic" concerns of a writer working in the tradition of nineteenth-century Romantic idealism.

Many critics have mentioned imagination in Victorian literature, but I know of none who has offered a definition of imagination and related imagination to basic ideas in Victorian culture and to the particular details of literary works. Imagination is usually mentioned in passing, its meaning taken for granted and its relation to the critics' real concerns left vague. I have of course indicated in my notes where critics have discussed ideas related to mine, but because I am doing something rather different, I have not gone into detail about their arguments. The critics whose work is closest to mine are those who have worked toward finding an alternative set of terms to those based on realism. Of these, the one who has most influenced me (and, I think, most critics) is Northrop Frye, in *An Anatomy of Criticism*. More recently, there has been a tendency—which my work here shares—to look at Victorian literature not as a movement toward realism but as a continuation of Romanticism, influenced by spiritual concerns inherited from Romanticism. Among critics who discuss the Romantic currents in Victorian thought are

Harold Bloom and Donald D. Stone; among those who are concerned with nonrealist tendencies are Chris Baldick, C. N. Manlove, and Tobin Siebers; and critics who have examined Victorian spiritual concerns include Hilary Fraser and Barry Qualls. J. Hillis Miller's *The Disappearance of God*, with its distinction between ideas of God as immanent and transcendent, seems to me especially illuminating.

Among Dickens critics who have been sympathetic toward his antirealist and idealist concerns, those I find myself most in agreement with are Edwin M. Eigner, Fred Kaplan, and Harry Stone. I should mention one other work on Dickens, Garrett Stewart's *Dickens and the Trials of Imagination*. I trust the reader will find that, despite initial appearances, my work here has a different focus from Stewart's; he is primarily concerned with the imagination of Dickens's characters and not, as I am, with the way Dickens relates imagination to the search for spiritual belief.

In these times when ideology seems to have taken refuge in the academy, it may unfortunately be necessary to explain to the reader why this book tries to remain free of the current ideological orthodoxy. It is often objected that every attitude is an ideology, that it is impossible not to be ideological. But there are open and closed ideologies; an approach that seeks to sympathize with the writer's viewpoint is not commensurate with one that seeks to impose an alien set of standards.

A critical approach that assumes the critic's main job is to get at the ideological assumptions underlying a work of literature, though it can be quite illuminating, has certain shortcomings of which we should be aware. For one thing, because ideological criticism has been taken up by academics seeking some substitute for the political expression denied them during a period of conservative ascendancy, it has tended to take on the dogmatism and intolerance of political ideologies, which exist largely in an adversarial relationship with other ideologies. Critics have sometimes assumed a prosecutorial stance toward the work of literature, trying to show up its assumptions as if they were political opponents. If we are trying to expose and even condemn writers, we are implying that we are superior to them, that our assumptions are the correct ones. I think there is no greater intellectual danger than being certain one has possession of the truth. Error is usually a matter not of being wholly wrong but rather of catching hold of one small piece of the truth and thinking it is the whole thing. Truth about something like the human mind and its creations is much too complex for us to be certain about it. Nor does this mean that we cannot understand anything about literature; those who assert that everything is uncertain are asserting a certainty of their own, and are using that assertion as a pretext to forgo the difficult, never perfect task of

working gradually toward an increasingly complete understanding of literature. The value of any approach to literature lies in how fully it helps us
understand the whole work; the more exclusive and intolerant an approach
is, the more it leaves out and the more it fails to achieve the sympathy necessary for understanding.

Another danger of ideological criticism with a social tendency lies in its
bias in favor of realism. As Northrop Frye and many others have pointed out,
we can understand certain kinds of literature only by accepting them on their
own nonrealistic terms. But the more political a critical ideology becomes,
the more it tends to judge literature not as literature but as a statement about
reality. If we are concerned to show that writers are compromised by their
acceptance of a social power structure that oppresses victims, we are assuming that the standards of judgment that really matter are those concerned not
with the quality of a work of art but with our idea of what society should be
like. Yet surely both matter; judgment should be multifaceted.

One reason it is dangerous to give precedence to realist criteria is that
we may be mistaken about reality. For instance, I am ill at ease with the
idea of society implied by condemning it as an oppressive power structure.
This not only seems a gross oversimplification but also seems based on some
naive assumptions—that all control is bad, that it is desirable (and for that
matter possible) to do without forms of control. Surely the truth is more
complicated; surely social control can sublimate as well as repress, can enable
people to channel energy into less selfish outlets and provide forms that enable self-expression to become more ordered and graceful—forms in which
our modern indulgence in self-liberation has left us sadly deficient. This is
not of course to say that social control is never oppressive, but an intelligent
judgment would have to face the probability that some of that very oppres-
sion may be the price one must pay for art—that sublimation cannot exist
without repression and that self-expression and control interact in ways more
complex than a Romantic idealization of self-expression takes into account.

Furthermore, if we concentrate on writers' unspoken assumptions, we are
in danger of undervaluing other aspects of their work. For instance, criticism
can become so concerned with unmasking writers' unconscious attitudes that
it pays little attention to what they actually say they believe. Much Victorian
literature (including most of Dickens) arises out of the process of seeking
belief, and if we ignore what it says about belief, we cannot understand that
process. In addition, if we discuss only a writer's ideology, we may be left with
an analysis that fails to explain why a work gives pleasure—that fails to deal
with the fine details of language that give a work its distinctive quality. Ideological criticism seems to mistrust the whole notion of quality; if all that

matters is whether a work's assumptions are correct, aesthetic appreciation is irrelevant. The attack on the canon tends to become an attack on the idea of quality, and writers tend to be valued because of what they reveal about their society rather than because of their skill as craftsmen. No doubt any one critic's idea of quality is somewhat biased, but it seems to me that our job as critics is not to use our disagreements as a pretext for jettisoning the whole notion of quality, but rather to use them as a basis for trying to discuss what factors influence quality and how to arrive at a more nearly just estimate of a work. A criticism that fails to contribute to an understanding of what makes a work worth reading hardly seems to have a reason to exist; it may be sociology or philosophy, but I doubt that it is literary criticism.

I do not offer these strictures because I wish to reject all ideological criticism but rather to clear a space for what I am doing here—to tell readers how my approach differs from what they may expect. I too am considering a writer's underlying assumptions, but I am trying to do so in a way that respects his expressed intentions and the complex of details that give his work its quality. If I point out conflicts and contradictions in a work, it is not because I wish to condemn inconsistencies but because I hope to understand how those conflicts contribute to the complexity of the work.

As I have mentioned, I think a study based on the concept of imagination is consonant with these goals, since imagination is related to both the microcosmic and the macrocosmic view of literature. On the one hand, the particular details of a work are the products of the imaginative process. On the other hand, Dickens (like many nineteenth-century writers) frequently makes his concept of imagination central to the beliefs his works are concerned with. In addition, a concern with imagination makes it easier to deal with the nonrealistic aspects of literature.

The nineteenth century is a period for which the study of imagination is especially useful. No doubt imagination has always been of great importance to writers, but the Romantics give it a higher rank than their predecessors, treating it more self-consciously and giving their ideas about it explicit expression not just in philosophical works but in lyrics and narratives. Critics have of course written a great deal about the Romantic idea of imagination, but they have paid little attention to the way that idea was modified later in the century. Yet the history of imagination does not end with the Romantics; in fact, it is only with their successors that the problems inherent in the Romantic concept of imagination become fully apparent. Imagination continued to be of central importance for many writers; indeed it was the later part of the century that saw the flowering of new forms of literature based more directly and explicitly than ever before on imagination—fantasies such as ghost stories and children's fiction. But the Victorians did not simply repeat what the Romantics had done, though they often tried to. As the century progressed, writers became increasingly aware of the difficulties created by the Romantic attitude toward imagination. Thus as we look at their work, we can learn more about the tensions implicit in imagination and the ways a writer can try to deal with those tensions—tensions that, though they become especially apparent in the nineteenth century, are, I think, inherent in imagination in general.

When I began investigating nineteenth-century ideas on imagination, I discovered that writers repeatedly mentioned imagination in connection with a larger complex of ideas; along with imagination, partly contrasted with it but inextricably bound up with it, they talked about belief and reality. In other words, imagination is important to many nineteenth-century writers, including Dickens, not just for itself but also for its connection with spiritual matters. Idealists, for example, feel that reality provides them with no object worthy of belief, and so they turn to imagination in the hope that it can create an object they can believe in. (I realize that *reality* is a problematic term, but here as elsewhere I have tried to use the terms Victorian writers preferred. By *reality* they usually seem to mean, as I assume most of us do, the perceptible physical world, but often with a spiritual implication—either that what is real is what compels belief, or that reality is the realm of experience that opposes belief, that is felt as a negation of the ideal which belief seeks. "Reality" and "the ideal" often seem conceived in terms of each other, each the negation of the other; yet many writers also wish to see the ideal as real—a contradiction that implies one of the main tensions in their thought.) In light of this complex of ideas, it became apparent that I could discuss the Victorian idea of imagination only by including all these ideas—faith, fact, and fancy—and examining how they were related.

I begin, then, with a brief opening section in which I explain what I have concluded nineteenth-century writers mean not only by imagination but also by belief, and analyze the way these two are related. And since this relationship is especially important in Romantic ideology, in chapter 2 I briefly examine the Romantic theory of imagination and its connection with the spiritual concerns of Romantic idealism, and then relate it to the main tendencies in later nineteenth-century thought. The Romantic idealist concept of imagination underlies the thought of most Victorian writers, Dickens prominent among them; they attempt to preserve, rehabilitate, or transform the Romantic imagination. I can only touch briefly in that chapter on the main tendencies in Victorian thought, but since Dickens shared the concerns of many of his contemporaries, we can understand him fully only if we see his work in relation to Victorian concerns and the idealist attempt to use imagination to try to find or revive some form of belief.

I have chosen Dickens for this study because he probably wrote more on imagination than any other of the writers I discuss here, and his attitude toward imagination is not only quite complex but also continued to evolve throughout his career. Furthermore, he makes imagination central in much of his work, and he uses it in especially complex, interesting ways, ways that are not merely realistic and yet not simply antirealistic either, so that they are related to both the main tendencies—idealist and realist—in Victorian literature. Because Dickens works at the intersection of these two tendencies, we can learn much about their conflict in his fiction. An analysis of Dickens's works can thus be particularly useful in helping us understand how the tensions implicit in the nineteenth-century concept of imagination found expression in a writer's oeuvre.

Another reason for examining the work of one writer in detail is to show how to apply the method I have developed here. We can use an understanding of how imagination works to analyze much of what goes on in literature. The concept of imagination not only offers a key to the imaginative details of works but can also enable us to relate those details to the overall purpose and structure of many works. We can learn to see how the work of literature attempts to give expression to certain imaginative desires, and then see how that attempt can arouse feelings of both doubt and guilt, feelings that impel the work to seek various ways—often very complex ones—of dealing with these conflicts, of convincing reason, of placating conscience, or of evading those opponents. These conflicts and the mechanisms of defense to which they give rise account for many of the details we find in works of literature. To understand them, however, requires that we study particular works in depth. And Dickens is especially attractive for such an in-depth analysis because he offers a very rich example of the way the concept of imagination found expression both in the details of individual works and in their structure. The limitations of imagination generate much of the comic and pathetic detail of his characterization, and his novels often use a structure built on a discovery of those same limitations and an attempt to transcend them.

chapter 1

Imagination and Belief

Though the word *imagination* has other meanings, in nineteenth-century literature it is usually used to describe the faculty with which writers (and readers) create images in the mind. Although we talk of it as a discrete entity, we should probably rather think of it as a name we apply to certain aspects of our mental activity, an activity that is probably all one complex, interrelated whole having many manifestations, some of which (such as imagination) we separate out and label for our convenience. I am not qualified to speak of the actual nature of the mental activity involved; for our purposes here it is enough to be concerned (as nineteenth-century writers were) with its results. We shall have to content ourselves with accepting that there is some process that resembles perception but is different, some sort of partial imitation of perception akin to what happens in dreams and hallucinations.[1]

For many Romantics, the crucial quality of imagination is that it can envision things that are different from (preferably better than) perceptual reality. However, I must agree with those who hold that such images are nevertheless based on the perceptual. Though imagination can transform and combine perceptual images in such complex ways that it seems to create a new "reality," I think what it creates must always be based on and make use of the perceptual. Even if exceptions are possible, it is hard to see how they could occur in literature, since it must always make use of language, which, in order to communicate, relies on words whose original purpose is to serve the basic human wish to label reality and give it meaning in relation to ourselves. Even if a writer attempts to free language from this basic signifying function—as, for example, by talking about "slithy toves"—the words he uses can only activate the imagination (as Humpty Dumpty admits to Alice) by suggesting actual, similar words that do call up images based on reality. I wish to define *imagination*, then, as a mental process that attempts to imitate perceptual images and (almost always, probably unavoidably) to alter those pseudo-images in various ways.

The theory that best helps me understand the nineteenth-century treatment of imagination is Freud's. To account for the way we create mental images when we dream, Freud suggests a possible origin for imagination in infancy. The baby, he hypothesizes, learns to associate the visual image of his mother with the satisfaction of his hunger. When he feels hunger, he wants his mother to reappear. If she does not come, his mind tries to get satisfaction by calling up from memory the image of her that it associates with satisfaction; it has not yet learned to distinguish between that image and reality and so does not realize that merely picturing her image is not enough to give full satisfaction. Yet envisioning her at least offers a partial substitute for satisfaction; because of its associations, the mental image gives some illusion of fulfillment. Thus the mind learns that it can give itself some pleasure through imagination, even if only a simulation of the real thing.[2]

This description accords well with much of what we find in nineteenth-century literature. For one thing, imagination is usually (perhaps always) used in the service of desire, often in an attempt to envision some sort of an ideal—that is, some perfect fulfillment of desire. This search for the ideal is especially characteristic of the Romantics—hence their emphasis on imagination. But I would guess that for all writers imagination at least partly serves desire, since they use imagination to try to satisfy a desire to control and transform reality. No matter how negative the results, there must be some wish fulfillment in the very act of manipulating our mental representation of reality; control is pleasurable in itself, enabling us to regain some of the infant's sense of omnipotence.

In addition, there is a regressive tendency in the way nineteenth-century writers use imagination. They often envision a paradise in which the desirer can receive the kind of complete, effortless gratification an infant seeks—can be fed and warmed like Porphyro in Keats's "Eve of St. Agnes" or like Oliver Twist taken in by benefactors. In such idealized fictional worlds it is often possible to have a relationship like that of an infant with its mother, with the sort of idealized, desexed, nurturing woman who recurs so often in nineteenth-century literature. The regressive tendency of imagination is especially clear in the many Victorian works for or about children, works in which the writer uses imagination to try to become like a child, to regain a childlike way of seeing, as Wordsworth wishes he could in "Intimations of Immortality" and as Dickens often attempts through his child protagonists. Probably in all literature the object of desire bears some vestigial resemblance to the primal object of an infant's desire, though in deflected, rationalized forms; but in the nineteenth century these tendencies are especially clear because imagination is under less rational restraint.

Freud's theories can lead us to some further conclusions about imagination. If imagination is a function of desire, it is liable to come into conflict with what Freud calls the "reality principle" or "ego," which I would rather call by its traditional name, "reason" (these terms are not exactly synonymous, but are roughly equivalent if we take *reason* to mean the side of the mind that is concerned with reality, though not necessarily wholly rational). As Francis Bacon puts it in *The Advancement of Learning,* poetry serves "to give some shadow of satisfaction to the mind of man in those points whereof the nature of things doth deny it," thus "submitting the shows of things to the desires of the mind," unlike "reason," which forces the mind to "bow . . . unto the nature of things."[3] Imagination serves the desire for satisfaction, but reason tells us reality is unlike what we desire.

Desire thus resents reason and tries to decouple perception from it, using imagination in an attempt to find more satisfying objects than reality provides, trying to see what is desired, not what is real, reversing our normal adult tendency to grant authenticity mainly to reality. Imagination doesn't wholly reject reality; it uses perceptual images. But it tries to make them serve desire, hoping to get pleasure from them. Desire tries to co-opt and make use of the reality principle, tricking it by counterfeiting the reality principle's material (sensory data) but translating these into a form (pseudo-images) that desire can alter and control. By creating images, desire hopes to convince reason to accept imaginary objects of desire as real things, trying to sell the ego its version of reality.

I suspect desire tries to overcome our sense of reality in all our mental activity. Perhaps our idea of reality is always affected to some extent by our wishes and emotions. We are always concerned both with what we want and with what is real, and we are forever seeking compromises between the two. Desire and the reality principle seem implicit in each other, each a function of the other, trying to overcome the other. But in imagination desire can become more dominant than usual, and the concern with reality can decrease. Though the reality principle probably always retains some control over the image, since imagination's raw material is drawn from the realm of perception, nevertheless in imagination realism defers more to wish fulfillment than is possible with perception. Imagination's accessibility to desire is its strength, what makes it creative, driving it to alter the perceptual, to combine, distort, displace, magnify, or invert images, and to suppress or alter their parts. However, some imagining is clearly more realistic than other kinds. We can think of a continuum of different ways of imagining, from those which are bound closely to the perceptual to those at the opposite extreme in which desire is almost completely in control and the perceptual is merely material to manipulate as in dreams. But presumably neither desire nor reason can ever be wholly free from the influence of its opponent.

This notion of a continuum may help us understand the differing concepts of imagination writers have held. For example, Coleridge distinguishes between imagination and fancy. I would say that the process I have been describing is involved in both of these; in both, the mind is acting upon its images, but in fancy the mental process is more conscious and rational, and unconscious desires are less free to bring about dreamlike transformations. Thus fancy seems more mixed, a compromise between imagining and more rational processes. We can also distinguish between the kind of imagination Blake values, imagination as creator, giving us a vision of something that the poet asserts is not based on reality, and the kind of imagination Wordsworth uses, combining with and modifying perception, half perceiving and half creating. Here again I think these are two varieties of the same basic process. Once more the variation lies in the proportion between two interacting mental processes; Wordsworth does not subordinate the reality principle so completely to desire as Blake does. I think desire is still dominant for Wordsworth; his main concern is creating an ideal. But the reality principle is almost an equal partner; he is as much concerned to make his ideal seem real as he is to make it seem ideal. For a poet like Blake, however, the imagination shapes images as it wills, not much concerned with trying to convince reason of the verisimilitude of its vision.

One objection to the theory that imagination serves desire is that we often imagine undesirable things. This must occur partly because imagination is mixed, not wholly under the control of desire, giving expression also to our sense of reality's imperfections. But sometimes imagination produces images that are not realistic but grotesque. Freud offers an explanation for this phenomenon. Desires are not as simple as they may seem; they include forbidden, unconscious elements that can arouse guilt reactions in us. What seemed desirable can become frightening. This is apparently because desire originates in and retains a connection with the infant's desire for his mother. (At least this seems true for males; for females I suppose the process is similar but involves desire for the father.) Desire can thus arouse Oedipal guilt, which can be manifested in a prohibition of desire and in a kind of self-punishment whereby the desirable image is transformed into or replaced by something that negates or actively opposes desire. But even when desire is thus suppressed, its presence is implied by the very act of suppression. We can see frightening objects as a negative transformation of what is desirable; what we fear is the negation of what we desire, is what we desire to escape or overcome so that we can replace it with its opposite. It is probably this tendency toward negative transformations that accounts for much of the complexity in the imagined object; negative and positive expressions of imagination can combine in complex ways, creating compromise formations in which both desire and the reaction against it find partial expression, modifying each other.

If imagination exists at the intersection of desire and reason, it probably always has some tension in it, a conflict that is more overt than in more rational mental processes where desire is more fully restrained. It tries to serve desire but also to convince reason; and desire and reason can probably never be wholly reconciled with each other. Our desires are constantly resisting and altering our awareness, and reason is constantly trying to correct this influence and restrain desire. This tension becomes more acute in imagination, since it allows desire more freedom from restraint than in usual mental activity. Thus imagination is inherently precarious, never entirely satisfying. If it is an attempt to replace perception, it is doomed to failure, since it can never wholly do so and thus can never give all the satisfaction that we wish for.[4] The infant's sense of being loved and gratified by his mother may be the most unalloyed satisfaction we ever know, free from adult awareness and guilt; all later attempts to find fulfillment may partly be attempts to recapture that first perfect pleasure. But if that perfection is what imagination fundamentally seeks, it can never recapture it, can never give us all we desire. Perhaps it is because we cannot have that perfection that we desire it so much.

Because of this tension, the question of belief arises. Imagination probably always causes some concern with belief; when we imagine something, the conscious, rational part of our minds is faced with the problem of whether to believe in the imagined object. To understand this process, we can return to the infant imagining his mother. Perhaps at first he cannot distinguish between perceptual and memory images—between actually seeing his mother and picturing her in his mind. But he gradually learns that there is a difference. He develops an awareness of reality; reason learns to stand apart from imagination and recognize that its images are illusory. We can see belief, then, as an attempt to reconcile these opposing forces; we can define it as reason's acceptance of the mental image, seeing it as real. (There are other meanings of the word *belief*, but this is the one most related to imagination and thus the one I shall use here.)

In the infant's case complete belief is presumably at first possible because he has almost no awareness of reality. If an adult seeks belief, he must try to return to a state like an infant's. Belief thus tends to share the regressive nature of imagination. Religion asks us to become as children, to give up our adult reality-testing and submit unquestioningly like children to a parent; it plays on our desire for an ideal parent, all-knowing and all-providing, able to give us a paradise where we can have complete happiness without adult guilt. And belief can be regressive in trying to allow desire to control reason; if we see reality as signifying the divine, we are seeing it as serving desire, controlled by a force that exists to reward us.

One can attempt to recreate childlike belief either by turning off reason in some way or else by winning it over, convincing it to accept the image. Imagination seems to involve both these processes. To some extent it tries to get us to suspend rational awareness, as we largely do in dreaming. But it can also use various tricks to imitate reality and try to convince reason. Seeing is believing, so imagination tries to make us see. We could say, then, that the act of imagining is an attempt to create belief. Desire induces the mind to envision images that it wants to get reason to believe in, trying to make it take the desired object seriously. The more real that object seems, the more satisfying we can find it.

This concept of belief as rational acceptance of the imaginary is close to the formulations of John Henry Newman and William James. Newman calls the process "assent," by which he means that reason accepts the imagined ideal as real. And James talks about the way belief attaches a "sentiment of reality" to an unseen object, trying to make it seem objectively present as in hallucinations; he adds that this belief is created by what he calls "ontological imagination," which comes from the unconscious and opposes reason, as with primitive people who do not distinguish between reality and the imaginary.[5]

But if this is the way believing works, we must conclude it can virtually never be perfect. Perhaps we can never wholly regain the infant's total freedom from the reality principle, nor the prescientific innocence of a primitive animist. If belief cannot be based on our sense of reality, then it evidently must rely on imagination, in which case it cannot escape the conflicts inherent in imagination. If belief uses imagination, the mind has had to reject the rational sense of reality, which thus remains apart, unconvinced, aware of a reality that is separate from the imagined ideal and thus aware that what it is being asked to believe in is only imaginary.

This tendency toward doubt is aggravated by the reliance of imagination upon desire, which arouses guilt reactions. If imagination causes guilt, reason is likely to try to escape that guilt by refusing to believe in the imaginary. Religion has traditionally provided ways of dealing with this problem. If it is impossible to reach belief by convincing reason, the mind can seek another, nonrational route to belief; instead of dealing with rational doubt, it can try to overcome the guilt that accompanies doubt. If reason cannot accept desire, religion can try instead to make desire acceptable to the conscience. It has done this by providing a system of sanctions that allow the individual to indulge desires while simultaneously controlling and justifying those desires so that they do not arouse guilt. For this purpose it combines the desirable parent figure with an authority figure; God is seen not only as the giver of paradisal fulfillment, as in the infant's view of his mother, but also as a paternal figure to whom one must submit. The submission exculpates the desire; if we are submitting, we are not being selfish and can feel we have earned a higher sanction for our desires. In addition, making the ideal parent figure male removes the Oedipal guilt in desiring union with the parent (for a male). And removing the object of desire to another world provides a further defense against guilt. If the ideal does not exist in the realm of the senses, we can see desire for it as purified of sensuality and selfishness.

By removing guilt so that we can indulge desires of a strong, primal kind, religion offers a powerful incentive for accepting its control, making submission seem attractive. And if we accept the idealized control it offers us, we do not need to worry about rational self-control. Thus we need not be concerned with the doubts that accompany reason. For the believer, submission is evidently enough; doubt is irrelevant. The object of belief is given a special status that exempts it from doubt; indeed, to question its reality is seen as blasphemous. What matters is desire, not the reality principle—not whether the ideal is real but whether it satisfies our inner needs, whether it *should* be true. In a religious culture, people are primarily concerned not with what is real but with what is good. Thus religion enables a form of belief based on submission rather than reason.

This process of overcoming guilt through submission is embodied in the basic narrative of Christianity. The Eden myth shows how uncontrolled desire cannot remain innocent, how desire has sexual (associated with a woman) and rebellious aspects, and how rebellious desire can find expression through reason, inducing it to question authority. The myth asserts that there is an inherent human tendency to disobey the father figure. The story of Christ, on the other hand, is offered as an antidote to Adam's fall. Christ acts out a submission to paternal power, a complete giving up of self, even to death, which removes guilt and regains parental approval, showing us how we too should give up selfish desire and submit to a higher control. The Christian is called upon to reenact this pattern, overcoming doubt by overcoming guilty desires.

This pattern seems to be a version of the process Freud describes whereby the male child deals with Oedipal guilt by partly giving up his desire and accepting paternal control instead. To make this submission bearable, he transfers some of his desire for his mother onto his father; the father partly replaces the mother as an object of love. Thus he is idealized, like God, and acquires something of the double nature attributed to God, both frightening like a father and loving like a mother. In this way desire is balanced with submission and so made acceptable.[6] Religion institutionalizes this process of internalizing paternal control. It provides a ready-made version of the idealized parent that we can set up in our minds. Since this control is sanctioned by social institutions, it is easier to accept than self-control alone. Because religion's control comes from outside ourselves, it can seem objective; and if it has the weight of the culture behind it, it can seem all-powerful. Furthermore, it is probably easier to submit to a God than to one's own father because God is impersonal, not arousing the conflicts that one's father would. And setting God apart from reality makes it easier to idealize and thus submit to him. In these ways religion facilitates and supports the process of overcoming Oedipal guilt, enabling people to replace the primal object of desire with an acceptable object.

I have gone into some detail about the nature of religious belief because I think what happens in literature is closely related to this process. Literature too tries to get us to believe in the imaginary, though not as seriously as religion does. If we take something seriously, we accept it as equivalent to reality in its demands on us; something we perceive as real requires us to use our rational awareness to deal with it, often through physical action. Literature of course does not demand that kind of seriousness; we presumably always remain partly aware that what we are reading is separate from our physical life, that we can treat it as if in play, seeing it as what D. W. Winnicott calls a transitional object—like reality but not real.[7] Religion, however, tries to make us take its images seriously, setting aside that corner of the mind that asserts those images are not real.[8]

Nevertheless, despite this difference, I think literature aspires to create a similar kind of belief, asking us in a less serious way to accept its images as real. And much literature, especially in the nineteenth century, reinforces this attempt by working out a process of sublimation like that I have been describing, offering us not just an object of desire but an idealized one,[9] an object that embodies both the fulfillment of desire and also submission to some form of control that can purify that desire. Often the idealized object is presented as belonging to a realm above the ordinary world, so that desire for it is no longer physical and is thus unselfish. Literature frequently seeks to replace a repressive kind of control—usually parental or social—which opposes or even punishes desire, with an ideal control like God's, which can allow desire to be fulfilled in some acceptable way. But that control is still a control, and desire must partly submit to it. If writers can create belief in an ideal control, they can offer us a fulfillment free of guilt, making us feel that submission is fulfilling. This is probably never wholly possible, but I think it is the goal toward which much literature aspires.

Even realists, I think, are trying to induce a kind of belief. If realists cannot believe in any ideal—in the reality of any object that corresponds to their desires—they can at least try to create something that seems real; feeling that something is real is a version of belief, even though a less fulfilling one. Realists create a real-seeming world to provide a place in which desire, like Quixote, seeks an ideal, although the searcher is caught in a reality that opposes his or her desires. The work of realism thus tries to reconcile the desire for an ideal with a sense of reality—in other words, to create belief—even though it cannot do so. As it becomes harder to reconcile desire with a sense of reality and thus to hold onto belief that the desired ideal is real, realists displace the object of belief,[10] giving up more and more idealization—that is, restraining desire more and more—in order to retain the sense that the object is real. They have had to choose between believing it is ideal or believing it is real, and in a scientific age realness seemed the more convincing criterion. By making the imagined object oppose desire, as we feel reality does, they can convince reason that it is real.

We can see the structure of narrative (at least most narrative) as an attempt to create belief. The central action of most plots is an attempt to possess an object, which we can see as an attempt to make us believe the object is real. Plot conflicts thus represent attempts to overcome obstacles to that belief. Perhaps the very attempt to induce belief is what causes the work's conflict; that attempt rouses opposing impulses in the mind, impulses that resist belief or resent the submission belief normally calls for, and the work tries to deal with those impulses by locating them in imaginary objects that it can deal with. If it can overcome those objects, it can induce a related process in our minds, a conquest of the impulses opposing belief. Imagination has a role to play in this attempt to create belief. It is imagination that envisions the object of belief. In wish-fulfilling literature, imagination can create the image of an ideal parent; it can disguise the image of the mother so that desiring her no longer arouses guilt. Religion, by offering ready-made images, guides imagination in order to protect it from guilty desire; literature offers a similar, if weaker, form of control. Desire is still present; like religion, much literature appeals to our wish for a fulfillment better than any this world offers, inducing us to imagine various versions of paradise and of an ideal parent who will allow us to enter that paradise. But because literature lacks the seriousness and firm, institutionalized control of religion, it allows imagination more freedom to move away from simple idealization and so gives more expression to the conflicts within imagination.

The very fact that imagination cannot wholly make us believe in its visions impels writers to try to make the imaginary more real-seeming and satisfying. Writers also try to give us other forms of satisfaction—aesthetic or moral—to make up for the fact that imagination cannot give us actual physical satisfaction. We can see literature as a series of attempts to overcome imagination's handicap, developing techniques to make the imaginary seem real or to justify it in other ways. At the same time, literature exploits the ways of controlling desire that imagination offers it. The very act of imagining is a way of restraining desire, getting it to withdraw from reality, to give up a physical object and accept an imaginary substitute. And that displacement facilitates further displacements that can transform the imagined object into rationalized forms, seeing it as a signifier representing some principle of control to which desire can submit. This can be a moral control to which one submits by giving up the rebellious Oedipal aspect of desire; it can also be an aesthetic control, accepting the way art distances and depersonalizes desire, making it symbolic.

Imagination thus offers an attractive compromise; it allows some fulfillment of desire, but in a form that is safely insulated from reality and fairly exempt from guilt. It enables us to give expression to desire and yet prevent it from finding direct physical expression. Some conflict with the sense of reality and some guilt remain, but the skillful writer can deflect both desire and the forces opposing it into forms that we need not take too seriously. Thus imagination offers a way of having your cake and eating it—of simultaneously accepting and disowning desire by simultaneously feeling its object is real and admitting it is not real.

chapter 2

The Romantic Idealization of Imagination

In order to understand the Victorian attitude toward imagination, we need to begin with the Romantics, whose ideas the Victorians inherited. We especially need to understand the relation of the Romantic concept of imagination to religious belief, since that relationship is at the heart of Victorian concerns. The Romantic poets—and many of their Victorian followers—place special emphasis on imagination mainly because they hope it can replace or revive religious belief, creating some ideal they can believe in.[1] They evidently feel that the traditional basis of belief is no longer adequate and hope imagination can provide a new foundation on which to build belief.

We can guess various reasons for this dissatisfaction with traditional religion. I emphasize that these are only guesses, and about a very complex phenomenon—the gradual change in European society as it evolved from medieval to modern. This change seems to have built up pressure as the effects of economic modernization increasingly conflicted with inherited social structures, like tectonic plates pressing each other, until that conflict led to eruptions, as it did for example in the French Revolution. It seems likely that the new form of literature that came into being at the same time was affected by many of the same forces that caused that revolution as well as the equally great, though less violent, changes that occurred in English society. One of the main changes was that people were evidently becoming less willing to accept social control, probably because of what Ian Watt has called economic individualism.[2] One result of that individualism was probably an increased emphasis on reason. The commercial world made people value a hard-headed concern with physical reality. But if a culture encourages people to emphasize the reality principle, it will be harder for them to set reason aside as faith demands.

In addition, Christianity retained a belief system based on the structure of feudal society, on the ideas of hierarchy and submission, and that system came to be more and more at odds with a capitalist system that rewarded individual initiative. For a feudal peasant it was practical to believe in a control one should submit to, but for a self-made tradesman submissive belief and practical independence would be in conflict. As a result, people probably began to feel religion was something apart from everyday reality, even opposed to it. The power of the church had seemed an objective fact as long as it was reinforced by social control, but once these came into conflict, religious authority no longer seemed absolute; it became a subjective fact—one for which it grew difficult to find objective correlatives outside the self to guarantee its absoluteness.

This shift would tend to make people feel that there were two distinct entities, a "reality" that rewarded individualism and an ideal world, apart from the competitive social world—a realm that was often identified with the subjective and with areas like the family and religion in which people preserved traditional belief in a control one should submit to. In contrast to that idealized area, people came to see reality as negative, opposed to the ideal. And they also came to see the ideal as unreal, abstract, separate from ordinary life. Puritans, for example, did not believe that the ideal could be incarnated in reality in the form of icons; they could no longer accept that a real object could signify the divine.[3] They could see the divine only as transcendent, not immanent, and so as something to be reached through subjectivity.

This sense of separation caused a new attitude toward symbols. In traditional religion, believers apparently accepted symbols such as icons not as merely symbolic but as in some way equivalent to the object represented, containing the divine within them as it was thought to be incarnate in bread and wine. They evidently had little or no sense of a separation between reality and the ideal—no sense that the object in reality only represents the ideal rather than being identical with it. They were in a culture that accepted the act of representation, that believed in signifying and saw emblems as holding absolute meaning. Religion demands acceptance of the act of signifying; the world is seen as signifying its creator. And religion provided communally accepted signifiers that one need not question as long as one accepted social control in general; the acceptance of meaning was reinforced by one's submission to the whole social system. That submission was itself part of a belief in signification; society was seen as signifying a higher, absolute authority. But as the social order became more obviously different from the abstract version of its hierarchy offered by religion, the actual social representatives of authority (king and pope) were no longer seen as having godlike authority and goodness. And as people lost belief in these concrete, social representations of divine control, religious belief was no longer supported by a social

sanction and it became more difficult to believe in the reality of the divine—
that is, to find objects in reality that one could see as signifying the divine.
Thus people began to see religious objects as merely symbols, which implies
an admission that the object is separate from and not identical with what it
represents—that the ideal and the real are opposed.[4]

This rejection of public, conventional bases for belief must be one of the
reasons for the increased concern with imagination. As Puritans wish not to
have an object of belief presented to them by the church but rather to find it
by looking into their own souls, so Romantic writers call on imagination to
replace conventional, communal images with private ones. The tendency to
replace public with private can be seen in the shift from a communal form of
literature like the drama to more private forms like the novel, written to be
read in privacy. When we watch a play, objects are presented to our perception in a social context; when we read, we must imagine things for ourselves.
And traditional poetry drew on a store of public, conventional iconography,
largely presented ready-made to the imagination; in contrast, relatively realistic fiction and Romantic poetry both try to reject the conventional and get
readers to imagine objects based on their own experiences. To envision a
Clarissa or a scene in nature, one must draw on experience of a more private
sort, requiring more imaginative participation, than in picturing a Greek god
or a conventional Petrarchan lover.

Thus an increased concern with imagination coexisted with the increased
concern with reason. Indeed the increased emphasis on reason and reality-
testing probably made people more aware of imagination as a separate entity;
only when one asks whether a mental image is realistic does one becomes
conscious (and critical) of imagination's unrealistic images. Reason and
imagination are thus felt to be in conflict. And though the Romantics try to
resolve this conflict, I think their very effort exacerbates it. In traditional
religion the idealized object could be accepted unquestioningly, but when a
Romantic poet tries to create a private version of the divine, he cannot count
on ready-made acceptance. He must appeal to reason, trying to make us
believe his image is real. But if he sets up reason as an arbiter, he has conceded
authority to it and thus given it more power to resist conviction. The effort
to create belief makes belief more difficult. The very fact that the Romantics
wish to use imagination to counteract reason implies that reason is strong
and skeptical enough so that they see it as a threat.

We can see this tension, for example, in Coleridge's idea of "poetic faith"
as a "willing suspension of disbelief."[5] This definition implies there is something one must suspend, a side of the mind that still opposes belief. And if
that suspension is willed and conscious, it is hard to see how it can be com-

plete; Coleridge seems to be relying on reason (the will) to suspend reason, and if he does this, then reason is still present. If one is conscious that one is suspending disbelief, one has not entirely escaped the conscious side of the mind that resists belief. And if faith is only "poetic," one remains aware that it is merely imaginary, a "delusion," a "*negative* faith" that does not ask for "denial or affirmation" of the "real existence" of its images.[6]

To convince reason, Romantic writers usually try to locate some sort of ideal in reality, to find some version of the divine in the physical world from which empiricism had seemed to banish it.[7] Locating the ideal in reality means trying to convince reason to believe it is real. A clear example of this process can be found later in the century in William Hale White's *Autobiography of Mark Rutherford*, recounting a disillusionment with religion; he says "the God of the Church" had come to seem a dead "idol," "artificial, remote, never coming into genuine contact" with him, and so he "transferred" his "reverence" from that God to "the abstraction Nature," a "God" that seemed "real," an "actual fact present before" his "eyes" (24; ch. 2).[8] We can see here the appeal to the reality principle, which cannot accept the conventional version of the divine as real and thus seeks some real-seeming alternative. But although Rutherford, like the Romantics, tries to find a new ideal in reality, he is also forced, like them, to rely partly on imagination. His initial inspiration comes not from reality but from Wordsworth's poetry, and the Nature he believes in is not merely perceptible reality but rather an abstraction based on perception but created in his mind.

This attempt to find an ideal in reality usually leads to disappointment. Perhaps the most notable version of such a disillusionment is the failure of the French Revolution to provide the expected paradise on earth. Those who had high hopes for it began by seeking an ideal in this world, and it was perhaps this failure to find such an ideal that caused Blake, for example, to turn to imagination as a substitute, seeking through it to find the ideal he could not locate in reality. Thus the very emphasis on the reality principle can lead a writer to value imagination, reacting against reason's failure to create a fulfilling belief.[9]

The Romantics often try, then, to enable imagination to supersede reason, to give it a power that can overcome reason's doubts. In attempting this, they redefine imagination. Earlier writers tend to take a patronizing attitude toward imagination, feeling that art's main job is to imitate reality and that therefore imagination should be under the control of perception, merely decorating it. Even Milton, though he is closer to the Romantics than are most earlier writers, since he values imagination's "surmise" (as he puts it in "Lycidas") as a way to gain some "ease"—to fend off despair—nevertheless sees that that surmise is "false," merely something to "dally" with (ll.152–53), not to take seriously. He is aware it is only imagination and so he seeks to move beyond it to belief. Thus he sets belief in opposition to imagination rather than trying to combine the two. I think earlier writers do not need imagination as much because they can accept belief more fully, finding reason compatible with it. But the Romantics no longer feel reason can reach belief, so they try to replace reason with imagination and define imagination as the capacity to envision the divine. They reject the view that imagination should serve reason, seeing that as a lower kind of imagination—what Coleridge calls mere fancy—and raise imagination to the seriousness of belief, using it to create the ideal that belief seeks. It is "Imagination," Coleridge says, that enables us to "see our God."[10] If reality opposes belief, they hope imagination can transform reality or overcome the sense of reality, reuniting the real and the divine as religion had once done.

The Romantics also try to reverse the desacralization of symbols I have described.[11] If traditional symbols have come to seem artificial and arbitrary, the Romantics want to replace them with "natural" ones that they can accept as real. If religious symbols have lost their power to signify, the Romantics want to create new ones that they can believe represent the ideal. Coleridge, for example, talks in the *Statesman's Manual* of "imagination" using the "symbol," which "is characterized by a translucence . . . of the Eternal through and in the Temporal"; the symbol both "partakes of . . . reality" and "renders" it "intelligible." That is, it draws upon the perceptual but gives it meaning, preferably by making it signify the divine, turning its images into symbols that show "the eternal" in "Reality."[12] The poet wants to locate the ideal in reality, and he does so by offering an image that can both seem real to us and simultaneously represent the ideal. He can do this by taking advantage of imagination's intermediate status; it creates an image that seems real but is not. Thus the image can be a symbol, a compromise formation apparently existing in reality but also signifying something beyond reality. Earlier writers had preferred metaphors, which admit that an object is not identical with another but merely resembles it—that is, metaphors do not try to create belief. In contrast, the Romantic symbol typically tries to make us believe that the image in "reality" is the ideal—that Shelley's West Wind is a divine spirit, that Keats's nightingale is immortal. However, if one can see the divine only through symbols, one is implicitly admitting that one cannot actually see it as real.

Romantic poets typically choose their symbolic imagery from areas that facilitate this dual sense. Most Romantic symbols are drawn from nature, which, as the Romantics conceive of it, is itself a compromise formation, in reality yet also in some way beyond reality. Shelley's skylark, for example, is both a bird and not ("Bird thou never wert")—both real and unreal. Nature (at least as the Romantics define it) lends itself to this attitude because it is to some extent alien to the human, something we can see as the Other. Yet at the same time it is of course part of perceivable reality; thus it seems both real and better than real, a contradiction papered over by thinking of it (like heaven) as some sort of higher reality. Making a compromise formation of this sort is an attempt to circumvent our sense of reality, trying to convince reason the ideal is real while at the same time admitting its unreality so that reason won't have to subject it to reality-testing.

In order to see nature as beyond reality, the Romantics use the concept of another opposing entity, society. I think the main reason for conceiving of society as a distinct entity is to enable them to set nature against it, negating society and replacing it with its idealized opposite. By defining society as what is real in the ordinary sense of the term, they can think of nature as something beyond reality, an alternative form of reality. And by locating the negative aspects of reality in society, they can make nature seem ideal. In addition, by locating the ideal in a realm separate from the social, the Romantics can justify their rejection of society. Similarly, they try to authenticate the concept of an ideal by setting it against an opposing entity, reality— which also seems to be a concept originally created in order to give value to its opposite.

The other symbolic images that nineteenth-century writers usually idealize similarly lend themselves to such compromise formations, being drawn from areas that can be seen both as part of reality and yet in some way outside it. The sea and sky, for example, though of this world, are also beyond our own part of the world. The sea in Wordsworth's "Intimations" ode, for example, is associated with what is "immortal" but is "far" away (lines 165–66). And women and children, who are often idealized too, can also be seen (by an adult male writer) as Other, not part of the competitive adult male world. Writers also try to make idealized objects seem both real and outside reality by locating them in the past (for example, in an idealized Middle Ages) or the future (the Victorian idealization of progress).

Perhaps one reason the Romantics seek some form of belief is to counteract and justify their rebelliousness. One of the traits they share with the middle-class rationalists whose values they wish to reject is an unwillingness to accept social control. This Romantic rebelliousness is likely to arouse guilt analogous to Oedipal guilt. One way they can deal with that guilt is by trying to do the same sort of thing religion traditionally did—find (or create) some ideal form of control, justifying their rebellion by asserting their submission to that higher control. As the Puritans replaced external ecclesiastical control with a rigid self-control,[13] the Romantics replace social control with various private versions of God. I suspect that the eighteenth century developed the sentimental idea of the innate goodness of the human heart as a way of justifying middle-class rejection of quasi-feudal forms of social control, just as the Hobbesian view of man's badness was developed to justify a strong social control. If we are naturally good, then society need not control us; we should be left to follow the dictates of our hearts, since those are virtuous. And if the heart is good, then the imagination that expresses its impulses must be good also. As Shelley puts it in *A Defense of Poetry*, the "most enlarged imagination" creates a "state of mind" that is "at war with every base desire."[14] Romanticism asserts that the imagination proves its goodness by envisioning the divine. If the imagination naturally tends toward the divine, then the poet is justified in rejecting social forms of religion, since he can find a better, natural object of belief within himself. He can assert he is not really rejecting authority but rather replacing false authority with a higher form of control, although what he is submitting to is actually an idealized projection of himself. And it is through imagination that he can make such a projection, creating a private object of belief.

But although the Romantics try to make imagination replace belief in this way, their very attempt to do so exacerbates the conflicts that seem inherent in imagination.[15] As I have said, their efforts to make the imagined ideal seem real tend to rouse reason's doubts. We can see the conflict between imagination and their sense of reality, for instance, in the way they often feel separate from the imagined ideal. Wordsworth cannot regain the union he once had with idealized nature; Coleridge can only wish for his lost vision of Xanadu; Shelley prays to become one with the West Wind, betraying his feeling of separation from it; and Keats is ultimately forced to accept his inability to be with the nightingale. These failures suggest a sense that the ideal cannot seem fully real, part of the ordinary perceptible world. The price the poet pays for idealizing nature is that he separates it from himself, locating it on a level beyond reality, making it unattainable. In other words, he has to protect the imaginary from reason's doubts by separating it from the world reason is concerned with. Reason, like the speaker in "Ode to a Nightingale," remains apart, unable to enter into the world of imagination, to believe in the imagined ideal.

One reason the Romantics run into difficulty is that they believe in the innate goodness of imagination and the desires it serves. As a result, they try to free imagination from restraint and allow it to serve desire wholly, assuming that desire (which they idealize as the heart) naturally gravitates toward the divine. But if we cannot share their assumption—if we must agree not only with Freud but with traditional religion that desire, far from being naturally innocent, has a lustful, guilty aspect—then the Romantic indulgence of desire seems self-defeating. They arouse more desire than they can satisfy or control. And the more they encourage imaginative desire, the more likely it is to arouse guilt and cause reason to react against it. Their sentimental ideology makes it difficult for them to recognize the rebellious nature of the desires they are expressing and thus to control those desires. They try to overcome guilt by idealizing imagination, but that strategy merely causes them to allow desire more expression, since desire for an ideal is especially strong. Believing that to be childlike means to be innocent, they try to counteract guilt by becoming childlike, but that very attempt to escape self-restraint allows desire to become more demanding and unsublimated. The Romantic concept of imagination thus contains implicit conflicts of which their Victorian heirs were forced to become increasingly conscious.

chapter 3

Imagination and the Victorian
Search for Belief

Many Victorian writers continue the Romantic attempt to reach belief through imagination, and consequently they inherit the conflicts I have been describing in Romanticism. They respond to these conflicts in different ways, some preserving Romantic idealism, others reacting against it. I think it is useful to categorize them in terms of their attitudes toward imagination and realism.

One group of writers is primarily concerned with reproducing what they consider to be reality; we can distinguish them from those who value imagination and are using it to create some alternative to reality. We can also make a second distinction between those who try to hold onto Romantic idealism as much as possible and those who have become disillusioned with it. These two sets intersect, producing four possibilities. Among the realists, there are those who are also idealists, who seek some sort of ideal but hope to find it in reality, not through imagination. In addition to these idealist-realists, there are also disillusioned realists, writers like Hardy, for whom realism means showing the absence of the ideal in this world. Among the writers committed to imagination there are idealists, such as Bulwer-Lytton, who believe, as did many of the Romantics, that imagination can lead one to an apprehension of the ideal. But there are also some writers who, like many realists, have become disillusioned with idealism but who nevertheless seek to hold onto imagination as the basis of their art even though they are thus forced to make art out of imagination's failure to fulfill its Romantic purpose. In this group we can place writers of horror stories, among others. Dickens includes elements of each of these kinds of writing—realism and fantasy, idealism and skepticism—within his fiction, and so it will help us understand his relation to his culture if we take a brief look at them and at these different kinds of writers and at the attitude toward imagination they imply.

In the nineteenth century, as religious faith weakened, the conflict between reason and the wish to believe increased. Reason became more scientific, materialist, and skeptical, and the idealist imagination, seeking something like religious belief, became harder to reconcile with reason. Thus many writers felt compelled to choose one or the other. I think, as I have said, that reason and imagination can never be wholly separated, but many nineteenth-century writers tended to move toward one pole or the other, so that by the end of the century we find them embracing either a fairly negative, uncompromising realism or else an equally uncompromising imaginative escapism. Wordsworth had striven for a synthesis of imagination and perception, the mind half creating and half perceiving ("Tintern Abbey," lines 107–8), seeing nature and sensing the divine through imagination.[1] But already in Wordsworth one loses that synthesis as one ages, and in later writers imagination and perception are more strongly opposed; both realists and antirealists can see the real and the ideal only as separate. Realists gave up trying to convince reason to accept an imagined ideal—that is, trying to find any ideal in reality. Most antirealists, on the other hand, felt a strong enough need for belief that they were willing to reject reason in order to hold onto imagination's visions, seeking belief even if it was unsupported by reality. Realists try to keep belief by finding something they can accept as real, antirealists by finding something they can feel is ideal. Either reality is seen as unideal or the ideal is seen as unreal.[2] Each of these attitudes is only half of belief; complete belief would combine the two, seeing the ideal as real.

This conflict affects Victorian idealism. By *idealism* I mean a commitment to belief in some version of the divine, at least in some ideal (often a vague one), which is thought of as existing beyond reality and is felt to be more important—more "real"—than reality. The desire for an ideal makes many nineteenth-century idealists oppose an acceptance of reality and so tend toward an antirealism that relies heavily on imagination.

One of the main Victorian exponents of Romantic idealism is Thomas Carlyle. But if Carlyle expresses the idealist scorn of mere rationalism, he also reveals the conflicts implicit in idealism. On the one hand, in the "Symbols" chapter in *Sartor Resartus*, he says that "not our Logical, Mensurative faculty but our Imaginative one is King over us; I might say, Priest and Prophet to lead us heavenward"; thus he echoes the Romantic idea that imagination can enable us to discern "the Godlike" (book 3, ch. 3). But in his essay "Biography" he speaks of the difficulties imagination creates. "Imagination," he says, "is . . . a poor matter when it has to part company with Understanding, and even to front it hostilely in flat contradiction. Our mind is divided in twain; there is contest." In other words, imagination comes into conflict with reason's sense of reality. This split prevents belief: "only in so far as Imagination, were it but momentarily, is *believed*, can there be any use or meaning in it." Belief is produced by a union of imagination with understanding, creating a "united soul." Like the Romantics, Carlyle wants to base belief on imagination, but he is more aware than they are how much reason resists that belief. And so, unlike the Romantics, he partly turns against imagination, doubting that it can win reason over. It is because he demands so much from imagination—wanting it to be priest and prophet—that he is forced to see it as separate from and opposed to reason and thus to turn against it. Carlyle cannot be satisfied with imagination if it is a mere playing at belief, picturing an ideal without taking it seriously. He asserts that we must make a choice—either imagination (fiction) or reality (biography).

This ambivalence about imagination foreshadows a division among Victorian idealists. On the one hand, there are those idealists who agree with the Carlyle of *Sartor* and seek to find the ideal through imagination. On the other hand, there are the idealist-realists who agree with the Carlyle of "Biography" and hope to find the ideal in reality; these writers are descendents of Wordsworth, trying like him to find the divine through perception.[3] As Carlyle puts it in "Biography," literature should "*transcend*," be "sacred, prophetic, and the inspiration of a god," and this should be done not through imagination but "by working more and more on REALITY," which he thinks can provide something the "soul" can "believe." Whereas Wordsworth thinks of perception and imagination combining to create belief, Carlyle here feels the two are polarized and we must choose one or the other.

Many nineteenth-century writers are idealist-realists, trying to reach a sense of something like the ideal through reality. They run a gamut from a writer as Romantic as Whitman to one as close to negative realism as Tolstoy. For example, John Ruskin in his chapter on the pathetic fallacy in *Modern Painters* says "fancy" makes us "see things falsely" (vol. 3, pt. 4, ch. 12, sec. 4; and see sec. 8), and the "highest" kind of writer keeps "his eyes fixed firmly on the pure fact" (sec. 11).[4] It is not that he is too realistic for imagination but rather that he is too idealistic; his criticism of imagination is not that its visions are too idealized but that it fails to convince reason of the reality of its visions.

Gerard Manley Hopkins is an especially clear example of the attempt to combine idealism with realism. Like Wordsworth, he feels that one can reach a sense of the divine from a perception of reality. But Hopkins's confidence that perception can lead to belief is unusual among Victorian writers. Even for Hopkins this path to belief is evidently difficult, judging by the intensity of the effort he makes (and pushes us to make) in his visionary poems, and also by the sense his poems of despair give us that the effort can fail. The problem with an idealism based on reality, of course, is that it is hard to find anything in reality that seems divine; Tennyson's feeling in *In Memoriam* that there is no sign of God in Nature is more typically Victorian than Hopkins's late-Romantic confidence.

Robert Browning is a good example of how idealism like Hopkins's can be combined with an acceptance of reality like Tennyson's. Since Browning usually cannot find the ideal in reality, he typically presents the imperfection of reality in a way that tries to force us to wish for the existence of an ideal beyond this world and so to infer that what we desire must exist.[5] By showing Cleon and Caliban, for example, groping for a god, he tries to make us see their limitations and so go beyond them, envisioning the God they cannot believe in. Browning thus combines his Romantic wish to locate the ideal in reality with an anti-Romantic insistence on the way reality resists our desire for the ideal. By using dramatic monologues, he can locate the subjective search for belief in characters whom he treats objectively, thus showing us an unideal reality but also showing the search for an ideal taking place within that reality. The rational awareness of reality's imperfection can stand apart from the desire for an ideal (as Browning stands apart from his characters) and so coexist with it; Browning can both accept the failure to reach belief and also insulate the desire for belief from reason's doubts. Yet this does not entirely reconcile the two; within the monologues, though it is distanced, their struggle continues.

Other realists are farther from idealism than this; yet many of them retain some residual idealism. George Eliot, for example, though she refuses to offer any transcendent version of the ideal, tries to find a secular version, thus attempting to reconcile idealism with realism by moderating her idealism. Matthew Arnold seems to attempt something similar, seeking a substitute for religion in a secular version of the ideal; he believes not in a transcendent object of belief but in a state of mind that resembles religious belief—in the act of belief as an end in itself.[6]

All these writers, comparatively realist though they are, retain some attraction to imagination. They do so, I would argue, because of their need for some form of ideal—that is, for more than reality can give them, for something they thus hope to find through imagination. Ruskin values a "sacred imagination of things that are not" as opposed, he says in his essay "Benediction," to the "infidel eyes" of the modern materialist unable to imagine the sacred.[7] Hopkins, whose faith is strongest, feels less need for imagination, but he does say in a letter that one needs to use "an inward eye" to see the value in nature,[8] implying that imagination plays a part in perception. Indeed he uses poetry to impose much more of an imaginative transformation on perception than Wordsworth does. Browning is more critical of imagination, but he shows characters such as Bishop Blougram (line 183), Abt Vogler (line 73), and especially David in "Saul" (lines 280–81) needing to supplement their realism with imagination's dream. Arnold speaks of the importance of imagination in *God and the Bible* (377–78) and shows he values the imaginative search for the ideal in "The Scholar Gypsy" (see for example line 158).[9] And even George Eliot, though she is usually critical of imagination, also betrays considerable sympathy with it. It is imagination that enables Maggie Tulliver to conceive of an ideal, to value love and beauty, and at the end of *Mill on the Floss* Maggie seems to attain an imaginative vision of the ideal (552–54; pt. 7, ch. 5).[10]

Dickens shares many of the attitudes we find in these writers. He too places considerable emphasis on what he presents as reality. He mainly shows reality as opposing the effort to reach an ideal—for example, Little Nell finds herself in a world that largely opposes her and that she must leave behind to find what she seeks. Yet though Dickens is thus partly like the anti-idealist realists who show how reality denies us any ideal, he is also quite a bit like the idealist-realists; though he often sees reality as quite negative, he also wishes to locate some version of the ideal in it. He feels the need to take reality into account, but he does not want to give up his belief in some quasi-religious form of ideal. Even in the case of Little Nell, we can see this ambivalence. Dickens almost gives her a paradise on earth with the Schoolmaster—that is, allows her to attain an ideal in this world. He seems divided, half believing (or wanting to believe) that the ideal is real—in reality—and half believing it is only transcendent—to be found after death. Thus his negative versions of reality are supplemented by idealized versions (like Dingley Dell, for instance).

This ambivalence affects Dickens's attitude toward imagination. He is partly like the negative realists, mistrusting imagination because it is unrealistic. But he is more like the idealists who desire a stronger sense of the ideal than reality alone can provide and so try to supplement or modify perception with imagination. The tension between these two attitudes finds expression in the way his novels are divided, one part relatively concerned with showing an unideal reality and another allowing more imaginative wish fulfillment.

Dickens also has considerable affinity with the strain in Victorian thought I would call antirealism, and to understand him fully, we need to examine the nature of that school of thought. Unlike the idealist-realists, many idealists try to base belief on an imagination that they conceive of as mostly opposed to perception. These writers react more or less directly against realism as they understand it. The main characteristic they share is a wish for some version of the divine, which they cannot find in reality and which they thus seek through imagination. For most earlier writers, belief was strong enough so that they did not need to emphasize imagination; for most modern ones, reason's sense of reality has become too strong for them to believe fully in imagination's vision of an ideal. But in the nineteenth century, reason and the need for belief were both strong, neither able to overcome the other completely, and so imagination took on greater importance, trying to reconcile the two. What reason accepts as real seems unfulfilling to the antirealists, and so reason seems negative—that is, opposed to desire, which seeks something more fulfilling than reality and so resents rational realism. Antirealists fear that spiritual belief may be destroyed by a narrow rationalism based on economic individualism and unable to accept the existence of anything beyond material reality. The reactive (and reactionary) nature of this kind of idealism is typified by Edward Burne-Jones's remark, "The more materialistic Science becomes, the more angels shall I paint."[11] In a world in which materialism was dominant and reality seemed increasingly unfulfilling, idealism became defensive, not trying to win reason over but to escape it, to fight off rationalism and preserve some sort of belief, however weakened.

The most extreme antirealists like George MacDonald and Bulwer-Lytton assert that imagination alone is enough to create belief. Such writers tend to distort their worlds in sentimental ways, allowing desire an unconvincingly easy victory over doubt, not facing the difficulties that reason would raise. Because they believe imagination is innately good, they tend to ignore or falsify its darker aspects, not acknowledging the opposing forces in it that create interesting tensions and make a work more convincing.

The main tendency I see in nineteenth-century idealism is a gradual attenuation of belief. As the initial Romantic optimism is followed by a sense of how unideal reality is, the first response (which we find in most of the earlier Victorians) is to redouble one's efforts to believe in some ideal despite reality. But most later Victorian writers seem less willing or able to make that kind of serious effort. Writers lost the Romantic confidence that imagination could provide a basis for belief.[12] Those that remained idealistic gradually fell back to positions of less certainty, admitting at least implicitly that the ideal they envision is only imaginary, so that they cannot fully believe in it. They largely gave up trying to convince reason and instead sought ways of evading it. They stop taking imagination seriously—that is, trying to convince reason to accept the imaginary as if it were real—and instead become increasingly playful. What belief they retain becomes self-conscious and partial, coexisting with an awareness that its object is not real, an awareness expressed by undermining seriousness, making the imagined ideal less real-seeming so that reason need not worry about believing in it. And as belief weakens, the later writers emphasize imagination more, since it is all they have to put in place of belief. They still try through imagination to create an ideal more or less like a religious one, but it is admittedly imaginary, not much believed in—idealism for art's sake. Imagination becomes a way of playing at belief.

This tendency is already apparent in some Keats poems that no doubt influenced Victorian writers. "The Eve of St. Agnes" offers a vision of the ideal, but its ending distances that vision, making us feel it does not exist in the narrator's reality but rather in the realm of imagination—"faery land" (line 343). Keats seems to be trying to set aside reason's need for belief and to accept imagination's vision of beauty as enough in itself. I think this effort to do without certainty—without any truth other than beauty—is what he is expressing at the end of "Ode on a Grecian Urn." We find a similar, but less conflicted, attempt to make imagination replace belief in the works of Dante Gabriel Rossetti.[13] A poem like "The Blessed Damozel" does not, I think, try very hard to make us believe in the ideal it describes but rather allows it to remain beyond the realm of reality-testing—that is, to remain implicitly imaginary.

Algernon Charles Swinburne goes farther, consciously rejecting "realism" and choosing to be "fanciful";[14] even if he doesn't believe in imagination's visions, they are too attractive—or reality is too unappealing—for him to give them up. He turns to "the world of dreams" in a self-conscious attempt to escape reason's unfulfilling, impossible quest for "truth" ("A Ballad of Dreamland"). And William Morris expresses a similarly attenuated sense of imagination's power. When he calls himself the "idle singer of an empty day," a "Dreamer of dreams," in the prologue to *The Earthly Paradise*,[15] he is admitting that imagination is not serious, cannot compel belief and so fill life's emptiness. In a civilization emptied of religious certainty, the artist can only give us "dreaming in idleness,"[16] offering visions that are admittedly imaginary. If belief is impossible, imagination is idle, unable to lead to belief, segregated from our sense of reality, and thus reduced to a mere plaything. Yet more emphatically than Swinburne, Morris holds onto imagination, as if trying to defy this sense of ineffectuality. He writes antirealistic stories that admit they are only imaginary and dreamlike but that nevertheless keep using imagination to try to create a vision of an ideal and thus induce some simulacrum of belief in the reality of that ideal.

This gradual decrease in seriousness is especially apparent among minor writers. When we look at popular literature and the various minor genres that developed in the nineteenth century, we find a great deal of antirealism and attempts to create some sort of belief based on imagination, but that belief rarely seems very serious. Whereas in mid-century idealism occurs in serious literature, toward the end of the century we find it mainly in popular fiction, adventure stories, fantasies, and children's stories—works whose format and genre expectations assume that we are childlike or in an escapist mood, that we are not going to take what is said too seriously and rationally, that we are not going to demand to be convinced that the imaginary is real.[17] It seems likely that the rise of fantasy and similar genres in the nineteenth century is largely caused by the decay of spiritual belief and the resultant search for substitutes, even though these are less serious. As the century progresses, writers who feel nostalgia for Romantic idealism increasingly choose to write fiction that is more or less avowedly escapist, not pretending to face up to the complexities and doubts of reality with much seriousness.

In mid-century a writer of popular fiction such as Charlotte M. Yonge still claims to be taken quite seriously, but already there is a tendency for idealism to occur in mass literature aimed at a less high-brow audience than, say, George Eliot's. Popular purveyors of idealism appeal in clichés to ready-made response, offering a conventionalized Romanticism their readers could respond to without effort. And they appeal to their audiences with a high degree of wish fulfillment, softening the sense of reality's resistance to desire and making fulfillment acceptable to their audience by sugarcoating it with plentiful doses of quasi-religious idealization. By the end of the century the split between serious and escapist fiction is much wider, and idealism is usually relegated to works that do not seriously claim to deal with reality.

The escapist attitude of late Victorian idealists is typified by Hall Caine, writing in 1890 that he values an "idealism" that is *false to fact, true to faith.*"[18] He has given up trying to reconcile fact and faith, reason and belief. If reality and idealism are totally opposed, then one must choose either an unidealized realism or else (like Caine and other romance writers) offer an unreal ideal. Nineteenth-century antirealists invented various kinds of fantasy in order to free imagination from rational skepticism and diminish the reality principle's hold on narrative.[19] Fantasy takes many forms; there is a wide variation, for example, in how much realism a writer combines with his fantasy, and in what ways he does so; and there is also variation in whether a fantasy is idealist or disillusioned. But I think idealism is implicit in most Victorian fantasy.

The objects imagined in fantasy are often ones we cannot take very seriously because they are clearly unreal, and they are typically supernatural rather than divine, so that we are not asked for serious religious belief. Thus the writer—though seeking, as other idealists do, something like belief—also accepts that imagination can only partly replace belief, imitating it in a rather playful way. But imagination's lack of seriousness can enable writers to evade reason's concern with certainty. If writers accept that the ideal is only imaginary, they need not try to convince reason to believe in it. Insofar as they can allow the imaginary to be an end in itself, they can enjoy its freedom from seriousness and play with it.

Among the popular writers who seek something like religious belief through imagination, I would include H. Rider Haggard, whose fiction describes journeys into the wilds of Africa that resemble a journey into the imagination,[20] and that turn out to be journeys in search of some ideal in which to believe. Rudyard Kipling is another late Victorian who occasionally tries to use imagination as a route to belief,[21] most clearly in "The Brushwood Boy," which is about using imagination to escape to a better world. However, the ideal world that Kipling describes here is admittedly imaginary; he is not asking us to believe in it but rather offering a playful substitute for belief, which reason need not attack because it keeps "a clear understanding that it was all make-believe." Making believe is playing at belief, imitating it without asking reason to take it seriously. Many late-nineteenth-century writers try to salvage belief in this way, not seriously trying to convince reason; they feel it is better to keep some idealism, though in an admittedly imaginary form, than to try to convince reason and force it to reject the imaginary entirely. Partial belief is better than none at all. As Kipling puts it in the poem "To the True Romance," "Enough for me in dreams to see" the ideal; if belief is impossible, imagination is the best substitute available.

Other idealists are more completely antirealist, less willing to balance imagination with a sense of reality. Of these fantasists, perhaps the most extreme is George MacDonald.[22] In his essay "The Imagination: Its Functions and Its Culture," MacDonald endorses the Romantic idea that "Imagination" is what directs the "intellect" to "God" (*A Dish of Orts* 11), leading us "beyond dull facts" "into the region of the true, of the eternal" because it comes from God (27). MacDonald is an example of the tendency of idealism later in the century to retreat to children's literature. Many later writers were attracted to children's literature, no doubt influenced by the Romantic idealization of children. They evidently felt that writing for children (and trying to become like a child in doing so) could enable them to escape from adult awareness of reality and return to a childlike state in which they could be closer to the divine, more able to believe in imagination's vision. As I have said, imagination seems rather regressive in any case, a loosening of the reality principle's hold over us, but writing for children offers an excuse to loosen that hold more than usual.

An adult writing for children, however, is not so much regaining a child-like state as self-consciously imitating it. Such a writer deliberately sets reason aside, and because the act is deliberate, reason remains conscious of its exclusion. Thus although the idealist hopes to recapture childlike faith, that attempt seems self-defeating; he must reject the rational side of the mind, which he would have to convince if he were to create full belief. Here again we see the attenuation of idealism, its retreat to a less serious form of literature. The writer is tacitly admitting that he cannot convince adult reason to believe in what he imagines. Yet this lack of seriousness enables him to evade doubt and be more idealistic than he could be if writing for a more skeptical audience. Some writers probably turn to children's literature because they have found it impossible to attain full belief; a playful imitation of belief is the best they can hope for, suspending reason because they cannot convince it. If they cannot believe in the ideal, they can at least imagine it.[23] As idealism becomes less serious later in the century, no longer struggling so much to overcome the sense that the ideal is unreal, later writers of children's literature are willing to be more playful, not trying to push us toward belief.

During this period—the turn of the century—there was a last flowering (a rather forced, hothouse flowering) of Romantic idealism, and one of the ways this found expression was in the many fantasies, both for adults and children, written then. Kenneth Grahame's *The Wind in the Willows*, for example, seems to be an attempt to escape into an imaginary world where the characters, being animals not humans, can be part of idealized nature.[24] One sign that this world is a product of imagination is the fact that the characters are anthropomorphic animals—unrealistic and therefore exempt from much of reason's concern with realism. Other turn-of-the-century children's books that offer a similar escape to idealized and admittedly imaginary worlds are E. Nesbit's *The Enchanted Castle*, Frances Hodgson Burnett's *The Secret Garden*, and J. M. Barrie's *Peter Pan*.[25]

In the comic literature of the later nineteenth century, idealism reaches its vanishing point. Oscar Wilde, for example, echoes the antirealism of his contemporaries, but in a more defiant way than the writers we have been examining.[26] Whereas they mostly betray at least some wish to regain belief, Wilde not only accepts this as impossible but mocks the wish. Instead of trying to make the imaginary seem real, he asserts—for example, in "The Decay of Lying"—that one should accept imagination as an end in itself, as a way of showing that we do not need belief (169, 180, 192, 195).

Edward Lear takes this escape from seriousness the farthest.[27] Even in Lear some Romantic idealism survives; especially in his longer poems he wistfully indulges in something like the Romantic quest for an ideal, going through the motions of seeking escape to some sort of paradise. But there is nowhere to go that he can believe is real; the Romantic quest has become nonsense. The fact that the desired object is imaginary has completely eclipsed the fact that it is ideal, so that instead of being a means toward belief in an ideal, imagination now prevents that belief. Recognition that the object is not real, however, results mainly in pleasure, not anxiety, because we need not take the question of realness seriously. Poetry is freed from the signified and can become mere play, a retreat to childlike irresponsibility, like children playing with words. This escape from reason's concern with reality is exhilarating, since it frees us from having to worry about belief—about whether any ideal can be real.

The weakening of idealism I have described in these writers shows how precarious and vulnerable a belief based on imagination is. Inheriting the Romantic wish to convert imagination into belief, the Victorians found that conversion more and more difficult, if not impossible. The writers I have been discussing here clung to their commitment to imagination, but by the end of the century many were forced to give up the attempt to build a serious belief on that foundation. Would-be idealists more and more had to settle for imagination without belief. This tendency too is reflected in Dickens. Although like realist-idealists he often tries to locate some version of the ideal in reality, his sense that the ideal may not be real after all frequently finds expression in the way he diminishes those versions, making them playful, childlike, less serious, and thus implicitly admitting they are only imaginary. Little Nell may not seem realistic (certainly not if you think of realism as anti-idealism), but Dickens tries to make us believe she is real. Dick Swiveller, on the other hand, attains a version of the ideal (a happy ending with the Marchioness) which may seem more realistic to us, since it is less fulfilling and much less idealized, but which is also kept playful and shown to be a product of imagination (Dick's, acting as a stand-in for Dickens). And as with Lear, this retreat from seriousness instead of disappointing us offers a pleasing escape from the doubts aroused by Nell's serious search for belief.

Dickens thus seems divided, partly trying to hold onto Romantic idealism but at the same time, in other parts of his work, allowing imagination largely to free itself from the need for belief and—if not to replace—at least to supplement idealism. Presumably this movement toward free, playful imagination occurs in his work for much the same reason it does in the writers I have mentioned above—because serious belief has become increasingly difficult. Like several of the writers I have just mentioned, he is attracted to the childlike—not just because of a Romantic belief that children are close to the ideal (a belief that remains strong in an early work like *Oliver Twist*) but also because of a wish to escape from adult seriousness and doubt. But though Dickens's fiction often resembles the more explicitly antirealistic works I have touched on here, he mixes antirealism with more realistic elements, pitting imagination against a sense of reality because unlike the pure antirealists he wants to find some serious form of belief—one that takes reality into account. Thus although he allows imagination some of the free play we find in those writers, he ultimately seems committed to converting it, putting it to the service of his deeper concerns.

One reason imagination seems unsatisfactory by itself is that, as I have said, it tends to undermine the faith writers try to build upon it. But there is apparently another reason for the mistrust of imagination, which we can discover by examining another kind of antirealism that also arose in the nineteenth century.

As idealism declines, one offspring it engenders is its own negation, a reaction against its faith. This tendency is manifested in the rise of negative antirealism, a mirror image of idealism—a literature in which imagination discovers not an ideal object of belief but its opposite. Instead of dreaming of paradise, writers have nightmares of hell.[28] Perhaps they do so because they have lost faith in any form of control able to sublimate the desires in imagination, so that those desires find guilty, frightening forms of expression. Perhaps they feel guilty at having rebelled against religion to seek some god of their own (a version of the Oedipal rebellion against the father, and therefore likely to cause guilt). Guilt may find expression in an unconscious reaction against imaginative desire, turning imagined objects into something undesirable or forbidden. Whatever the psychological process involved, the result shows us again the close relationship of imagination with religious belief, and shows especially clearly the difficulty it encounters in seeking that belief.

Why indulge imagination even when it turns nightmarish? Perhaps writers do this partly because they cannot help seeking an ideal even if they no longer believe in it; and partly because they are fascinated by the depths of imagination and get pleasure in discovering its secrets—probably the pleasure of overcoming inhibition. They evidently find reason even less fulfilling than imagination and want to escape its dominance whatever the costs. As people came to think of belief and realism as opposed, they felt that overcoming realism was desirable as an end in itself, as a weak substitute for belief (as ghosts are a weak substitute for gods). They could at least hold onto some version of the supernatural, even if they could no longer believe it was good.

We can see the entrance of horror into literature, then, as a result of the decay of faith. That decay is also evident in the way this negative antirealism is pervaded with uncertainty. Tzvetan Todorov, discussing fantasies of this sort, holds that their distinguishing characteristic is a refusal to let us be certain about the reality of the imagined object.[29] This uncertainty, however, is not restricted to the fantasies he discusses; it is also common in idealist fantasy. It seems to be just one more manifestation of the inability to convince reason to believe in the imaginary—an inability that may be endemic to all literature, but that becomes much more prominent in a period like the nineteenth century in which belief is weakening, creating strong tensions between reason and imagination. It is as if the loss of religious certainty infects the mind with generalized doubt, creating a mental climate in which it is difficult to be sure about anything. Uncertainty about whether a ghost is real can be a displaced, more manageable version of uncertainty about whether God is real. But Todorov seems correct in noticing that this uncertainty is especially strong in negative fantasies. I suspect this is so because negative fantasy is a product of greater religious doubt; it expresses an inability to believe in the ideal. The uncertainty may also be a result of the guilt reaction I have described. One way the conscience can punish desire is by denying it possession of the object—that is, not letting the object seem real to it. Thus in negative fantasies the object that desire calls into being is not only made unfulfilling, opposing the desire it should fulfill, but is also uncertain, evasive, constantly withdrawing from the desirer. The more guilty imaginative desire becomes, the more likely it is to create objects like this that the mind cannot fully accept.

Perhaps the most interesting Romantic treatment of the guilty, unfulfilling side of imagination is in *Frankenstein*. I find the book poorly written, but there is an undeniable attraction in the concept on which it is based. That concept can be understood in various ways, but the useful interpretation here is that the novel is a description of the dangers of the Romantic indulgence of imagination.[30] We can read the story as a kind of allegory in which imagination becomes a monster, out of control and destructive. The monster seems to be an embodiment of Frankenstein's imagination; like a Romantic poet, Frankenstein is "guided by an ardent imagination" which seeks "the secrets of heaven" (28, 32; ch. 2), trying to use imagination to create an ideal he can believe in. But by giving imagination free rein, he lets loose uncontrollable forces—forces embodied in its offspring, his monster, but which we can see as representing the negative side of his imagination.

Mary Shelley suggests that it is because the mind cannot restrain the rebellious, passionate forces in imagination that imagination cannot create a Romantic ideal. Instead it creates the opposite; the monster is the negation of the ideal, man as the reverse of godlike. It destroys what Frankenstein loves, suggesting that the rebellious forces released through imagination can destroy the ideal and belief in it. Neither Frankenstein nor the other people from whom the monster seeks love and a parentlike acceptance can respond to his wishes, suggesting that there are forces in the psyche that reason or conscience cannot accept, or that cannot accept their control. The monster's search for an ideal—an object to love—reenacts the Romantic attempt to reach belief from imagination, as his creator tried to do at the start. But imagination (at least after rebellious impulses have made it monstrous) cannot reach belief. Some force in imagination seems to prevent the very belief it seeks.

We can also associate Frankenstein with reason, since he is a scientist. It is as if the monster is his imagination and he acts for reason, trying to control that imagination. But the two have become radically separated from each other, located in two separate selves, and so reason cannot control imagination. Therefore belief (reconciling reason with imagination) is impossible, and imagination, out of control, cannot reach the ideal. Thus it becomes negative and rebellious because it cannot accept control; and thus reason, like Frankenstein, can only reject and fear it. Shelley seems disillusioned with the Romantic belief that heart and imagination are naturally good. Romanticism asserts that if one allows imagination freedom, it will lead to the ideal; the monster shows that a free imagination leads in the opposite direction. Imagination is frightening.

Like idealist fantasy, various types of negative fantasy, especially ghost stories, became increasingly popular late in the nineteenth century, but at the same time became less serious. If the horror expressed still has a spiritual dimension, it is diminished. The genre conventions of fantasy enable us to avoid taking it very seriously. Writers who use negative antirealism in popular fiction often seem to be appealing to stock responses to titillate an increasingly wide and undiscriminating audience. They enable us to play with fear without feeling seriously threatened, knowing we are not in a world like reality. Nevertheless, these writers—notably Sheridan LeFanu and Bram Stoker—exploit Victorian religious anxieties,[31] if only in a vague form that is no longer clearly associated with its original cause but is more easily exploited because of its vagueness. I suspect this kind of fiction became popular because it reflects real spiritual concerns, but also because it deflects those concerns into a form that need not be taken too seriously.

Dr. Jekyll and Mr. Hyde is a more serious work showing that the impulses that can find expression in imagination, far from being innately good as in Romantic ideology, are just the opposite. Dr. Jekyll, like Frankenstein, indulges imagination in the hope that it will lead him to the ideal but finds its opposite instead.[32] Hyde, like Frankenstein's monster, seems to represent destructive, uncontrolled imagination, which instead of enabling Jekyll's "soul" (108) to reach belief leads him into "despair" and "blasphemies" (81, 83, 90, 96, 109).

The Picture of Dorian Gray offers a similar revelation of the guilty forces in imagination.[33] Like Jekyll and Frankenstein, Dorian starts out seeking a version of the ideal and relies largely on imagination in doing so (for example, 213, 229, 236); here again, however, imagination is taken over by guilty desires that prevent attainment of the ideal (for example, 301, 338). The destruction of Dorian acts out not only the destruction of innocence but also the death of a belief that the imagination can be innocent.

One other writer who might at times be considered a disillusioned antirealist is Lewis Carroll. Carroll is too complex to put in any simple category, and the more conscious, public side of him (what I would call the Dodgson side) espouses a fairly conventional Romantic idealism. But though he may send Alice into the realm of imagination in search of a Romantic ideal, what she actually finds is an almost complete frustration of her desires. I don't think Carroll is consciously saying there are frightening forces in the imagination that prevent belief, but I do think he shows (probably to some extent unintentionally) that to be true. Carroll evidently feels that imagination is negative because it is opposed to reason; Alice keeps seeking rational comprehension, and Carroll's imagination keeps creating things that defy comprehension. I would say that this conflict between reason and imagination reflects the breakdown of any form of belief (especially religious belief) in the nineteenth century. Insofar as belief involves reason's accepting an imagined ideal as real, we could say that Alice's adventures are about the search for belief—that is, about reason's attempt to find something in the realm of the imaginary that it can accept as real and thus find fulfilling. But Carroll shows us the impossibility of reaching belief.[34]

These writers show that underneath Victorian idealism there were forces in the post-Romantic imagination that were strongly opposed to that idealism. Perhaps the idealism was mainly a defense against those impulses, an attempt to conceal them or make them acceptable, freeing imagination from guilt. But we can also see these negative writers as reacting against idealism, unable to accept the control it tried to impose on imagination, pushing Romantic rebellion toward its logical extreme, trying to free imagination even if that meant it fell prey to guilty desires. In any case, as idealism weakened, it became harder to control imagination, to force it to envision an ideal, and the desires that found expression through it thus became increasingly uncontrolled and frightening. Imagination turned out to be considerably more problematic and full of conflict than Romantic ideology had assumed.

Some of this anxiety finds expression in Dickens, who was quite attracted to ghost stories and nightmarish states of mind—for example, Jonas Chuzzlewit's. His attraction seems the result of his fascination with imagination in and of itself. But I think it is likely that his discovery of the frightening forces in imagination was one of the main causes of a mistrust of imagination he often expresses and of his consequent need to modify or replace imagination in order to reach belief. If imagination can be taken over by rebellious and destructive impulses (like those in Jonas), it can contribute to spiritual fulfillment only after it has been purified in some way.

To understand the ways Dickens and his contemporaries dealt with the problems created by imagination, we can look at one last group of writers. The nineteenth-century writers I find most interesting and powerful are those who cannot be categorized simply as either idealists or anti-idealists. Though partly retaining Romantic idealism, they also feel doubts that lead them to make concessions to realism. They try to hold onto belief that imagination can lead them to the ideal by combining it with reason's awareness of imagination's dangers and limitations. This mid-century synthesis of idealism and realism, however, was precarious; before long writers could no longer reconcile the two. As the sense of reality's unidealness increased, the idealist imagination became increasingly embattled, forced to make more and more concessions to realism, to retreat into escapism, or to express disillusionment and even horror.

Victorians' disillusion seems to result mainly from the fact that they inherit the Romantic assumption that one should be able to find some ideal in reality, an assumption that people increasingly found incompatible with the unideal nature of the reality they saw around them. Many mid-Victorians, still comparatively idealist, try to overcome this difficulty by falling back on some version of religion that can allow them to hold onto belief even though they cannot find the ideal in reality. They console themselves with the assertion that the ideal must exist somewhere beyond this world, replacing the ideal they originally sought with a surrogate, which they endow with some of the qualities of the abandoned ideal. Thus they attempt to salvage belief by transferring it to an object beyond the reach of rational doubt, letting reason keep its concern with reality but making that concern irrelevant to their belief.

This act of giving up an earthly paradise for one beyond this world reenacts one of the basic patterns of Christianity, Adam's loss of Eden followed by Christ's offer of a paradise after death. I suspect that many Victorians are especially influenced by the ending of *Paradise Lost*; as Adam gives up paradise, they give up the Romantic hope for an ideal in reality, and like Adam they turn to the workaday world, but do so fortified by belief that the lost ideal can be regained in an afterlife. However, this solution involves a sense of loss, giving up the Romantic confidence that one can fully possess the ideal, can convince reason of its reality. They feel the need to give up that desire because they feel it leads to Byronic disillusion and resentment of reality. And to counter their sense of loss, they often try to make the substitute ideal they offer seem real after all; after giving up earthly desires, characters are often allowed earthly fulfillment, though in some purified form. Thus writers seek a compromise, simultaneously giving in to reality and holding onto idealism, trying to paper over the contradictions between the two.[35]

This process of giving up desire is often expressed as a transformation of imagination, freeing it from the desire to possess an ideal in this world and teaching it to serve a spiritual purpose instead. By locating the object beyond reality, one need not feel selfish and guilty for desiring it. This transformation resembles the process of dealing with Oedipal guilt by giving up the wish for actual possession of the desired object and replacing that with an object that is more acceptable because it combines desire with submission to a higher control. We can see imagination being refashioned like this already in *The Prelude*; imagination is "impaired" but then "restored," a lower, childish form of it replaced by a more spiritual form. The Victorians share Wordsworth's sense that imagination is weakened by one's awareness of reality, but they are less confident about how fully it can be restored and so are more likely to try to go beyond it, to seek some form of belief that they can see as higher than imagination. Yet what they present as rising above imagination often sounds more like a retreat. As a result, they are more likely to end up not with belief but merely with hope; if they cannot believe the ideal is real, they assert that some day they will be able to, deferring belief to somewhere beyond reason's reach. This is another strategy for shifting the ideal to a realm that seems real but is exempt from reality-testing.

The contradiction between idealism and realism reaches the surface, as I have mentioned, in Carlyle.[36] In Wordsworth that conflict is already implicit, but he still believes it is possible to fuse reason and imagination—to find a version of the ideal that, though reached through imagination, seems to exist in reality. But in *Sartor Resartus* the two seem increasingly opposed. He wants to overcome reason's conflict with imagination by reconciling the two— "Imagination, wedded to the clearest Intellect" (1:4). If "Fantasy" could be superadded "to sight," he could manage "a discerning of the Infinite in the Finite, of the Idea made Real" (2:5). Natural supernaturalism seeks to locate the supernatural—the divine—in the natural—reality. But though Carlyle asserts that he can reconcile reason with imagination, strong tensions remain. The very attempt to reconcile the two admits that they are opposed. Partly he tries to assert that this conflict does not matter and allows tension to remain. He also tries to make it seem his belief is not based on imagination by replacing imagination with another term, saying belief is based instead on the "heart" (for example, *Sartor*, book 2, chs. 7 and 9) and asserting that this is superior to imagination, which he disparages as mere "fancy," the debased form of imagination serving selfish desires that make us think we have a right to earthly happiness.

Like many later Victorians, Carlyle wants to see belief as higher than imagination or to translate imagination into a form that reason can take seriously. Our mere "imagining" can be blinded by dependence on the perceptual, and so should be replaced by "pure spiritual Meditation." But since this is in the "mind's eye" (book 3, ch. 8), it seems to be merely another version of imagination, put into more impressive terms in order to overcome reason's misgivings, appealing to belief in a higher plane of existence to obviate questions of reality. I think he is also trying to purify imagination of physical desires so that it will not arouse the guilt that causes reason to react against the imaginary. If we can see imagination as serving a power higher than reason, we can see it both as innocent and as beyond reason's doubts.

The tension between imagination and reason is especially strong in Emily Brontë. Despite her idealism, she shares the Victorian ambivalence about imagination.[37] *Wuthering Heights* expresses both an awareness of reality (the world in which we are mortal) and an unwillingness to give up imagination's vision of something higher; the awareness of death is in tension with a vision of life beyond death. Nelly and Lockwood speak for the rational side of the self, which cannot believe in imagination's visions; Lockwood, for example, is afraid of Catherine's ghost, seeing it as merely imaginary (a dream) and rejecting it. In contrast, Heathcliff, like imagination, tries to make her become real—that is, seeks to believe in the imaginary. The novel balances these two attitudes by offering two stories, one restricted to the physical world that reason perceives (the second Cathy and Hareton find fulfillment in that world) and one that goes beyond that reality, finding fulfillment on the transcendent level that imagination pictures. It is as if reason writes one version and imagination another version of the same story. Reason can accept one ending as realistic, not involving the supernatural; the other ending offers hope that imagination is right, that there is a life beyond death, even though that possibility lies beyond what reason can accept. Brontë is more willing than most writers to admit that she cannot reconcile the two and to accept uncertainty, like Keats. She values both the desire for an ideal and the acceptance of reality and does not try to pretend that they can coexist without conflict.

We can see a similar tension in the works of Charlotte Brontë, but she reacts against imagination more strongly than Emily, showing more awareness of the way reality is unideal and forcing herself to accept the absence of the ideal. Where Emily resents reason's control over imaginative idealism and yields to it only reluctantly, her sister seems to fear imagination's challenges to her self-restraint, her hard-won acceptance of reality, and though she cannot help sometimes giving way to imagination, she does so only under protest. She evidently feels that the desires that imagination indulges are too opposed to reality and probably guilty. She thus forces her protagonists to suppress their desires more than Emily does. Nevertheless, those desires remain quite passionate, often find expression through imagination, and, as in *Wuthering Heights*, seek some ideal form of fulfillment.[38]

Jane Eyre, for example, starts out, like the youthful Brontë, allowing imagination too much freedom, not accepting reality enough. Because her imagination is too uncontrolled, desiring the ideal and refusing to accept reality, she becomes rebellious and guilty and needs to restrain imagination, as Brontë taught herself to discipline her own Romanticism. But Brontë does not want to give up imagination and accept an unideal reality; like other Victorians, she hopes to transform imagination in order to create an ideal she can believe in. Rochester embodies the undisciplined imagination that Jane must learn to control so she can lead it to belief; her education of Rochester acts out the process of transforming imagination. To transform him, Jane must also transform herself, going through a process of self-sacrifice and suffering to purge herself of the excessive, selfish desires that threatened to take over her imagination (for example, 140; ch. 16). Once she has suffered enough, she can attain her version of the ideal, though a diminished ideal (Rochester is no longer the ideal Romantic hero he once seemed). Brontë seems to be expressing a belief that the ideal (if not wholly ideal) can exist in reality; and imagination (though it must be strictly restrained) has a part to play in reaching that belief.

In *Villette*, however, belief is no longer possible, and imagination's desire for the ideal remains opposed at the end to reason's sense of how unideal reality is. Reason and imagination remain in unresolved tension throughout the novel. Brontë seems to keep fighting her own imagination, preventing it from making the novel wish-fulfilling, and it seems to keep demanding expression despite her opposition, continually seeking an ideal and continually being denied by the work's reality. At the end, all Brontë can do is leave realism and the desire for the ideal in tension, implicitly admitting that she cannot reconcile them as she did at the end of *Jane Eyre*. She gives us a happy ending, but then reason steps in and says it is only imaginary.

Although this ending is more pessimistic and unresolved than in most Victorian fiction, it nevertheless uses a typical Victorian strategy. Brontë gives up trying to find the ideal in reality (that is, trying to convince reason), but only in order to salvage some version of belief by transferring the ideal to a plane safely beyond reality, holding onto a half-belief that imagination may ultimately prove right after all. Even though Paul is presumably dead, he is transferred to a plane of existence from which he can continue to inspire Lucy, giving her "a hope for the future," a hope that the ideal can eventually become real; that hope gives her "a motive for persevering" (594; ch. 42). That is, she holds onto some belief that the ideal may exist, though beyond reality, and that belief enables her to bear the unidealness of reality. Despite her realism, Brontë thus cannot help hoping for something more, for a "reprieve from the dead" (596; ch. 42), and I would add for a reprieve from spiritual doubt. She cannot actually believe in the imagined ideal, but she retains some hope that she may become able to.

Tennyson exhibits a similar conflict; he feels that imagination cannot lead to belief as the Romantics hoped, but, like the Brontës, because he cannot find a firmer basis for belief, he is unwilling to abandon imagination entirely.[39] This attitude is perhaps most explicit in "The Palace of Art," where he feels he must reject the paradise imagination has created. Imagination is too subservient to desire, creating a selfish version of the ideal, one that is too earthly. This arouses guilt that prevents him from fully believing in the imagined ideal; he sees it as artificial, set apart from reality. Yet Tennyson wishes at the end of the poem that he could return to imagination's paradise, which is like wishing he could regain belief in the imaginary.

We see him trying to resolve this problem most clearly in *In Memoriam*. He wants to overcome his sense that there is no ideal in reality, an absence represented for him by Hallam's death. That death is like the death of belief in the ideal, a belief he is trying to revive by translating it from a Romantic form—which tries to locate the ideal in reality—into a religious form. Since his sense that there is no ideal in reality keeps undermining belief, he turns to imagination. But it cannot create belief as it could for the Romantics; his "dream" cannot "resolve the doubt" (68:8; and see 94:10, 14 ff., and 49:6, 13). Like Carlyle and others, Tennyson tries to deal with this failure by replacing imagination with a higher kind of vision; but here again this vision still seems to be a form of imagination, though now transformed. The transformation culminates in poem 103, where imagination seems able to create a convincing "vision" (line 3), a dream in which he reaches what seems to be heaven, thus through imagination reaching something like belief in an afterlife. But because he has tried to base belief on imagination (122:4 ff.; 123:10), reason remains unconvinced and can only be set aside (120:6–7), leaving him like a child (124). He thus accepts that the ideal is merely imagined: "I dream a dream of good" (129:11). Admitting this, however, enables him partly to evade rational doubt, not seriously trying to win reason over. Thus imagination can have some success where a demand for serious belief—for full acceptance by reason—would fail. This unresolved tension and the continual effort to overcome it are the organizing principle of *In Memoriam*, the cause of its continual fluctuation between doubt and desire for belief.

Dickens resembles these uncertain idealists more than he resembles any of the other writers I have mentioned. They reveal a conflict that I think is basic in Victorian thought and important in Dickens—the conflict between the wish for belief in some ideal and the strong sense that reality opposes that belief, the sense Tennyson expresses, for example, when he talks about "Nature, red in tooth and claw" (*In Memoriam* 56:15). Just as *Wuthering Heights* is divided between two halves, one more visionary, the other more willing to accept the limitations of reality, so there is a tendency in Dickens, as I have already mentioned, to split his novels into more idealized and more realistic parts, a tendency most apparent in *Bleak House*. We could describe this combination of idealism and realism as an attempt to have one's cake and eat it too, simultaneously trying to believe in the reality of the ideal and admitting it is not real. Logically this may be untenable, but imagination has ways of cirumventing logic; I suspect it always tries to combine an illusion of reality with an evasion of reality-testing.

Similar divisions occur in other Victorian novels. *Vanity Fair* is divided between Amelia, whose idealizing imagination is felt to be inadequate by realistic reason, and Becky, whose anti-idealist rationalism is felt to be inadequate by the idealistic heart that wishes for some object of belief. In one part of the novel, Thackeray uses Becky to give reason's view of how unideal reality is, while in the other part he uses Amelia to express the imaginative desire for an ideal to believe in. Thackeray seems unable to reconcile these; his reason sees Amelia as foolish, but his idealism sees Becky as selfish and unfulfilling. *Middlemarch* and *Daniel Deronda* are similarly divided, the "realistic" stories of Lydgate and Gwendolen, stories that deny the ideal can be found in reality, contrasting with the more idealized stories of Dorothea and

Deronda, stories in which imagination tries to alter realism in order to offer some version of the ideal in this world, even if a diminished, secularized version. Like *Wuthering Heights,* these novels seek to keep idealism despite an opposing sense of reality by letting the two impulses coexist, though in unresolved conflict. As in Tennyson and Charlotte Brontë, the conflict between realism and the idealizing imagination forces the writer to become critical of imagination—to feel it is unrealistic.

In the following chapters I give many examples of a similar critical attitude in Dickens; even in a novel that endorses imagination as much as *Hard Times* does, as I argue, there is also a sense that imagination is weak. I also describe the way Dickens tries to overcome that weakness. Like these other writers, he tries to purify imagination, to raise it from a selfish form to a higher one. Such a process, which I believe we can see taking place in *In Memoriam,* is especially clear in *Jane Eyre.* Like several Dickens characters (especially David Copperfield), Jane disciplines her imagination by forcing herself to accept the fact that reality opposes her selfish desires. She (like analogous characters in Dickens) goes through a process resembling that in *Sartor Resartus:* she must first utter an Everlasting No, rejecting a false, selfish belief—a belief that the imagined ideal can exist in this world. She does this when she gives up Rochester. Once imagination has been purged of selfish desire and has made this concession to the sense of reality, Jane can move on to an Everlasting Yea, a new, chastened belief: she can have Rochester after all. We shall see how this kind of process works, and what else Dickens does to try to move from imagination to belief, in the chapters that follow.

chapter 4

The Development of Dickens's Imagination: The Early Novels

Dickens is arguably the best example of a Victorian writer committed to imaginative idealism yet also giving expression to the conflicts that idealism engenders. His work exhibits an especially strong conflict between Romantic idealism and a realistic attitude which sees the fictional world as quite unideal and which is concerned with making us feel that world's reality. On the one hand, as he puts it in a speech about watching a play, he values the chance to escape from "the real world" into a "fleeting fairyland"; but he also realizes that that fairyland is only imaginary and that one must return to one's awareness of this "cold" world.[1] He can neither give up the desire for an ideal nor escape the awareness of reality, so he can only let the two coexist. And in the area between them, attempting to find ways to resolve their conflict, lies imagination.

Like the other complex writers mentioned earlier, Dickens is seeking to use imagination to move away from realism to belief, but as in their works, that attempt creates problems. He sees reality as mainly opposed to the desire for an ideal, unlike the Romantics and their idealist-realist successors. But his sense of reality prevents him from simply escaping to a fairyland like the extreme idealist antirealists, and so he must seek to envision a version of the ideal in reality, despite his sense of how unideal reality is. Thus he must try to work out compromises that both accept reality to some extent and simultaneously use imagination to try to transform it. The tension between idealism and realism drives imagination to generate the complexities of his work. We can see those conflicts and his attempts to deal with them as the basis upon which he structures his mature novels. We can thus use his work to gain a fuller understanding of this complex process and how imagination functions in it. He uses imagination in particularly complex and interesting ways, and in my final chapter especially I examine his works to see how the tensions in the idealist concept of imagination find expression in the actual texture of literature, in the complex details through which imagination works.

Dickens also provides a good example of the way a concept of imagination can evolve. Perhaps because he started young, his writing reveals more growth than does the oeuvre of most writers; to the end of his life he remained willing to face conflicts in his thought and try new solutions to them. He began by largely accepting the mockery of imagination one finds in eighteenth-century imitators of *Don Quixote*. He did not take imagination very seriously and so tended to express it in playful ways, often through comic characters, in the form Coleridge would call fancy. (Dickens uses the two terms interchangeably, though like most of his contemporaries he tends to use the word *fancy* for less serious forms of imagination.) In his later work he becomes increasingly concerned with using imagination seriously.

As his need grew for some sense of spiritual meaning, he turned to imagination not simply for a playful escape from reality but for a transformation of reality, trying to give reality meaning and to find some version of the ideal in it.[2] For example, he moves from an emphasis on metaphor to an increased concern with symbols. In his earliest work he laughs at the contrast between the real and the imaginary, but later he tries to deal seriously with the way reality opposes imagination's desire for an ideal. He does not wholly overcome his earlier feeling that the imaginary is merely fictional, not able to alter reality. But he comes to feel that reality and realism are a threat to imaginative idealism, and in reaction he values imagination more. Yet like many other Victorians he feels forced to make increasing, if grudging, concessions to realism. Like other comparatively antirealistic writers, however, he responds to his sense of the unidealness of reality not by giving up idealism but rather by seeking ways to salvage it, to modify it so that it can withstand his doubts. And in that modification he still finds an important role for imagination to play.

Imagination and the sense of reality thus remain in conflict for Dickens as for the other writers I have been discussing. He imagines an ideal—usually an idealized parent-child relationship—but at the same time he remains aware of a reality that he sees as strongly opposed to that ideal. These imaginative and realistic visions interact. Imagination transforms reality so that we see it not merely as neutral but rather as something actively opposing imagination's desires and therefore grotesque or frightening. And his sense of reality also reacts on the imagined ideal, seeing it as unrealistic. His version of the ideal is less convincingly a part of reality than in, say, Wordsworth; rather it is set in opposition to what his novels present as reality. An idealized heroine like Little Nell is shown as too good for her world; his idealized homes are set apart, refuges from the outer world. He thus intensifies the contrast betwen an anti-ideal reality and an antireal ideal. But unlike a simple antirealist, he tries to work out a balance between these two. The strong conflict between them is caused by the intensity of his effort to find some way of reconciling them; it is because he tries to put the ideal into the real— putting a heroine like Nell into a grotesque "reality"—that he causes each of these to oppose the other. And it is his very attempt to face reality that causes imagination to react against it, envisioning an ideal with which to oppose reality. His novels thus become battlefields on which realism and antirealism fight for supremacy.

This attempt to reconcile the imagined ideal with a sense of reality, here as in other writers, represents an attempt to create belief—to get reason to believe the ideal is real. The nature of the belief Dickens seeks is not very clear; he values not some explicit set of beliefs but rather the state of mind (he would say heart) in which one can believe in some ideal, no matter what. This vagueness about what the object of belief should be is common among Victorian writers; they wish for belief even though they do not quite know what to believe in. But like other Victorians, Dickens does not let this vagueness daunt him; whatever his doubts, he continues to value the search for belief, making it central in most of his novels.

In his early works Dickens is not yet very self-conscious and does not talk about imagination much. He seems unaware of the conflict between comparatively realistic elements in his work and unrealistic elements derived from such sources as melodrama, romance, fairy tale, traditional comedy— forms that influenced the shape his private fantasies took, combining with those fantasies in distinctive ways. These disparate elements coexist in Dickens's early fiction without much indication that he feels a need to reconcile them. His early statements on imagination are fairly conventional, like many of the other elements he was beginning to absorb into his work, and consequently do not seem consonant with what he is doing in other areas.

If we look, however, at what Dickens does with imagination in *Pickwick*, we can see him beginning to work out his ideas on how to use it. Pickwick begins the novel by feeling the inadequacy of reality; he is not "content with examining the things that lie before" him and does not want to "gaze on Goswell Street for ever" but rather hopes "to penetrate to the hidden countries" beyond (73; ch. 2). At first Dickens sees this quest—which we can see as a parodic version of the quest for the ideal—as comic. He began the novel with the conventional intention of mocking imagination as do his eighteenth-century models; he conceived of Pickwick as a Quixote, led into various contretemps by imagining that things are different from what they really are. But this passage is prophetic; as the novel progresses (and indeed throughout Dickens's career), the question of whether there is anything better than Goswell Street becomes less and less a laughing matter. Dickens came to feel how unfulfilling reality is (and for Dickens reality usually means the city) and how much it threatens idealism (a discovery Pickwick makes in prison). As a result, he no longer laughs at idealism's failures, and Pickwick's imaginative idealism no longer seems foolish.

I think his imagination seeks a more serious, full, and idealist expression than Dickens has originally allowed it because there are strong desires seeking an outlet through it. The strongest, most basic desire driving his fiction, which begins coming to consciousness during the writing of *Pickwick*, is the desire for loving parents able to provide a stable home (like Dingley Dell), parents in whom he can believe, free of resentment.[3] The ideal he imagines is usually an idealized parent of this sort and an idealized child (often a daughter) able to win the love of such a parent. He comes to see his version of reality, the city, as more and more opposed to that ideal, probably because he associates it with the slum streets to which his parents abandoned him in his childhood; it is that unhappy childhood that his idealized home evidently seeks to cancel out or compensate for.

We can see his attitude toward imagination changing in his treatment of Sam Weller. As Garrett Stewart says, Sam is mainly an agent of imagination.[4] However, I think that is an oversimplification. As long as Dickens mocks Pickwick and imagination, he uses Sam primarily as the voice of reason, telling Pickwick what reality is actually like and correcting his naive idealization of it. But as Dickens increasingly accepts a desire like Pickwick's for an ideal, he gives imagination greater expression in Sam. This acceptance of idealization is related to the need for a good parent; Dickens and Sam accept Pickwick because they want a father to believe in. At the same time that Dickens gives Sam an ability to make fictions, he creates a fiction for Sam, imagining for him the good father (Pickwick) he lacks in his "reality." We increasingly see Pickwick not as a fool but as an idealized father figure, and we thus see Sam as a surrogate son, and one who like Dickens replaces his actual, ineffectual father with an imagined ideal. Sam becomes the subject of imaginative desire, and Pickwick becomes the object of that desire.

Dickens can ally Sam with imagination because he has given him some capacity for imagination from the start; Sam is never merely a perceiver of reality but joins to his realism an ability to make reality more bearable by imaginatively transforming it. Unlike Pickwick and like Dickens, Sam expresses awareness that he is using imagination, that what he is creating is playful; thus he can use imagination without being deluded by it. The main way he uses imagination is to create fictional characters, comic alter egos to whom he can attribute his utterances—precisely what Dickens himself does. By transferring imagination to such characters, Sam distances himself from it and doesn't fully accept it, so that he can balance it with his awareness of reality. At the same time, by replacing reality with fictions, Sam (again like Dickens) can keep from taking reality too seriously.

Dickens's increasing acceptance of imagination is also reflected in the interpolated tales. Early in the novel the main form in which he allows imagination expression is through these tales, thus segregating it from his main story, where imagination is mistrusted.[5] Evidently he is somewhat attracted to it and wants to give it an outlet but does not trust it enough to give it too much expression in the main story. Even in the tales he is still rather critical of it, as he is critical of Pickwick's imagination. "The Madman's Tale" shows how "realities" become "distorted" by a "diseased imagination" (220–26; ch. 11), just as the Pickwickians, in this same chapter, are unable to perceive reality clearly when they misinterpret Bill Stumps's mark. (Later Dickens is more sympathetic toward delusions.) We take imagination less seriously in these tales because it has been cut off from the work's reality.

But if Dickens has not yet worked out a way of integrating imagination with his sense of reality so that it can enter into his fictional world and act in the main story, he can nevertheless take advantage of the fact that imagination is less serious when thus segregated from reason. Because it is set apart, it is not threatening, and so he can let it take on more uncontrolled, rebellious, grotesque forms. In contrast, his later novels express this dark side of imagination in their main plots, locating such rebellious impulses in villains upon whom the story can act so that Dickens can reconcile imagination with the idealized control in which his central plots try to make us believe.

In the later interpolated tales Dickens begins to accept imagination more, evidently because (as with Sam) he has learned how to use it in a more playful way. "The Bagman's Story" takes pleasure in the way Tom Smart's "imagination" creates an "illusion" and asks us half seriously to "believe" in that illusion (259–73; ch. 14). In "The Madman's Tale" Dickens rejected imagination because it demanded a total belief, which reason could not give; but if (like Sam) imagination is willing to compromise, asking only for a playful half-belief, we can accept its visions. Similarly, we can accept Pickwick's belief in the ideal because Dickens (like Sam) does not take it too seriously. Belief can coexist with a more realistic awareness because he disarms reason by implicitly admitting the ideal is only imaginary.

We can see Dickens beginning to combine imagination with a more realistic attitude (as he does in his later fiction) in "The Old Man's Tale about the

Queer Client," when the old man talks about how "romance" can be found in the "common-place" (361; ch. 21). We can also see this acceptance of imagination in "The Story of the Goblins Who Stole a Sexton." The goblin is "fantastic" (483; ch. 29), admittedly imaginary and playful, and because imagination is thus not taken too seriously, reason can accept it. Whereas Dickens began the novel by accepting the opposition of imagination and reality, he is now using imagination to challenge realism as the goblin challenges Gabriel Grub's skepticism. Like imagination, the goblin shows Gabriel "pictures," and these lead him to believe in "a bright and happy Heaven" (487–88; ch. 29). Dickens has tamed imagination; it is no longer uncontrolled and frightening, and so it can lead to belief. Once he has done this, he no longer needs to segregate it in separate tales; imagination can now interact with reality by overcoming reality's unidealness. Thus in the later part of *Pickwick*, he abandons those tales and instead expresses imagination through Sam and Pickwick, through whom it can lead to a more serious belief than it can in a goblin tale.

The prison scene also shows how Dickens's attitude toward imagination is changing. The novel begins by showing how reality defeats Pickwick and the idealist imagination, but by the end Pickwick and imagination triumph over reality. When Dickens puts Pickwick in jail, it is not to disillusion him but rather to act out idealism's confrontation of reality, proving that Pickwick can keep his idealism despite this exposure to reality—and probably also to prove to Dickens himself that his imagination can rescue Pickwick from falling into the condition his real father fell into, can keep belief in an ideal father despite reality. He is no longer mocking Pickwick and the ability to imagine an ideal because he needs that ability in order to deal with his sense of reality.

This sense of imagination's strength also finds expression in Sam's strength, his ability to ward off reality—to face it without losing belief in an ideal, as Pickwick does in prison. It is because imagination is so strong and idealistic in this novel, apparently, that the good father Dickens imagines here (Pickwick) can be quite idealized, not as disabled as Dickens's later father figures are by reason's doubts about such an ideal. By allowing Pickwick to triumph, Dickens seems to be forcing realist reason to give in to imagination. He presumably wants to overcome his awareness of reality because that awareness includes his knowledge of his own father's imprisonment and thus works against his believing in his father. In his fiction he can reverse that situation, imagining an ideal that can withstand reality, just as Sam's imaginative play can resist the pressures of his world.

Instead of mocking idealism in the later parts of *Pickwick*, Dickens embodies cynical, anti-idealist realism in Jingle so that he can reject that attitude and allow Pickwick's idealism to overcome it, as the goblin converts Gabriel Grub. Dickens began by mocking idealism as Jingle does, so he is using Jingle's conversion to reject his own unbelief. Though Jingle exhibits an imaginative playfulness like Sam's, he shows that when imagination does not serve idealism, it can be taken over by rebellious, potentially guilty impulses. Jingle rejects idealism, seeing Pickwick as a fool. There is some potential rebelliousness like Jingle's in Sam's imagination; he mocks his father, as Dickens (and Jingle) initially mock Pickwick. In Dickens's later novels this tendency to resent parent figures becomes a serious problem, and so it becomes harder to reconcile imaginative play with belief in a higher power; but here imagination remains playful enough so that Dickens does not feel a need to purify it as much as he does later. By replacing Jingle with Sam as the main comic character, Dickens replaces rebelliousness with Sam's playful ability to keep such irreverent impulses from becoming too strong, his ability to accept reality in a way that is not so serious it will destroy belief in an ideal. Like Dickens, Sam uses imagination to transfer rebellious, skeptical impulses to fictional characters, thus expressing those impulses in a merely playful form, distancing them. And when other characters threaten Pickwick, Sam can also reduce them to the comic, thus protecting Pickwick's idealism. Dickens values Sam's imaginative playfulness, then, because it offers a defense against impulses that threaten belief.

Thus Dickens makes imagination serve belief, as Sam serves Pickwick, not mocking but accepting the ideal. We can see Sam's capacity for belief—though in a diminished, comic form—when he imagines "some other world" (811; ch. 51), an afterlife for donkeys, and when he sees Pickwick as an "angel in tights and gaiters" (734; ch. 45). Putting an angel into gaiters is a way of trying to locate the ideal in reality, to make it convincingly real, but this also represents a compromise with the sense of reality, a willingness to accept a diminution of the ideal, combining belief with a diminished version of mockery like Jingle's. Sam embodies imagination's ability to compromise like this, balancing realism with belief in an ideal (unlike Pickwick, who is too idealistic for this world). Dickens is using this compromise to reconcile imagination with rational doubt; imagination wants to envision the ideal—an angel—but realism modifies that by putting gaiters on it. We do not take an angel wearing gaiters as seriously as a full-blown specimen.

By keeping the ideal playful in this way, making concessions to realism, Sam (and the imagination he speaks for) can evade rational doubt and create at least a diminished belief. Similarly, Sam teaches Pickwick to accept reality not in order to destroy Pickwick's idealism but to save it (though probably this was not Dickens's original intention), modifying that idealism so that reason can accept it. But though Pickwick needs Sam, Sam needs Pickwick too, and it is Pickwick who is the master, as Dickens wants belief to control imagination. Dickens even comes to value Pickwick's lack of realism, seeing it as a childlike innocence that protects him from the awareness that would threaten belief, enabling him to remain exempt from the dangers of reality. Yet by protecting Pickwick, Dickens is tacitly admitting he cannot fully reconcile belief with his sense of reality.

We should not, however, see the union of Sam with Pickwick as a total resolution of imagination with idealism. Though Sam serves Pickwick, he retains some mischievous independence—some diminished irreverence, implying that there are impulses in imagination that resist complete belief and submission. If Sam were no more than an idealist, he would stop being funny; and if Dickens's fiction were totally idealist, there would be no room left in it for imaginative play like Sam's. The two impulses can coexist here, but they remain somewhat separate, even potentially in conflict, and this tension continues to affect Dickens's later novels.

Dickens is moving here as he was to do throughout his career, from imagination as something merely playful to a more serious use of it, able to see beyond Goswell Street and envision an ideal. We can see this in his idealization of Dingley Dell, with its ideal family reunited in "pure and unalloyed delight" that is "incompatible with the cares and sorrows of the world," an ideal whose attainment induces something like "religious belief," a belief in something better than reality. Because he cannot escape a sense of the world's sorrows, he cannot fully believe in this vision of the ideal; rather he must at least partly see it as imaginary—one of "the delusions of our childish days" (458; ch. 28). But if imagination cannot compel complete belief, it still largely overcomes the sense of an unideal reality; the cares of the world may be real, but they are not at Dingley Dell—that is, not in the realm of imagination. We can see imagination similarly defying reality at the novel's end. Dickens pictures Pickwick in "unmixed happiness," the "sunshine of the world . . . blazing full upon" him. At the same time he admits that sunshine is "brief," that "There are some dark shadows on the earth," and thus that this idealized picture is "visionary." But he defies this awareness, saying that earth's "lights are stronger in the contrast" and that he prefers to look at "the light" (896; ch. 57). Dickens is asserting that he believes in the ideal despite reason's awareness of an unideal reality, since that reality merely makes the ideal more desirable.

In Dickens's later works the darkness threatens that vision more seriously and cannot be so easily defied, but perhaps all of his novels are striving for this same vision of the light, trying to overcome disillusionment. His later novels continue to act out, though in increasingly conscious, serious ways, the pattern he discovers here: reality seeks to disillusion idealism (as with Pickwick in prison) and imagination helps idealism fight off that disillusionment.[6] Here, however, Dickens is able, through Sam, to harmonize realism and imagination with an ease that is not possible for him later on. Perhaps he can do so because he does not take either too seriously yet. He continues to use the comic parts of his fiction as he does here, to make his idealizations more acceptable, but later on imaginative play and idealization are in greater conflict, not as easy to reconcile as Pickwick and Sam.

We can see *Nicholas Nickleby* as continuing this process of working out a relationship between realism and imagination. Here as in *Pickwick* Dickens begins by expressing mistrust of imagination. He mocks "imagination" in various foolish characters: Mrs. Nickleby's "imagination" gives her foolish "visions" of social success (342; ch. 27); Mr. Mantalini's "imagination" is equally selfish (124; ch. 10); and "imagination" is parodied in Romantic poseurs like Mrs. Wititterly (353; ch. 27) and Curdle (311; ch. 24). But *Pickwick* has taught Dickens that characters who are misled by imagination can be entertaining, and he is less concerned with condemning them than with enjoying their delusions, the escape from reality they offer. He asks us to enjoy Mantalini's "playfulness" (124; ch. 10) more than condemn him. He is continuing the movement toward accepting imagination that began in *Pickwick*. Thus he also locates imagination in more sympathetic characters like Newman Noggs, whose "imagination" may make him comically forgetful of what is "real," but who is also "warm," generous, and opposed to the villains (373, 420; chs. 28 and 33). In other words, Dickens mocks imagination for being unrealistic but feels it can also foster idealism (implied by Newman's wishing to fight villains who oppose attainment of the ideal).

We can see Dickens's sympathy with imagination in his treatment of Crummles's theatrical troupe. They offer the pleasure of imaginative role-playing, temporarily replacing the story's serious conflict with a comically unrealistic version of it, and they offer Nicholas a refuge, as imagination offers some escape from a serious concern with reality. But they also imply Dickens's sense of the limitations of imagination. They can help Nicholas only temporarily; he must go beyond play-acting, as Dickens seems to feel the need to go beyond imagination, at least when it is playful like this. Like imagination, they can only offer Nicholas a substitute for reality; they cannot help him deal with the outer world. And their play-acting is unrealistic (300 ff.; ch. 24), suggesting that imagination cannot compel belief. The escape imagination offers is combined with an awareness that it is only imaginary. As Dickens puts it, "Dreams" are "bright creatures," but they "melt away," leaving us facing "stern reality" (146; ch. 13). He mainly thinks of imagination as something childish, not to be taken seriously, as in Crummles's plays. Yet Dickens is relatively content to enjoy the imaginary here for the playful pleasure it gives, not worrying about its conflict with realism but allowing the two to coexist.

His sympathy with imagination is clearest in the conflict between Nicholas and Ralph. Whatever his misgivings about imagination, Dickens finds it much more valuable than Ralph's narrow concern with "fact" and intolerance of "romance" and "fancies" (594, 764; chs. 45 and 59). Just as imagination has helped make Newman an idealist, its absence has made Ralph a selfish materialist. And at the end Ralph is driven to suicide by the "imagination" (802; ch. 62) he has tried to deny in himself. While he locates realism in his villain, Dickens endows his protagonist with a "sanguine imagination" that gives him "visionary ideas" (41, 27; chs. 4 and 3) of being a romance hero. Though Nicholas, like Pickwick, is shown to be partly deluded in these visions, Dickens also values them.

Nicholas must learn to reconcile his imagination with reality (as Sam Weller has) so it is not delusive. He goes through a process of education similar to what happens in later Dickens novels, though it is less serious here and rather perfunctory. The theatrical troupe, for example, teaches him the difference between playing the hero and actually being a hero. Once his imagination has been made unselfish through his sufferings, it is what leads him to idealism and a capacity for love that are impossible for Ralph. Nicholas's "warm and active imagination" enables him to have "a vision" of the ideal, as embodied (all too conventionally) in Madeline (519; ch. 40). At first he is too "sentimental" (519; ch. 40), like the Romantic poseurs or a play-actor. To become worthy of Madeline, he must transform imagination, making it serious and changing his "passion" into "reverence," a belief in the "purity" of the ideal. He makes this transformation by seeing her as "far above his reach" (635; ch. 48), giving up the selfish desire to possess the ideal. Dickens rescues the ideal from the sense that it is unreal by locating it on a level where the question of reality no longer applies, setting aside the rational concern with reality. At the end, imagination has been transformed so that it now has a spiritual function: it can give Smike "dreams" of heaven (762–63; ch. 58). It has been raised to a higher level, where (Dickens hopes) it can overcome the sense of reality, as Nicholas ultimately overcomes the realist Ralph.

In *Oliver Twist*, though he is less concerned explicitly with imagination, Dickens begins to alter his narrative stance in a way that was to have a strong effect on the way he expressed imagination, allowing him to channel it more through his narration itself rather than having to rely almost entirely on his characters. Locating imaginative desire in characters distances it and thus lets us take it less seriously. In *Twist* Dickens rediscovers the child in himself; he begins to learn how to assume a childlike persona, altering the way he looks at the fictional world.[7] This enables him to get at strong desires (and equally important, the reflex of those desires, strong fears) like those a child feels, less restrained and rational than in an adult. He is able to get more direct access to the desire that he found most powerful, the one that typically impels his plots—the child's desire for parental love. Because that desire is so strong and irrational, it has a strong effect on his imagination. Insofar as he is able to see the world as a child, full of desires and fears, would see it, he can distort that world, as he does in *Twist*, into dreamlike—often nightmarish—forms. He puts himself into a childlike state of mind in which he can allow imagination to color his sense of reality.

At one point in *Twist* Dickens describes such a dreamlike state, in which "reality and imagination become so strangely blended" that we cannot separate them, and our perception of reality becomes assimilated to "our visions" (216; ch. 34). Thus, for example, he here presents Fagin as both real and dreamlike. Fear influences the imagination by making it see as evil whatever opposes the protagonist's desires. By allowing this imaginative influence, Dickens can create characters more frightening and villainous than in *Pickwick*—characters who are seen as if by a child, a child who wishes for loving parents and therefore sees the reality that denies that wish as negative, even terrifying.

Dickens can also allow desire to influence imagination so that it idealizes the protagonist and what he desires. He is building on what he learned to do in *Pickwick*, using imagination to envision an ideal. More directly than in *Pickwick*, however, he is locating that ideal in a "reality" with which it interacts, showing how his embodiment of childlike purity, Oliver, is threatened by a world that opposes him and the desire for an ideal he represents. Thus the conflict between Oliver and the city works out the interaction between Dickens's wish to believe in an ideal and his sense that reality opposes that belief. And here again imagination overcomes realism by envisioning idealism (in Oliver) overcoming reality. Imagination creates an idealized home to fulfill the desires expressed through Oliver, and it pictures that ideal world replacing the negative one that opposed Oliver's desires.

In *The Old Curiosity Shop* Dickens returns to this conflict, creating another innocent child embodying the ideal—Little Nell—and surrounding her with a grotesque version of reality that exists to oppose her and thus to threaten belief in the ideal. But in this novel, as in *Twist*, Dickens is moving toward increased seriousness, and here for the first time it becomes evident that his seriousness arises from spiritual concerns. These concerns were apparently influenced by the death of Mary Hogarth, on whom Nell is based. Her death evidently made Dickens feel something like what Hallam's death made Tennyson feel, doubts about an afterlife and divine justice, which impelled him to seek ways to reaffirm faith. This spiritual desire from here on supplements and modifies his desire for ideal earthly parents, offering a way to believe in an ideal that is not contradicted by reality (as Nell desires her grandfather to be like an ideal father but must finally accept that the only ideal father can be in heaven). We can see him associating Mary with religious belief in a dream in which he asked her, "What is the True Religion?" In other words, he acted out the process of seeking belief through imagination, imagining (in a dream) an object and asking that object to give him belief. But because it was only a dream, he ended up (like Keats at the end of "Ode to a Nightingale") wondering whether he "should regard it as a dream, or an actual Vision."[8] I think Dickens does something very similar with Nell; he creates an imaginary version of this idealized person in order to try to obtain belief from that act of imagining. By making Nell confront death, he is using her to seek belief in an afterlife.

Because Dickens is seeking more serious belief here, more directly confronting his sense of how reality (especially death) opposes belief, he is asking more of imagination and causing doubts and conflicts that his earlier playfulness could evade. His attempt to make imagination serve a more serious function, since it insists on an ideal and thus opposes reality so strongly, ends up preventing complete belief. He has made Nell too good for this world, asking for more than his sense of reality can accept, and so he cannot reconcile the wish for belief with that sense of reality. He tries to reconcile them by locating his ideal beyond this world, but this leaves his sense of reality's unidealness intact and strongly in conflict with his wish for an ideal.

Nell is presented at the start as an "image" in the narrator's "imagination, surrounded and beset by everything that was foreign to its nature" (13; ch. 1). We can see in this image of Nell beset by an alien reality how imagination's attempt to envision the ideal calls into existence a sense that reality is foreign and opposes that ideal, polarizing the imagined world, dividing it into what is for and what is against desire and seeing whatever opposes desire as threatening (besetting Nell). Dickens seems to have tried to idealize her by removing from her any impulses that would oppose belief in that idealization, but as a result those impulses found imaginative expression in the world around her. And because he has separated them from Nell, they oppose her more fully; the purer and more ideal he makes Nell, the more anti-ideal her world seems, the more grotesque and villainous the characters around her. Making Nell innocent and sexless, for example, evidently causes him to make Quilp lustful and guilty in reaction. Dickens's sense of reality keeps trying to destroy his belief in an ideal by insisting that reality is grotesque, highly unideal, and able to destroy the ideal.

As when he puts Pickwick in jail and Oliver in Fagin's, Dickens puts Nell into this world hoping to show how the ideal can resist those impulses that oppose belief. Nell inhabits "cruel reality" because she embodies Dickens's attempt to find a belief that can deal with that reality. She is an expression of imagination's attempt to reject reality, seeing reality as negative because imagination wishes to rise above it as Nell seeks a better world. Dickens probably emphasizes how unideal the world is to make the ideal seem more desirable, making us sympathize with Nell's quest. However, Nell's story implies that Dickens cannot believe in any ideal in reality; he can find no fulfillment good enough for her and can only offer her a paradise after death. She finds an idealized rural sanctuary like Dingley Dell, but Dickens can no longer consider such an imagined ideal as convincing, a place where she can stay.

We can see Dickens's uncertainty in a passage in which he tries to base belief on imagination, overcoming the sense of reality. He is describing the thoughts of the bachelor, one of the idealized (and hence rather unconvincing) father figures Nell finds—thoughts about tombs in the church, and thus about religion as a way of dealing with the idea of mortality: "he was not one of those rough spirits who would strip fair Truth of every little shadowy vestment in which . . . teeming fancies love to array her" since these "airy shrines" appeal to "the human heart" even though rationalists question what he believes (400; ch. 54). Imagination is here closely allied to belief, but though this linking idealizes imagination, it weakens belief. Dickens is admitting that belief is separate from truth and may require one to defy reason's doubts rather than answer them. Thus, even in the most idealist part of the novel, complete belief is impossible.

In response to Nell's death—her failure to overcome reality—Dickens does the opposite of what he does in his later fiction: he retreats from this serious use of imagination to the playfulness of his earlier work. He gives up Nell and falls back on Dick Swiveller, who, like Sam Weller, embodies imagination that does not demand serious belief but is content to accept its own limitations and remain playful, thus coexisting easily with a sense of reality.[9] Through Nell, Dickens attempts to overcome reality and thus sees it as strongly opposing belief, but through Dick, he merely wants to evade reality, and thus Dick need not feel reality is so strongly opposed to him. Dick can balance a partial belief with a partial acceptance of reality because neither is serious. And it is his imaginative ability to transform reality into something unserious that enables this. Dick is "poetical," able to create a "pleasant fiction," a "flight of fancy" that can appeal to the "imagination," and able to "defy suspicion," reason's sense of what is "real"; he can use imagination to create a kind of "faith," even though we must simultaneously accept that that "creed" is only a "deception," requiring that one "reject all . . . reason, observation, and experience" (53–54; ch. 7).

Dick's ability to overcome reality in play is dramatized in the partial fulfillment he reaches; he uses imagination to transform the Marchioness, giving her her name and turning her into a playful version of a romance heroine with whom he can have a playful version of fulfillment. This playful version of belief that imagination offers is exemplified when the Marchioness says, "If you make believe very much," you can get a kind of fulfillment from an unideal reality—can even get pleasure from orange peel and water (481; ch. 64). She is a worthy mate for Dick because she can play at the same kind of make-believe as he does. As she makes orange peel seem fulfilling, he uses imagination to transform her into a fulfilling mate—and Dickens makes this come true (since Dickens too is playing at imagining fulfillment). Because Dick doesn't demand a serious ideal as Nell does, because he can settle for less, Dickens can allow him fulfillment, though in this diminished, childlike form. The Marchioness is the best substitute he can find for Nell and a serious ideal. (There is a similar, though less interesting, use of Kit Nubbles; he too is given a diminished fulfillment to console us for Nell's death.)

Dick's willingness to let realism and belief coexist, to admit with one side of his mind the reality of what the other side pretends to reject, exemplifies the difference between imagination and belief. Where belief, as in Nell's case, tries to convince reason, imagination, as in Dick's case, is satisfied with temporarily and playfully setting reason aside. Similarly, Dickens himself tries to get us to believe temporarily in something that we and he know is not real, for the pleasure that we, like Dick, can get from pseudo-belief in a "pleasant fiction." Yet Dickens seems less confident here than in Sam Weller's case that he can balance imagination and reality, seems more aware that imagination is only playful and that reality opposes its desires. Dick is weaker, more threatened by his world than Sam is, though still freer than similar characters in later Dickens novels. Whereas Sam (and Dickens's imagination) can save Pickwick, neither Dick nor Dickens can save Nell; imagination cannot overcome his sense of reality. The death of Mary Hogarth has evidently made Dickens more conscious that there are things in this world that one cannot overcome.

The conflict between imagination and the sense of reality creates a division in the novel; Dick and Nell live in separate worlds. In his world imagination can deal with reality; in hers, imagination, seeking serious belief, cannot overcome the sense that in reality we must die. This split between a wish that imagination could overcome reality and a sense that reality resists our wishes is embodied in the contrast between Codlin and Short. Codlin the materialist is "doomed to contemplate the harsh realities of existence" and cannot believe in the puppets, whereas Short can have a kind of belief in an imaginative creation (the puppet show) and see Punch as able to "triumph over the enemy of mankind" (130; ch. 17). Dickens would presumably like to integrate these attitudes, but they remain opposed here.

The two parts of the novel become increasingly separate as it progresses. At first Nell's world occasionally touches the one that Quilp and Dick inhabit, and with the puppet show and waxworks she is in contact with the realm of imagination. But as Dickens uses her more seriously to confront spiritual matters, he insulates her more and more from those areas of the novel that could undermine that seriousness. Dickens has not yet found a way to integrate the playful imagination of his earliest work with the more serious use of imagination, seeking belief, toward which he is now moving.

Yet despite his sense that imagination is in conflict with belief, he values it because it offers him a middle ground between Quilp and Nell—between complete belief and none at all, complete submission and total rebellion against control. Imagination as expressed through Dick is a compromise between these extremes, combining some belief with some acceptance of reality, some rebelliousness with some restraint so that the rebellion stays merely playful.[10] Whereas in the characterization of Nell, Dickens cannot allow expression to any Quilplike energy, in Dick's case he can find an outlet for irreverent, sexual, anarchic energy like Quilp's, but in a safely diminished, childlike form.

The compromise Dick offers, however, is not the reconciliation of reason and belief; rather, it is a willingness to let them exist in unresolved tension, as the two parts of the novel coexist. In his later fiction Dickens can no longer remain unbothered (like Dick) by the fact that the imaginary is not real; he feels a greater need to try to resolve this tension. Here already he is pulled between enjoying imagination for the relief it offers from realism in Dick's half of the novel and wishing in Nell's half that he could convert it into a form he could seriously believe in.

In *Martin Chuzzlewit* Dickens continues his tendency to take the concerns associated with imagination more seriously. In this novel he begins trying to find a way of dealing with the conflicts we have seen in *The Old Curiosity Shop*, though he is not yet very successful. The novel is mainly concerned with belief in the heart's natural goodness, one of Dickens's central concerns. His trip to America showed him that when men are allowed to be free and natural, they do not exhibit the innate goodness that his Romantic idealism had led him to expect.[11] Perhaps America was his heart of darkness; it did not destroy his idealism as Africa did Conrad's, but like Mary Hogarth's death it posed a serious challenge to his beliefs, forcing him to take more seriously the conflict between reality and what he wanted to believe in. He is no longer so confident about the mind's goodness; instead, in this novel he is more conscious of dangerous forces within the mind, forces that can pervert imagination. Perhaps he feared his own doubts and guilty impulses. Whereas in earlier novels he sees the misuse of imagination as mainly comic, here it is dangerous, allowing expression to dark forces in the psyche.[12] Pecksniff, for example, claims to be an "imaginative" idealist (391; ch. 20) like Tom Pinch (and like the Romantic poseurs in *Nickleby*), but unlike Tom he merely pretends to believe in imagination's "visions" (142; ch. 6), trying to trick others (especially Tom) into believing unselfishly in an ideal so he can selfishly exploit their belief. Dickens does give Pecksniff some "fancy" (540; ch. 30), but instead of simply enjoying his playfulness as with Swiveller, Dickens now sees such pretense as a dangerous perversion of idealism and makes Pecksniff a largely villainous character.

Dickens evidently no longer feels that imagination is naturally good but rather that it needs to be controlled by some higher belief. He embodies the absence of that belief in Pecksniff and his kinsmen, the Chuzzlewits, to whom he bears a family resemblance and who seem to represent fallen social man, corrupted by selfishness. Old Martin Chuzzlewit, for example, has lost faith in human goodness, as I think Dickens was afraid he himself might. Like Pecksniff, the Chuzzlewits have "no faith" (107; ch. 4), a failing that extends to their materialist follower Tigg Montague (157; ch. 7). Anthony Chuzzlewit believes only in money, and his son Jonas shows how this lack of spiritual belief can destroy the soul. Dickens uses the characterization of Jonas Chuzzlewit to show that without such belief imagination can be taken over by guilty, destructive forces. As Dickens puts it in discussing old Martin, "fancies" can become "sick" (82; ch. 3). Jonas's "fancy" especially is taken over by uncontrolled, guilty impulses (853; ch. 51) that give him a nightmare (798; ch. 51). Several other characters have nightmares also (436; ch. 22; 462; ch. 24; 481; ch. 25; 727; ch. 42). Even Mrs. Gamp shows how imagination can become selfish. Her playfulness lacks Sam Weller's innocence; though attractive, it is also deluded and self-serving.

Dickens dramatizes the dangers of imagination in the story of young Martin, who shares the family failing of selfishness, as if infected by his grandfather and Pecksniff. Perhaps Jonas is meant to show us what their teaching might have turned Martin into; inadequate father figures could have led him too to hate paternal control and give way to Oedipal rebellion. Dickens, however, keeps him safely insulated from Jonas's world and keeps his rebelliousness from becoming very serious. Yet Dickens dares suggest that his protagonist could fall prey to the same forces that have corrupted the rest of the family. Where Nicholas Nickleby was guilty of nothing worse than falling into delusion like Pickwick, Dickens is now for the first time willing to entertain the possibility that dark, selfish impulses can exist in his main character, his representative of what he feels himself to be or what he wishes or fears to be. The forces threatening the mind can no longer be kept at a safe distance, in minor characters. They affect Martin's imagination. He exhibits "selfishness" (416; ch. 21) like Jonas's, which perverts his "imagination" (275; ch. 13) so that he deludes himself that he can make his selfish dreams come true and find a self-gratifying ideal in reality—an Eden.

Martin's trip to America is like a Romantic attempt to escape ordinary, unideal reality. But when he finally reaches his "terrestrial Paradise" (584; ch. 33), it makes a mockery of his dreams,[13] as it did of Dickens's. What he discovers in Eden is the opposite of Eden—the absence of any ideal in this world. He finds man's fallen nature; the human family when left free like Americans is selfish, like the Chuzzlewit family. This absence of the ideal is like what Dickens found in Nell's case, but here he can no longer counteract it with an imagination that is free of guilt and delusion as he did with Swiveller. Dickens's disillusionment has affected his view of imagination so that he can no longer forgive it for evading reality, can no longer see that evasion as innocent and leave it free as in the case of Swiveller. The only character here who has Swiveller's freedom and innocence is Young Bailey, and he is much less important than Swiveller and is not allowed the same kind of fulfillment. Instead, imagination becomes corrupted in other characters as it does in Martin.

Dickens, however, is not primarily a realist; he doesn't simply want Martin to face the absence of an ideal in this world. Rather he shows us this unideal reality, as he confronted death in *Old Curiosity Shop* and prison in *Pickwick*, so that he can seek some belief able to deal with that negative vision. He tries to do this with young Martin and Mark Tapley, but though Martin moves beyond selfish imagination, he does not reach any spiritual belief. All Mark offers him is a rather defiant rejection of selfishness and despair, accepting reality despite its unidealness, an attitude that does not provide the kind of positive belief Dickens evidently wants. Instead, since the belief Dickens seeks is mainly opposed to his sense of reality, he must try to base it on imagination, and the character he creates to represent imagination seeking belief is Tom Pinch. In the later part of the novel, as Dickens becomes aware of the need for some belief to fill the void left by Martin's disillusionment, he increasingly emphasizes Tom, ending the novel by showing Tom as an embodiment of the belief he wishes to offer us. At first Tom seems another imaginative character, but because Dickens takes imagination's limitations more seriously now, he must try to overcome its shortcomings in more serious ways. Thus, though Tom is like Swiveller in being the character who offers the main alternative to the protagonist, he is given a much more serious treatment than Swiveller.

At first Tom, like Pickwick, is deluded by imagination. Like Martin, though in an unselfish way, he tries to have "faith" (75; ch. 2) in an ideal in reality, and that ideal (Pecksniff) turns out to be a false one. Tom's "visions" are childlike, seeking to escape from "surrounding realities" (125–27; ch. 5), and he is like a child in wanting to believe in an ideal father figure. But eventually Dickens values Tom, as he did Pickwick, for his capacity for belief. Tom's belief is based on imagination and so is unable to convince reason that its visions are true, yet Dickens asserts that such a belief, imperfect though it is, is better than none at all: "There are some falsehoods . . . on which men mount, as on bright wings, towards Heaven. There are some truths, cold bitter taunting truths . . . which bind men down to earth with leaden chains" (274; ch. 13). If realism is unfulfilling, preventing belief, imagination may be the best substitute for belief he can manage.

Dickens, however, wants to transform imagination so that it is better able to deal with a sense of reality like Martin's. He does this by transforming Tom, teaching him to balance imagination with rational awareness. Tom learns to reject his false "idol" Pecksniff (563; ch. 31)—a disillusionment that parallels Martin's in Eden; both characters discover the ideal they believed in does not exist in reality. For both, this disappointment could lead to despair and a materialist view that there is nothing but an empty reality. Tom's "idle dream" has "melted away" and he finds himself facing a "cold and bare" world (628–29; ch. 36). He comes to London, which is like entering reality for the first time, facing its unidealness.

Tom has reached an Everlasting No, rejecting false belief. He and Dickens are in danger of losing their faith in imagination's ability to reach the ideal, in the possibility of reconciling the ideal with a sense of reality. Reality, Dickens tells us, often "extinguishes the soul's bright torch" (286; ch. 13). Tom could fall into disillusion and cynicism like Martin's at the start. But Dickens protects Tom from this fate, as he protects Pickwick in prison and many other characters. Instead of being defeated by reality, the idealist imagination overcomes it, moving on to a higher belief, an Everlasting Yea.

Dickens transforms Tom by purifying him of selfish desires. In doing so, he is purifying the imagination Tom represents so that it can be made more acceptable to reason, made so noble that it can overcome reason's doubts. He has shown us that such a purification is necessary, since imagination can be taken over by selfish, guilty impulses like those we see in Jonas. Like other Victorian writers, Dickens hopes to convert imagination into something higher—something like belief—by rejecting that dark side of it. And here again, the process of purification resembles Oedipal submission; by giving up his desire for Mary, Tom can replace a repressive father figure—Pecksniff—with a forgiving one—old Martin, who is converted so that he no longer seems negative like Pecksniff but rather becomes like an idealized father. This substitution resembles a child's giving up its desire for the mother (unattainable and pure, like Mary) and accepting rather than resenting the father. We can see Tom giving up the desire that motivates imagination and accepting that imagination cannot overcome reality when he says that "someone who is precious to you may die, and you may dream that you are in heaven with the departed spirit, and you may find it a sorrow to wake to the life on earth. . . . It is sorrowful to me to contemplate my dream . . .; but the realities about me are not to blame. They are the same as they were" (846; ch. 50). Imagination fails to overcome the sense of reality, so that one can believe only in an imagined ideal that seems beyond this world and thus beyond the reach of reason.

Once Dickens has used Tom to reject selfish imagination, he can accept the imaginary. After Tom gives up his relatively selfish dream of having Mary, Dickens allows him a dream come true after all, when old Martin rescues him, becoming the ideal father Tom has dreamt of since the days when he idealized Pecksniff. Old Martin at first seems to exist in Tom's "fancy" (693; ch. 40); then Dickens makes the imagined ideal come true. Dickens is trying to make imagination overcome reason's doubts, its sense that there is no good father. And he makes this transformation sound like the sublimation of earthly desires into spiritual ones, replacing earthly fulfillment with submission to a higher control, thus joining desire for the ideal father with desire for God in a way that *Old Curiosity Shop* couldn't. Although Tom is reconciled with a father figure, he mainly seems to accept that the imagined ideal cannot exist in reality and instead is to be found somewhere "higher" than this world (845; ch. 50). Thus Dickens wants us to feel that Tom's acceptance by old Martin is analogous to a union with God, that imagination has led to belief in an ideal father like God.

We can see Tom acting for this belief when he teaches old Martin to "believe in better things" (888; ch. 52) and helps young Martin overcome his skepticism. Martin at first mocks Tom for not being "rational" (264; ch. 12), like reason rejecting imagination. Martin wants the ideal to be real, not imaginary. But belief depends here on giving up reason's wish to find the ideal in reality and accepting that the ideal must be imaginary, as Martin accepts Tom (816; ch. 48). We can see Martin's conversion to imaginative idealism like Tom's, for example, when, newly returned from America, he sees London not as bleak reality but as a "fairy" place (621; ch. 35).

At the novel's end Dickens implies that since we cannot find the ideal through reality, we should look for it through art, thus trying to get imagination to stand in for belief. He shows us Tom sitting at his organ like Abt Vogler, using the artist's imagination to reach a sense of the divine. He is still a "dreamer," but like Dickens, he can use his art to make the imagined ideal seem real, creating visions of "the divinest regions" (770; ch. 45). In the novel's last sentence his music (representing imagination, I think) "shuts out the grosser prospect of an earthly parting"—that is, overcomes reason's awareness of death in reality—and "uplifts" him (as Dickens hopes his art can uplift him and us) "to Heaven" (918; ch. 54).

Yet if Tom embodies belief, he also shows that a belief based on imagination is not very strong. He is a rather weak character, unable to overcome reality and thus (like Nell) forced to look beyond it for fulfillment, so that we feel Dickens still cannot fully reconcile the imagined ideal with his sense of reality. He admits this conflict when he tells us there are "fancies in Tom's mind, the folly of which his common sense could readily discover, but which his common sense was quite unable to keep away" (649; ch. 40). We see Dickens here wishing to believe in the imaginary but at the same time unable to overcome his sense of the way reality opposes it. Since reason fails to satisfy the desire for something better than reality, the mind cannot wholly give in to reason but clings to imagination.

Dickens also treats Tom too sentimentally, evidently trying to arouse conventional emotions in order to drown out reason's doubts, probably because he feels it is his duty as an artist to offer us a strong belief whether he fully shares it or not. It is hard to feel that the optimism he offers through Tom is a sufficient antidote for all the opposing forces the novel has expressed—that Tom's submissiveness could really overcome the kind of violent rebelliousness Dickens expresses in Jonas and that his idealism could withstand exposure to the anti-ideal world that Jonas and others inhabit. Like Pickwick, Tom is protected from the forces that could destroy his belief, suggesting that Dickens still must segregate the idealist imagination from his sense of reality and the skepticism it encourages. Thus the disillusion implicit in Jonas's story and in Martin's trip to Eden remains largely unconnected to and unreconciled with the idealized ending. Because Dickens must purify Tom's imagination to convert it into belief, he must also segregate it from the uncontrolled, playful aspect of imagination he expresses through characters like Mrs. Gamp, just as Swiveller and Nell remain separate.

We can find this unresolved tension between imagination and an awareness of reality, the two coexisting without being able to convince each other, in Dickens's metaphors.[14] But here Dickens can reconcile the two more fully, as he could earlier through characters like Sam Weller. A metaphor accepts the "realistic" object but simultaneously induces us to supplement our simulation of realistic perception with an imaginative way of seeing, a vision that is not constricted by our sense of reality, a momentary subversion of realism. The metaphor both entertains an imaginary vision and (like Sam) accepts that it is not real; it can do this because it does not assert that the imaginary is real but merely speaks of it *as if* it were real, remaining playful rather than demanding serious belief as Dickens does through Tom. A phrase like "as if" does not try to convince reason and so can evade its reality-testing. This enables us to feel that even though imagination cannot abolish reality, it can circumvent it. Reason still pictures something it takes to be realistic, but at the same time we partly set aside our concern with realism and, as if in play, entertain the fanciful image. Thus we partly accept reality and partly escape it.

Once reason has been bought off by admitting an image is only imaginary, imagination is free to let desire (or fear) alter the perceptual. This can make reality more bearable, since we no longer need feel it is all there is and is beyond our control. Metaphors, then, enable Dickens to balance imagination with realism. He can give us imagination's (for example, Tom's) vision of an ideal and at the same time can see that this is only an "illusion" that seems "as if" it is true "in Tom's glad mind" (117–18; ch. 5); what is merely "as if" true to the narrator (and reason) seems true to Tom (and imagination). If Dickens cannot fully believe, he can let imagination (and Tom) believe for him. He remains aware he is telling us only what "one might fancy" (186; ch. 9), that his novel is "a dream within a dream" (361; ch. 17). It is as if he is telling reason what the dragon on Mrs. Lupin's sign seems to say: "Don't mind me—it's only my fun" (77; ch. 3). By admitting that the imaginary is only playful, he prevents reason from seriously questioning it, so that like Mark Tapley he can "almost delude himself into the belief" (902; ch. 53) that the imaginary is real.

This combination of imagination with partial disbelief also finds expression in the novel's comic characters, in whom survives some of the same playfulness we saw in Sam Weller and Dick Swiveller. For example, young

Bailey's "genius . . . eclipsed both time and space, cheated beholders of their sense, and worked on their belief in defiance of all natural laws" (489; ch. 26), which is much like what Dickens himself does. This is another instance of imagination's disarming doubt by remaining childlike and playful. Similarly, Mrs. Gamp, the most imaginative character in the novel, like Dickens creates a fictional character, Mrs. Harris, and using her imaginative world as "a talisman against all earthly sorrows" (838; ch. 49) transforms or defies reality with her "imagination" (824; ch. 49). She resembles Bailey in using imagination to defy reality, but in both cases Dickens's awareness of that reality coexists with imaginative escape, as in his metaphors. However, a balance between realism and idealism is fully possible here only for the metaphor-making narrator, not for a character within the story, like Sam Weller—not even for Bailey, whose fate suggests that imagination is more threatened and corruptible here than in earlier novels. And I have already mentioned the corruption implied in Mrs. Gamp and Pecksniff. No character except Tom keeps imagination free from the materialist desires that make it too demanding to be balanced with a sense of reality. The more Dickens wants imagination to be serious enough to lead to belief, the more he becomes aware of ways in which it resists belief and is not ideal.

In *Chuzzlewit*, then, Dickens has taken a step toward reconciling imagination with belief in Tom Pinch's case. But in this novel the corrupt social world of Jonas and others and the idealized world of Tom's imagination are even more separate than Quilp's and Nell's worlds, and playful imagination is unable to bridge their gap, since it is free and uncorrupted only in the narrator and not embodied in any character like Swiveller, able to enter the story and offer us a middle ground between unideal reality and an unbelievable, unreal ideal. Dickens has not yet found a way to integrate the various aspects of his work, to reconcile imagination with realism within the story, through its action. The more seriously he seeks to make imagination lead to belief, the more he must deal with the sense of a reality opposing it. But at this stage of his evolution, he has only discovered that conflict; he has not yet found a way to resolve it.

In *A Christmas Carol* Dickens puts into practice the idea of the artist's role he worked out for Tom Pinch at the end of *Chuzzlewit*. He no longer sees the artist primarily as an entertainer, a Sam Weller or Dick Swiveller, but rather as someone who purifies imagination, overcoming rather than playing with the uncontrolled forces in it and thus transforming it into belief. Thus we find him continuing his tendency to express imagination less through characters and more through his narrator and also through a stronger, more conscious narrative control. When expressed through characters, imagination tends to become more playful and irresponsible, since the writer has distanced himself from it and need not feel responsible for it. By expressing it through his narrator, Dickens imposes more serious control on it. From here on he also tends, when he expresses imagination through characters, to use more serious, idealized characters like Tom Pinch, characters through whom he also controls and idealizes it more, rather than leaving it mainly to fools and rogues like Mantalini and Mrs. Gamp. He has become too aware of the dangers of imagination to give it so much freedom.

One reason Dickens now emphasizes his narrator more is that he has become aware of a moral, even spiritual, purpose for his art, and so he is more concerned with acting on his audience, hoping to waken belief in us. In *A Christmas Carol* he wants to convert us by converting Scrooge, to take us through a mental process like that by which he reawakens Scrooge's imagination and so leads him to belief.[15] In using Scrooge as the representative of the doubt he seeks to overcome, Dickens is facing up to the problems I have discussed in *Chuzzlewit;* writing that novel evidently made him aware that there were conflicts in his fiction he needed to resolve, that he needed to exercise a stronger control over his work. If Tom Pinch fails to deal with the forces opposing belief, here Dickens sets idealism in direct, conscious opposition to materialism, basing his story on a confrontation between representatives of the two attitudes. Scrooge is as skeptical a materialist as any Chuzzlewit, and in opposition to him, the spirits are a much stronger embodiment of idealism than Tom. They speak for the idealist imagination with godlike power, a power given them by the narrator with whom they are closely allied. If they can convince Scrooge, then idealist imagination must be able to overcome rational doubt.

We can associate the spirits with imagination both because they are imaginary (seeming imagined by Scrooge) and because they have imagination's power to call up visions. Dickens uses imagination here to picture the ideal he wants Scrooge to believe in. Scrooge has refused to believe he needs familial love, and the spirits show him visions of that ideal. Like imagination, they show him what he desires or fears—his child self needing parental love; loving families like the one he could have had; people who are suffering because they have lost this love (especially in the vision of himself dying). Dickens hopes that these visions of the ideal and of its absence, even though they are only imaginary "shadows" (70; st. 5), will be so vivid that he can lead reason (embodied in Scrooge) to believe in the ideal. Scrooge lacks "fancy" at first (14; st. 1), but Dickens induces him to give up adult rationalism and rediscover the child's ability to believe in the imaginary, as when Scrooge pictures Ali Baba (28; st. 2). Perhaps imagination and even belief are only a means toward an end for Dickens, and what he really wants is the feeling of love that these can induce, a feeling of loving and being loved by a perfect parent, whether that parent seems real or not. I think he wants such a feeling in order to overcome his resentment of his parents; by converting Scrooge into a good father figure at the end, he seems to be trying to convince himself to believe in an ideal father, as he so often does in his novels.

He chooses a Christmas tale for this conversion because he especially associates Christmas with imagination, as we can see by the fact that his Christmas stories are fantasies. In a later Christmas piece, "A Christmas Tree," he describes Christmas as "a short holiday . . . from the great boarding-school, where we are for ever working at our arithmetical slate"—in other words, a holiday from rationalism, a return to a childlike state in which one can use "fancy" and still believe in its vision of "Fairy immortality" (12, 10). As this last phrase suggests, he associates Christmas not only with imagination but with belief. He can use this double association to connect imagination with belief, making us feel imagination can bring about a Christmaslike rebirth of belief.

A Christmas Carol points the way to Dickens's later fiction. In the novels from here on, as in the *Carol*, imagination serves a more serious, spiritual purpose than heretofore, confronting the forces opposing it more directly and acting through the narrator and the central plot rather than primarily finding expression through comic characters who are not integrated into the main action.

The Christmas stories that follow *A Christmas Carol* similarly try to transform reality through imagination. Of these, *The Cricket on the Hearth* is the one that reveals most about Dickens's attitude toward imagination. Though it attempts to do what *A Christmas Carol* does, using a cricket instead of ghosts to convert unbelievers, it is much more ambivalent about imagination. Caleb Plummer creates a fantasy world for his blind daughter, Bertha, and Dickens shows this as a mistaken use of imagination. Caleb is a toy-maker, using "poetical license" and creating "grotesque figures" (184; pt. 2), as Dickens himself does, suggesting that what Dickens is criticizing here is his own use of imagination, reacting against the lack of seriousness in his earlier fiction. Caleb has used his "fancy" to make the world seem "transformed" (189; pt. 2) to Bertha, creating a "picture in her mind" of an "enchanted home" (185, 182; pt. 2) that is quite unlike their real one. He has done this to induce "belief," giving her "dreams" of a better world in which she can see "light" and so bless "Heaven" (183, 187; pt. 2). Like Dickens, he is trying to create belief through imagination. But that belief is based on blindness to reality. Like his daughter, Caleb has lost track of reality, becoming "dreamy" (184; pt. 2), always looking at "some other time and place" as if seeking "the Philosopher's stone" (172; pt. 1), trying to possess an ideal.

If one is unaware that reality is different from the imagined ideal, one may seek the ideal in reality, and when reality fails to live up to one's dreams, one is in danger of falling into disillusion. For example, Caleb makes Bertha fall in love with old Tackleton by falsely idealizing him; when she discovers he is not what she thought, she could fall prey to despair. Dickens is dealing with a problem analogous to religious doubt; Bertha fears that the "images" her heart sends to "Heaven . . . might not be . . . true" (201; pt. 2)—she fears that she believes in a false ideal. When disillusioned, she laments that Caleb has filled her "heart so full, and then come in like Death" to "tear away the objects of [her] love" (222; pt. 3); a kind of belief has been killed. Her brush with disillusion is paralleled by John Peerybingle's; he momentarily loses faith in his wife. Dickens associates this loss with "toys" that have "run down" (207; pt. 2), suggesting that imagination, like a toymaker, has failed, defeated by the sense that reality is unideal.

As usual, Dickens raises the possibility of disillusion in order to repudiate it. Caleb's misuse of imagination does not discredit imagination entirely but rather shows the need to convert it into a higher belief that can face reality without being destroyed. Bertha rejects her "fancies" (222; pt. 3) only to replace them with a higher "sight" that enables her to see not reality but a godlike "Presence" that leads her to "reverence" (223–24; pt. 3). Dickens implies that this belief comes from imagination. He embodies the spirit leading to belief in the cricket, and he suggests it represents a higher power able to inspire imagination; it gives Peerybingle "visions" of the ideal as he gazes into the fire (180–81; pt. 1), an act Dickens often associates with imagination. And he later describes it "suggesting his reflections by its power, and presenting them before him, as in a glass or picture" so that he sees an "image" of the ideal, purged of any "shadow" (211–12; pt. 3). Like Scrooge's spirits, the cricket works by activating imagination. But the story implies that imagination can be led to the ideal like this only after it has faced an apparently disillusioning reality. Perhaps the fear of disillusionment drives imagination to desire belief more seriously, curing it of mere playfulness. Bertha's acceptance of reality enables her to look beyond this world, and John's case shows that spiritual belief like hers enables one to defend against seeing reality as wholly unideal.

At the story's end Dickens leaves us with nothing but "a broken child's-toy" (234; pt. 3). Unlike Caleb at the start, Dickens is here admitting that his "glimpse" of the ideal is only imaginary, beyond our certainty. By doing this, he can protect the imaginary from disillusionment like Bertha's, accepting that it cannot overcome reality. But if he is accepting imagination's limits here, I think he does so because, like Bertha, he wants to go beyond imagination. He wants to be more than a mere toymaker—to transform imagination so that it can carry out the spiritual mission he undertakes in these Christmas books, leading us to a glimpse of something beyond the merely imaginary.

The Cricket on the Hearth, then, shows that Dickens does not feel imagination can lead to belief as easily as it seems to in *A Christmas Carol*. The forces opposing belief are not as easy to overcome as in *Carol*; imagination must (like Tom Pinch) face an apparently disillusioning reality that sobers it, curing it of mere playfulness, so that it can be converted into a higher belief that can face reality without being destroyed. If Dickens is to organize novels around imagination overcoming realism like Scrooge's, then that process must be a longer, more painful one than for Scrooge. In his novels from here on, Dickens thus makes imagination serve a more serious, spiritual purpose than heretofore, confronting the forces opposing it more directly.

The Christmas stories, however, do not offer a complete blueprint for the kind of fiction Dickens was moving toward. For one thing, works so short do not leave enough room for the playful, rebellious side of imagination, and although Dickens wants to bring that aspect under control, he does not want to give it up entirely.

chapter 5

Dombey and Son

We can consider all the works I have so far discussed, wonderful as they are, as an apprenticeship for the more serious, controlled, self-conscious novels that begin with *Dombey and Son*. *Dombey* differs from its predecessors in many ways. It is evidently the first novel Dickens wrote with a clear idea of the whole novel in mind from the start. He seems to have decided after his problems with *Chuzzlewit* that he needed to concentrate carefully on one main unifying idea, and everything here is subordinated to that idea. There is virtually no imaginative play simply for its own sake, uncontrolled by a larger purpose; even in his prose he has pruned away playful elaboration. I think he does this here because he has finally discovered what he wants to concentrate on, a concern serious enough to engage him deeply and complex enough to base a whole novel on. *Dombey* is the first novel in which he is able to connect individuals and their problems to general concerns and fundamental questions that provide a unifying idea for his work.

The concern he focuses on here is the one he has been moving toward in the preceding works: the problem of belief. *Dombey* is his first novel to be centrally and pervasively about a spiritual problem, as I hope to show here. (It was right after *Dombey* that Dickens wrote a life of Christ.) But equally important, Dickens has also discovered a dramatic form in which he can deal with his problem. Here, in contrast to what he does in preceding novels, he does not separate the idealist part of the novel from the part that faces what he presents as reality; Florence Dombey is rather like Tom Pinch or Little Nell, but unlike them she has to stay in a world that challenges her idealism. And she is given a sensitivity to that challenge that the simpler characters of Pickwick and Oliver Twist lacked. Thus Dickens can base his plot on the conflict between the heart—what he conceives of as needing belief—and the world—what he conceives of as opposing belief. Here for the first time he does this explicitly within the relation of child and parent. *Dombey* is his first novel to be based on a parent-child relationship; although such relationships are always central for Dickens, this is the novel that deals most basically, directly, and extensively with parents and children. The problem of spiritual doubt is evidently closely related for Dickens to the filial relationship, as I shall also try to show here.

This effort to use the work of fiction as a way to reach belief involves imagination. Dickens is trying to overcome the division between realistic awareness and idealistic imagination that we have seen in his earlier works and that I have mentioned in Carlyle and some other Victorians. From *Dombey* on, Dickens makes the conversion of imagination into belief a central organizing principle. As he becomes more concerned with that conversion, he becomes more aware of its difficulties. Whereas Scrooge can still return to a childlike state like Pickwick's without much effort, from now on Dickens becomes increasingly concerned with the necessity for leaving behind the childlike, however much he may still value it. This abandonment of child-hood is enacted in the death of Paul Dombey. When Little Nell dies, she can be replaced by childlike characters (Swiveller and the Marchioness), but when Paul dies, his sister Florence is left to grapple with the problems that defeated him, and she must do so by growing up at least to some extent. She does not have to give up imagination as much as a character in a realist novel would, but she has to reconcile it with a sense of reality. If she ultimately finds a faith like Nell's, it is one that (unlike Nell's) must remain in this world—that is, must be balanced with an adult sense of reality. Thus Dickens is more directly concerned with the way reality opposes imagination's desire for an ideal.[1]

Until now Dickens has been largely content to let imagination evade real-ism, coexisting with it by remaining playful and so not demanding serious belief. The parts of the early novels that seek serious belief, such as Nell's story, remain separate from the parts where imagination is mainly expressed; there is little play of fancy in Nell's life, and there is little serious searching for an ideal in scenes involving comic characters such as Swiveller. *Dombey*, how-ever, like *A Christmas Carol* but more seriously, tries to transform imagination so that it can better satisfy the need for belief. Other Victorians do this too, but perhaps the process is most complex and difficult in Dickens, if only because his imagination is more energetic and harder to bring under control.

Before examining the role imagination plays in the novel, I would like to begin by discussing the spiritual concerns that he wants it to serve. I think we can best understand *Dombey* as an attempt to work out a belief that can enable the characters (and us, and Dickens) to face death,[2] probably because Dickens was still trying to come to terms with Mary Hogarth's death, but also because mortality is the issue that makes the need for belief most urgent. The novel begins with a death, and its first quarter builds up to the death of Paul. From then on it displays two alternative ways of dealing with death, Florence's and Dombey's. Dickens tells us the novel is about Pride,[3] and clearly it is Dombey who embodies that pride. Critics have usually seen the pride as social and discussed the novel as social criticism. But although Dombey represents repressive social power, it is also clear, especially at the novel's end, that Dickens also thought of pride in spiritual terms. In fact his social criticism is fundamentally spiritual; what is wrong with society is that it induces a pride that prevents us from looking beyond the self to seek belief in something higher. Dickens is mainly using Dombey, then, to show the inadequacy of social pride as a way of dealing with death and the despair that death can cause. He is thus using Dombey (like Scrooge) to embody the spiritual condition he wants to overcome in order to create belief.

Dombey's pride makes him set himself up in place of God, as Dickens implies with the phrase "Anno Dombei" (60; ch. 1). But Dombey does not so much worship himself as worship society in himself—himself as the representative of social power. Like the other social characters, he believes in the material values he has learned from commercial society; his materialism cannot conceive of any object of belief beyond this world. His belief is shown by his answer to Paul's question: "Money . . . can do anything." In other words, it replaces God. It possesses the power and the glory, since it can make someone like Dombey "powerful and glorious." It can "even keep off death," or so Dombey tries to believe. But Dickens uses death to show the weakness of this materialism. In this conversation, Paul is seeking something to believe in because he needs help facing his mother's death; he asks what money is "after all," suggesting a need to believe in something after life, and asks, "Why didn't money save me my Mama?" (152–53; ch. 8), suggesting a wish to believe in salvation. The belief Dombey offers him gives him no way to deal with mortality and nothing to live for, so his death is like the spiritual death such materialism can cause.

By making Paul die, Dickens forces Dombey to face this weakness in his belief. Dombey's idol cannot save Paul, and it does not help Dombey accept death. Instead, death calls into question his assumption (which is society's) that earthly success is fulfilling and gives life meaning. Death makes him feel "the feebleness of wealth." Remembering Paul's question about money, "he could hardly forbear inquiring, himself, what *could* it do indeed, what had it done?" (345; ch. 20). Dickens gives Dombey this doubt so that he can eventually be redeemed; one side of him, the heart he has suppressed, seeks something better than material things. This side of him echoes his namesake, Paul, whose conflict and need for belief he has inherited; he too must now face the death of a loved one and seek a belief that can enable him to bear it. But the death of Paul corresponds to the way Dombey represses the child in himself, denying his own heart as he virtually kills Paul by denying him the love and belief his heart needs. Dombey does this because he can find no spiritual belief; thus he clings to material possessions, feeling that if he loses them, he will be left with nothing. As a result, here as in traditional Christian thought, pride causes despair; Dombey sees himself as replacing God and so cannot believe in any being higher than himself, any being able to overcome death. He can only fear death; if material reality is all there is, there is no life after death.

Dickens uses the railroad here to represent this view of death. The railroad is a complex symbol; it is mainly associated with Dombey, society, and death, suggesting that Dickens wishes to equate these. I think it is primarily meant to represent the mechanistic view of the world held by materialist society—the rationalist view that the world is controlled by mechanical forces that only bring death. Dickens uses the railroad to make us feel this kind of materialism is mechanical, not truly alive, and also to associate it with destruction, making us feel materialism destroys traditional belief—as the railroad destroys Staggs's Gardens, which its inhabitants hold "sacred" (122; ch. 6)—and also, like Dombey, destroys the capacity for life and love. But although it kills, the railroad is not so much a symbol of death as it is a symbol of the way death appears to the materialist—to Dombey.

Because of his feelings about death, Dombey sees everything tinged "with the morbid colours of his own mind": "All things looked black, and cold, and deadly upon him, and he on them." Reality is "a wilderness" in which there is no sign of God. As the train has created this wasteland (or made it seem a wasteland to the observer), so death makes reality seem empty. All the earthly things Dombey has valued are lost in death, just as "houses, mansions, rich estates" are "left behind" by the train and so shown to be "insignificant." When the train has passed, as when life has passed, there is "no trace to leave behind but dust and vapour." And because death negates all material fulfillment, Dombey can only see death, like the train, as a "power" that goes "inexorably to its foredoomed end," "dragging living creatures of all classes, ages, and degrees behind it." Like the train, death seems "indomitable" because he cannot believe in any higher power able to overcome it; and because he cannot believe in divine pity, it seems a "remorseless monster" (354–56; ch. 20). As he associates the train with "darkness," "plunging down into the earth," so he cannot think of death as rising to heaven and finding light.

The idea of death, like the train, might be redemptive; it too can "let the light of day in" on the world, revealing the vanity of earthly things and thus the need for God. But Dombey cannot see this; he can only see death, like the end of his journey, as "the end of everything" (354–56; ch. 20)—a dead end. Death seems "ruthless" because it has "crushed his hopes" of earthly fulfillment (346; ch. 20). It is not, of course, that Dickens himself believes death is like the train, though he may fear he could share Dombey's view. To those capable of spiritual belief, the appropriate symbol for death is rather the sea—natural, beautiful, and allowing a glimpse of something on its further shore, a belief in something beyond this life so that one need not fear death. The train, after all, is manmade, implying that Dombey's view of death is his own creation, not a natural view.

Because he has rejected the side of himself that resembles Paul, instead of turning (as Paul would) to Florence and the belief she could offer him, Dombey here journeys away from her and toward her opposite, Edith. In choosing Edith, he is choosing the social values his materialism endorses. Since he can see death only as frightening, he tries to overcome his thoughts of it by seeking social fulfillment, marrying Edith, who he hopes will make "the monster of the iron road" seem "less inexorable" (371; ch. 21). He is trying to reassure himself that his social values are right after all. But instead, what he finds in Edith, as in society, is a reflection of his own pride and inability to love and believe. This recognition forces him to confront his false beliefs, to see how unfulfilling they are. Edith shows the hopelessness that results when one denies the heart's needs as Dombey has. Thus, ironically, his very attempt to escape despair leads him deeper into despair. He has only postponed his day of reckoning till the novel's climax.

Dombey is finally forced to begin confronting what is wrong with himself at the point when he once more encounters the train, in the scene where Carker dies. In facing Carker, Dombey is facing the negative side of himself. He and the society he worships have made Carker what he is; Dombey has taught Carker to ape his materialism and lack of belief in any higher power. Dickens pushes these attitudes to an extreme in Carker to show Dombey how dangerous they are, how the absence of belief leaves one with no ability to restrain selfishness, leaves one at the mercy of the rebellious and lustful forces within the self. Like Dombey, Carker has pinned all his hopes on earthly fulfillment, and now that is shown to be empty, all his schemes "frustrated." Thus, like Dombey, he is left facing a world that he can see only as physical, without God, negative, and "pitiless" (861–62; ch. 54), since he has "no hope" (873; ch. 55) of anything like divine pity. Nothing is left but "Death," of which, like Dombey before, he can only feel "terror" (863; ch. 55). He too sees death (for example, in his premonitory visions) as like a train, mechanical and thus remorseless; as in Dombey's view, the train, like death, is "cruel" and "irresistible," a "devil" rather than an agent of salvation

(872–73; ch. 55). Carker's destruction by the train, then, symbolizes a spiritual destruction caused by his inability to believe in a God able to make death redemptive.

The main reason for Carker's death, I think, is to show Dombey how this lack of belief leads to death (meaning spiritual death). It is as if Dombey kills Carker, not only because he frightens Carker onto the track but also because, by being inexorable (like the train) and unforgiving, he has taught Carker the values that cause the despair that here destroys him—the belief that the universe is governed by a mechanistic control like the train that brings only death and thus that there is no forgiveness, only vengeance. Dombey is playing God here: vengeance is his. But here at last Dombey is shown the consequences of his false religion. The train reveals how his materialism destroys people, and Carker's death reveals how horrifying vengefulness is. His change of heart begins when he sees Carker die; his face changes "from its vindictive passion to a faint sickness and terror" (875; ch. 55).

Dickens makes the death wholly physical, since these men believe only in the physical, and thus makes it wholly horrifying, so that he can use it to begin Dombey's revulsion against his own denial of pity. Seeing death as like a train is inadequate; he needs to find something better than that destructive monster. It is as if Dickens embodies Dombey's negative, materialist side in Carker so that by killing off Carker, he can purge Dombey of that side and so transform him. The transformation begins when Dombey faints here, as if he too has died, so that he can be reborn. He has reached something like Carlyle's Everlasting No, a rejection of false belief, of belief that he can attain the ideal in this world. Now he needs a new belief to replace his old one, belief in an ideal beyond reality.

Just before Carker's death, Dickens evokes the divine forgiveness Carker has cut himself off from, letting us see what he needs to believe in if he is to accept death. Since death has finally forced Carker to give up his rationalism and accept imagination's vision, he is able to glimpse the God he has hitherto rejected and that death—too late—shows him he needs. The divine is represented here (as it is several other times in the novel) by the sun, "so transcendent in its beauty, so divinely solemn," and associated with a "sense of virtue upon Earth, and its reward in Heaven" (874; ch. 55). But the sunlight, and the revelation it represents, only show Carker what he has missed in life. This revelation, however, is not too late for Dombey; I believe it is put here to show us what Dombey needs to learn. But Dombey cannot reach this new belief on his own; he needs something like divine grace. Dickens must appeal to a state of mind beyond Dombey's rationalism, and for that he turns to the character he has set in opposition to Dombey, Florence. Whereas Dombey lives by reason and thus believes only in the things of this world, Florence lives by the heart (that is, the desire for belief) and so can believe in a world beyond this one.

To understand the relation of this belief to imagination, we need to consider Florence's precursors, Paul and Walter. In the first quarter of the novel, it is mainly Paul who seeks some belief, so that he can accept the thought of death. Since the materialism Dombey has offered does not fulfill this need, he must look beyond the rationalist realism that Dombey believes in. Thus he turns to imagination, which eventually leads him to a vision of the divine, perhaps because he is a child, still able to believe in the imagined ideal. Yet that belief does not come easily. We can see Paul as embodying not belief but rather the doubting mind that seeks belief. His father and sister compete for his allegiance, like materialism and belief. When Dombey fails to convince him money is God, he turns to Florence. She has not yet reached the point in her development where she could offer him a definite belief, but she can at least teach him to value the heart, whose capacity for love and belief she embodies. To Dickens (as to other idealists) the heart means that part of the self that seeks something to believe in, that feels the need for something more than material reality. Thus it can lead toward belief, an action symbolized by Florence's carrying Paul upstairs to the light, whereas Dombey (like reason) can only stand below in the dark (155; ch. 8).

Paul cannot wholly overcome the realist side of himself that reflects Dombey and so cannot reach complete belief (until he dies); therefore, he turns to imagination, since it can lead him toward belief. He has a tendency to "dream" (154; ch. 8) and has strong "fancies" (275; ch.14). But Dombey, like rationalism, imprisons him in a world that opposes imagination; Blimber's school, for example, destroys children's belief in "the fancies of the poets" (208; ch. 11). Finding no ideal in reality, Paul retreats more and more to his "musing fancy" (234; ch. 13). But since imagination alone cannot overcome his sense of the "real" world (226; ch. 12), he must transform imagination. Here again this transformation has a psychological and a spiritual dimension. There is an Oedipal element in Paul's desire; he wants his mother and desires Florence as a substitute for his mother, desires that are Oedipal and thus arouse his father's opposition. Dombey punishes Paul for his desire by cutting him off from Florence and thus, in a way, killing him. To deal with the Oedipal guilt here, Dickens replaces Paul's desire for Florence with a spiritual desire. Giving up Florence means giving up earthly desires, thus purifying desire so that it can be allowed fulfillment; he can attain union with his mother as long as he doesn't demand that that ideal exist in reality.

His death is like the death of earthly desire. It is as if Dickens is shifting the ideal away from reality so that reason need not question its realness.

One way Dickens shifts the ideal beyond reality is by equating it with the sea. The sea lies beyond this world, as belief lies beyond reason and our sense of reality, and as death lies beyond life.[4] When Paul tries to understand what the waves are saying, he is trying to find the meaning in (or beyond) death. He responds to the sea with his imagination, suggesting that it is through imagination's ability to look beyond this world that he reaches belief in an afterlife. It is his "fancy" that pictures the river going "to meet the sea" (293; ch. 16) as life moves to death. Since the sea is closely associated with death, Paul is using imagination to transform death, not seeing it as something frightening like a train but as something that will enable him to reach the divine, as imagination seeks to reach belief.

Shifting the object of desire away from reality to the area beyond it (the sea) is a way of shifting desire from reality to imagination, which is similarly beyond reality. Just as Paul's retreat to death enacts a process of giving up selfish desire for fulfillment in this world, retreating to imagination also means replacing real fulfillment with an imaginary substitute. Here again, imagination offers a way of evading the sense of reality in order to reach something like belief. As Paul approaches death, then, Dickens tries to make us feel imagination is enabling him to approach belief. Earlier, his use of imagination was rather childish, as when he saw animals in the wallpaper. But now his imagination becomes more serious, just as Dickens is moving toward a more serious use of imagination in his fiction.

By accepting death (contemplating the sea), he learns to have a higher vision. Accepting death means accepting that the ideal cannot exist in reality and giving up the selfish desire to possess it physically, an abnegation that is possible because Dickens (through his sea imagery) makes death the sign that there is a realm beyond reality where the ideal can still exist. At Paul's death, then, he no longer sees death as a dead end the way Dombey does but can "see" the divine, see what is on the far "shore," what lies beyond death (297; ch. 16). Reaching that shore is like going beyond imagination to belief. Dickens is trying to make the imagined ideal seem real, make us believe it can actually be seen.

Only Paul, however, can see this vision; we must take his word for it. And he can see it only by dying. This implies that Dickens cannot reconcile the ideal with his sense of reality and so must locate it beyond reason's reach, beyond reality. Because he has based belief on imagination, he cannot escape the doubts that imagination keeps causing—reason's sense that the ideal is only imaginary. The fact that Paul and Florence are two separate characters suggests that Dickens is divided, half trying to believe in an ideal located in this world (which he seeks through Florence) and half accepting that it can exist only beyond reality (where Paul goes). Paul may have found an ideal father in heaven, but the fact that he had to seek one there reminds us that he has none here on earth.

We can see how imagination causes these doubts more clearly during the novel's first quarter in the story of Walter Gay, whom Dickens sets up as an alter ego to Paul. Walter's story shows that, though imagination leads toward belief, there are also forces in it that work against certainty.[5] Because he has not yet faced death, Walter's imagination is less serious than Paul's, more in need of discipline (just as Dickens feels he needs to bring his own imagination under more control, moving away from the playfulness of his earlier fiction). In addition, Dickens can allow Walter to have a desire for Florence that is closer to the sexual than Paul's, so that there are more uncontrolled, potentially guilty impulses in Walter's imagination that need to be chastened.

At Walter's first appearance we see that he is largely dominated by imagination, daydreaming of adventures at sea. Since the sea is associated with death, this may suggest that Walter (and imagination) fail to take death seriously (not yet understanding what the sea means) and so are not aware of the need for spiritual belief. The Wooden Midshipman is like a little world created by the childlike imagination, a refuge from reality, a place where it is safe to remain playful. It is the kind of home the young Paul might imagine, with an idealized father figure who is the opposite of Dombey—weak, loving, impractical, no threat to a son. Dickens suggests the ship is a place where the "romantic" still survives amidst the "uproar" of reality (87; ch. 4), as imagination like Walter's survives here despite realism like Dombey's, which dominates the surrounding commercial world. And the shop is influenced by "fancy" (89; ch. 4), which tries to turn it into a ship—that is, make it belong to some realm beyond the surrounding world, as if to sail off in search of the ideal.

But the Midshipman also shows imagination's limitations. His "attraction towards the marvelous and adventurous" (96; ch. 4) makes Sol Gills weak; he sees reality "through a fog," not fully aware of it (89; ch. 4). He admits imagination's weakness when he tells Walter that running off to sea is "well enough in fiction . . . but it won't do in fact" (95; ch. 4). This childlike kind of imagination cannot accept reality and so seeks to escape it, like Walter wanting to run off. Sol tries to make Walter face reality by sending him to work at Dombey and Son, but if imagination alone is unsatisfactory, so is realism like Dombey's, which threatens to destroy idealism as Dombey nearly causes Walter's death. Walter needs to face reality, but not so that he will become a realist like Dombey; rather, he needs to do so in order to transform imagination. Facing reality forces imagination to accept the fact that its desires cannot be fulfilled, and so Walter can learn to purge his imagination of selfish desires that seek to possess the ideal in this world.

The desire Walter must sublimate in this way is his desire for Florence. She represents the ideal he would like to possess, and also embodies the "simple faith" (337; ch. 19) he needs; he wins her by becoming like her, a process we can see as the conversion of imagination (which Walter starts with) into belief (which Florence's example teaches him). Here again that conversion is not so much a process of convincing reason as it is an attempt to purge the mind of the potentially guilty, quasi-Oedipal aspect of desire; Walter must become worthy of Florence by proving his desire is free of any of the lustful rebelliousness we find in Carker. But the difficulties he encounters show Dickens's sense that there are forces in imagination that resist belief.

When Walter first meets Florence, he sees her too much through the eyes of "childish" imagination (567; ch. 34). The episode is like a fairy-tale rescue of a disguised princess from a wicked "witch" (137; ch. 6); things are "grotesque and exaggerated," seen with "childish" vision (567; ch. 34). Walter and Sol both respond to Florence with imagination (135, 139; ch. 6). Rescuing her from Dombey's world and taking her to the Midshipman is like a victory by imagination over reality, rescuing her from the nightmarish sense that she is at the mercy of repressive parents like Mrs. Brown and her father and replacing them with an idealized father figure (Sol) who seems rather imaginary. In his earlier fiction Dickens could accept such a playful, wish-fulfilling use of imagination, but here he treats it as childish and unrealistic. Florence must return to a reality that denies such dreams. Walter is too weak to save her, just as imagination can offer only a momentary escape but cannot vanquish the awareness of a world of "stern practical experience" (172–73; ch. 9).

As Walter grows up, he must learn to take Florence more seriously, which resembles learning to see the ideal not as merely imaginary, reaching a belief he can reconcile with his sense of reality. At first Florence is "the spoiled child of his fancy," something "agreeable to his imagination," rather than something seen as a "matter of fact" because his "love of the marvelous" has not yet been "weakened by the waters of stern practical experience" (172–73; ch. 9). One should accept reality in order to prevent imagination from indulging selfish desires like a spoiled child. The mention of waters here suggests that what will chasten imagination is the sea—that is, facing death.

The first experience that forces him to face reality more seriously is Sol's bankruptcy, just as Aunt Betsey's bankruptcy sobers David Copperfield and as his own father's bankruptcy must have opposed Dickens's Romantic vi-

sions. Like Dickens, and like Florence later, Walter must defend against losing belief in a good father figure. He is left facing a "strange and new" reality
(178; ch. 9) from which the ideal seems banished. He deals with this danger
of disillusion, again like Dickens and like Florence later, by trying to retreat
to imagination; he goes to Captain Cuttle, which is like seeking another version of the ideal father, but one that is less serious, more obviously imaginary.
At this stage in Walter's development, belief in an ideal father can only seem
childishly gullible, like the Captain; the ideal survives only in diminished,
comic form. Thus belief in this ideal is no longer strong enough to overcome
the sense of reality, as the Captain is not strong enough to overcome Sol's
problems. This experience, then, forces Walter to realize that imagination is
weak, that his "fancies" are "wild" and unrealistic (199; ch. 10). It teaches him
the need to transform imagination, taming it so it can lead to belief.

Dickens shows Walter trying to change his imagination in this way, to
purge it of selfish desires. Walter likes to "imagine" selfishly that Florence
could help his "fortunes," "but another and more sober fancy" tells him he
must give her up:

> Walter so idealised the pretty child . . . that he blushed for himself as a
> libeller when he argued that she could ever grow proud. On the other
> hand, his meditations were of that fantastic order that it seemed hardly
> less libellous in him to imagine her grown a woman. . . . In a word,
> Walter found out that to reason with himself about Florence at all, was
> to become very unreasonable indeed; and that he could do no better
> than preserve her image in his mind as something precious, unattain-
> able, unchangeable, and indefinite—indefinite in all but its power of
> giving him pleasure, and restraining him like an angel's hand from any-
> thing unworthy. (287–88; ch. 15)

He is struggling here to move from a selfish imagination that desires money
and physical possession of a grown, sexual Florence to a sober imagination
that allows the ideal to remain unattainable. By thus renouncing physical
desire and the unworthy thoughts that arouse guilt and make Walter feel he
is libelling Florence, he can replace the earthly object with an idealized one
that he can safely desire. Though the ideal still seems an object of desire here,
it is simultaneously something that negates desire, imposing restraint.

Walter replaces a desire for physical fulfillment with Florence (a desire
that could become sexual like Carker's and arouse Oedipal guilt, since Florence is rather maternal) with desire for a spiritual ideal, safely removed from
physical reality and thus from reason's doubts. He gives up physical desire by
leaving Florence and going overseas, just as Paul gives up earthly desires (at

the same point in the novel) by going across the sea of death; Dickens uses the idea of death to teach us to give up selfish desire. Dickens evidently intends us to see Walter's self-abnegation here as a movement toward a higher belief like that Paul found in death. Like Paul, Walter can transform imagination because he has faced death; Paul's death enables him to believe in a "solemn presence" beyond this world (337; ch. 19). He goes to sea as if to learn there what Paul saw, a belief that can enable him to overcome death and so return to life. Accepting death means accepting that the ideal cannot exist in reality and giving up the selfish desire to possess it physically. Dickens also makes death the sign that there exists a realm beyond reality where the ideal can still exist.

This self-abnegation offers a way of evading reason's sense that the imagined ideal is fantastic and unreasonable; Walter replaces a physical Florence with one who is an image in his mind so that he can preserve that image unchallenged by reality-testing. By accepting that the ideal exists only on a level other than physical reality, he can circumvent his sense of the unidealness of reality and protect the ideal from doubt. This is like the "Renunciation" Teufelsdröckh makes at the climax of *Sartor Resartus*, enabling him to reach a sense of "Blessedness" that is "HIGHER than Love of Happiness" (book 2, ch. 9). But although Dickens is trying to move from imagination to belief here, he has not been able to convince reason; he has had to set it aside. Though he asserts there is an ideal, he also must admit that there is no ideal (in any real, attainable form). He cannot resolve this contradiction; he can only set reason aside. He presumably hopes the mind can accept this evasion because it gives pleasure, allowing an illusion of fulfillment.

Despite these doubts, Dickens is trying here to move from imagination to something quite like religious belief, going beyond the "old day-dreams of [Walter's] boyhood" to a sense of the "purity and innocence" of Florence, who seems to "rise up, far above his idle fancies," as belief would rise above imagination (335; ch. 19). Walter frees his "soul" of "doubt" and reaches a "simple faith" like Florence's. Once reality has taught him that there is no ideal in this world, he can redirect imagination so that it envisions an otherworldly object instead.

Walter's movement here from fancy to faith reenacts the typical Victorian idealist attempt to move from Romanticism to religion, finding some belief able to allay the guilt aroused by Romantic desire. This effort to make imagination serve a serious purpose acts out the way Dickens is disciplining the childish tendencies that were not under so much control in his earlier work. Paradoxically, he moves toward this idealism by confronting reality. Like Walter, he wants to transform imagination because he has been forced to accept that there are things in reality, especially death, that a merely playful imagination cannot deal with. In *Pickwick*, when reality defeated imagination, that was merely a laughing matter and could be reversed fairly easily. But now the need to overcome disillusion has become so serious that the whole novel is organized around the attempt to do so. I think Dickens wants to do something similar to what Walter does here; after acknowledging the unidealness of reality, he wants to create an image of the ideal in our minds that we can use to counteract our sense of reality.

Dickens, however, does not find Walter an adequate center for the novel, suggesting that he still feels dissatisfied with the imagination Walter represents and wants to replace it with something higher. Thus he replaces Walter with Florence, representing a belief that lies beyond imagination. It is Florence's response to Paul's death that Dickens contrasts most strongly with Dombey's; her belief offers the antidote to the dark vision of death Dombey has on the train. Walter disappears from the novel immediately after Paul so that Florence can occupy center stage and we can focus on what she represents. Whereas Dombey's story shows the need for spiritual belief, Florence shows the belief he needs and shows that that belief, unlike Dombey's materialism, is fulfilling.

We can consider Florence the successor to Paul and Walter; their movement from imagination toward belief in the opening quarter paves the way for her, leading her to the belief that enables her to accept Paul's death as Dombey cannot. The first quarter of the novel leads up to Paul's revelation that there is an afterlife, creating belief in it in order to bequeath that belief to Florence. The "light" she sees at his death gives her a sense of "eternity" that can "fill" the "void" in her heart (313; ch. 18) and so sustain her through the rest of the novel. This faith enables her to accept not only death but also the unloving world she finds herself in. She carries on where Paul left off, trying to hold onto the vision of the ideal that he purchased for her with his death, but unlike him she keeps that vision in reality, maintaining it despite an awareness of reality. Moving from Paul to Florence is like moving from childish imagination that cannot accept reality to a faith that can resist the awareness of how unideal the world is.

Through Florence, Dickens is trying to solve the problem that Paul's death poses, to overcome the despair that could be caused by his discovery that the ideal cannot exist in this world. Florence's job is to try to reconcile belief like Paul's in an ideal beyond reality with a sense of reality like Dombey's. It is as if Paul is transformed into Florence, as Catherine Earnshaw is reborn in her daughter; in *Wuthering Heights*, as in *Dombey*, one protagonist can reach the ideal only by dying, transcending reality, but that protagonist is supplemented by a successor who can find a version of the ideal in this world. Like Brontë, Dickens wishes to counteract his sense that there is only a transcendent ideal by finding some version of the ideal that he can see as immanent.[6]

The novel tries to translate the act of finding belief into a process of becoming reconciled with one's father. Dickens evidently hopes that learning to believe in an ideal father will enable belief in God—or that belief in God will enable acceptance of the father. Perhaps his own father's inadequacy threatened to undermine his belief in a heavenly father; perhaps he also wanted to believe in some perfect parentlike being to overcome his resentment of his actual parents. He almost always uses a parentlike (usually fatherlike) character as the object of desire in his fiction—the embodiment of the perfect love his protagonist seeks. He probably does this partly to make spiritual belief more convincing by giving it a more real-seeming object, but I think he is also using belief to try to suppress its opposite, resentment of his parents, overcoming that resentment by transforming the image of the parent from a resented to a forgiven one. He often acts out that transformation on a more conscious, rationalized level by associating the idealized father with God and the resented one with society. The transformation in his attitude is displaced into a replacement of repressive, punitive social control with the forgiving, loving control of God.

Dickens evidently needs this belief to help him deal with death; *Dombey* combines coming to terms with death and coming to terms with one's father. Mary Hogarth's death may have affected Dickens so strongly because it reactivated his sense of having lost his mother's (and perhaps sister's) love, which could have aroused Oedipal resentment of his father, a resentment that could cause guilt. He could then deal with that guilt by replacing his sense of his father's inadequacy with belief in an idealized father who could forgive him. His novels often act out the process of forgiving a father so that one may receive a father's forgiveness.

Dickens typically embodies the ability to forgive an erring parent in female characters. Replacing Paul with Florence as protagonist is like trying to get rid of the masculine side of himself, which would feel Oedipal resentment. But if the origins of the novel's conflict are Oedipal, he can deal with it better by shifting it to a more conscious, rationalized level, translating it into spiritual terms. Thus he replaces sorrow at the loss of perfect maternal love with sorrow about mortality and sees the process of dealing with that sorrow as a movement from resenting repressive social control to submitting to a loving God, a movement made possible by replacing imagination (Paul) with belief (Florence).

Having bequeathed Paul's vision to Florence, Dickens confronts her with Dombey's unideal world in order to test her belief. Here as elsewhere, Dickens seems to be testing his own idealism, seeing if it can withstand his sense of reality. It is as if Dombey, like materialism, tries to destroy Florence's belief, to make her see the world as he does and fall into despair like his. Dombey embodies the absence of love, which could make her lose hope. She must face the absence of any ideal in her world as much as Paul or Walter do. Yet she does not retreat from reality as Paul must. Through her, Dickens tries to hold onto belief in the ideal that imagination (like Paul) sees beyond reality and yet to accept reality even though it opposes that belief. He hopes to reconcile childlike belief with adult realism. Only by dealing with reason's sense of reality can he reach a firm belief.

In the first quarter of the novel, Florence shares Paul and Walter's uncertainty; for example, she cannot hear any meaning in the sea (171; ch. 8). And like them, she begins with imagination. We can see her imagination leading her toward belief when Polly Toodle tells her an imaginative story to teach her to believe in an afterlife (77–78; ch. 3). It is Paul's deathbed vision that enables her to move beyond this childish, primarily imaginative stage. Facing death forces her to believe that the ideal exists beyond this world, and that belief enables her to accept the absence of love in this world. Thus, although at first she gives way to despair like Dombey's, she is able to overcome it, freeing herself of the "taint of earth" in her desire (317–18; ch. 18), the earthly desire that would make her resent the absence of the ideal in reality. Since she is picturing something beyond this world, she is still using imagination, but an "innocent imagination," unlike Dombey's selfish and thus despairing thoughts (326; ch. 18). Dickens has tried to use her to purify imagination so that it can become belief. She has been purged of selfish desires by giving up Paul and Walter, who embody the desires and doubts she must rise above; their examples teach her to give up the desire to possess the ideal in this world.

Although Dickens tries to use Florence to move beyond imagination, he is unable to give her a belief based on reality and so must still rely on imagination. Thus, despite his efforts to reach certainty, doubts keep recurring. We are told she "imagined" an "enchanted vision" of Dombey loving her. Dickens admits that it is "fanciful and unreal" but says, "she almost believed it was so," and this partial belief gives her "trust in God." Yet though she strains toward belief, she cannot overcome reason's sense that her vision is only imaginary and so cannot escape her sense of the "desolation" of reality (396; ch. 23), though her belief is strong enough to resist that sense. Until the climax, she keeps seeking some version of the ideal (mainly a loving father) and keeps being disabused by reality, dreaming of the ideal but failing to convince reason it is real. Though she has tried to accept that the ideal exists only beyond this world, imagination cannot help trying to envision it as real, trying to convince reason to accept it, and thus reason is forced to reject it. Since reality appears so unfulfilling, she keeps returning to imagination, alternating between versions of belief and doubt like many Victorians. Each time reality breaks in, the ideal seems more remote. She is forced to retreat, giving up desire more and more. Yet imagination enables her to keep envisioning the ideal, and so even though it cannot compel full belief, it enables her to resist despair.

Dickens uses Edith to represent the despair Florence must avoid. Edith embodies what Florence could have become; she too has been denied parental love and as a result has fallen into a hopelessness that is exacerbated by Dombey and society, whose materialism fails to provide Edith with any belief able to overcome her weariness. Edith shows us the dark side of imagination, which Florence must not give in to, an imagination that cannot reach belief but instead gives "bad dreams" (700; ch. 43; and see 752; ch. 47), as Edith influences Florence to have unhappy "dreams" too (701; ch. 43). Edith's unbelief and guilt embody what Florence could feel, what an unpurified imagination could lead to. As Edith enters a dream Florence has, replacing Paul's vision of an afterlife with a vision of death (591–92; ch. 35), so doubt could enter the imagination and pull it away from belief in an afterlife. It is as if a dark, unbelieving side of Florence (and of Dickens) enters the dream, calling the imagined ideal into question. At the same time, Edith represents the maternal love Florence desires and cannot have, presumably be se Dickens feels it is Oedipally forbidden. This denial is projected onto Edith; she wants to give Florence love but is prevented from doing so, as if the doubt she embodies is preventing the ideal from becoming real. We can guess that Dickens locates doubt and guilt in her in reaction against the Oedipal and rebellious desires he associates with her.

The climax to Florence's disillusionment comes in the chapter entitled "The Thunderbolt" in which Edith runs away and Dombey strikes Florence, accusing her of being like Edith. The chapter—indeed the whole novel—is organized to lead up to this moment when Florence loses her last shred of faith in her father. Dickens begins the chapter with a meditation on the way social reality can destroy the mind's ability to rise up on "wings," leaving it "far away from Heaven" (737; ch. 47). The danger here at the novel's darkest point is that Florence may finally succumb to this same kind of influence, that Dombey's realism may prevail. Her "patient trust" can no longer "survive the daily blight of . . . experience." She cannot believe in "any lingering fancy in the nature of hope" that Dombey can love her, seeing that when she "imagined" this it was only a "delusion."

Yet despite reason's rejection of the imaginary, she is still desperately trying to hold onto some semblance of belief, loving Dombey not "as the hard reality before her eyes" but rather as an admittedly imaginary ideal, someone "who might have been," "a vague and dreamy idea . . . hardly more substantially connected with her real life, than the image she would sometimes conjure up, of her dear brother yet alive" (739–40; ch. 47). This resembles what Victorian idealists do with religious belief; she tries to salvage belief by admitting it is imaginary, giving up the attempt to convince reason. She tries to overcome "doubts" about her parents by converting them into "shadows of her fond imagination," "living, in a dream wherein the over-flowing love of her young heart expended itself on airy forms" that she cannot reconcile with the "real world" that rebuffs her desire (743; ch. 47). (Similarly, Dickens creates imaginary idealized parents to try to overcome his sense of his own parents' inadequacy.) But although imagination is an attractive defense against doubt, it cannot overcome reason's sense of reality, which remains in unresolved conflict here with the desire for an ideal. Thus Florence cannot fend off the disillusion that finally comes to her. When Dombey strikes her, her eyes are finally opened completely to reality, to the absence of a good father in this world, "murdering" her belief in the ideal she has imagined (757; ch. 47). When she runs out into the streets, it is as if she is leaving behind the imaginary home she has tried to believe in and is facing reality, the same urban reality Dickens found himself in as a child, when he too felt betrayed by his parents.

But here as usual, Dickens raises the possibility of disillusionment only to react against it. In order to overcome as much as he can the uncertainty Florence has not been able to avoid, Dickens must make her face reality as much as possible, just as he is trying to make his own fiction take reality into account more fully. When Dickens was working on a novel, he returned to the city streets. I think he did this to revive his childhood sense of abandonment by his parents, but in order to overcome that feeling by creating fiction. By facing the absence of a good parent, he strengthens his need to imagine one and uses that need to drive himself to renew his belief in that imagined ideal.

Thus when Florence runs into the streets, as when Copperfield is sent to work in the city, the experience is presented as a disillusioning exposure to reality, but it also leads to an imagined rescue from that disillusionment. Her rejection of Dombey is like Carlyle's Everlasting No, a realization that what she has believed in is false. As with Carlyle, that rejection has value because it leads to a new belief. And like Dickens, she moves toward that belief through a return to imagination. She runs from her father to Captain Cuttle at the Midshipman, reenacting her childhood escape from Mrs. Brown. As I have said, the Midshipman seems to represent the realm of the imaginary, a refuge from reality. It is fitting that the Captain lives there, since like a "child" he has a "credulity, and generous trustfulness" that enable him to believe in the "impossible pictures" and "romance" that imagination creates (776; ch. 49). He is also a product of wishful imagination, an attempt by Dickens to imagine an ideal father. It is as if Dickens is allowing Florence to retreat from her sense of the unidealness of her real father to belief in an imaginary father, escaping adult awareness and returning (as Dickens too tries to do through his fiction) to a childlike belief in the imaginary, in a fairy-tale world, as she did when escaping from Mrs. Brown. When she reaches the Midshipman, she is "like a baby" and is received with the fatherly "gentleness" Dombey has never shown her (760; ch. 48).

Although this seems like another retreat from reality, Dickens evidently intends it to be a step forward. Florence is not simply regressing to a childlike belief in the imaginary. Because of her disillusion, she is now aware that the ideal is merely imaginary; she (and we) cannot take Cuttle seriously as a substitute father. Rather, Cuttle seems like a merely playful, admittedly imaginary version of the ideal, like a child's version of a fairy godfather. Wanting Dombey to be an ideal father is a serious attempt to make the imagined ideal become real, but accepting the Captain as a substitute for Dombey means giving up hope of a real, serious ideal in this world. Imagination, however, can offer an area protected from reason, which belief can retreat to, as Florence finds refuge at the Midshipman. If Florence were not able to retreat from her real father to an imaginary one—if she felt reality was all there is— she could not have kept her belief.

Dickens is balancing imagination with reason's sense that it is only imagination, and I think he wants us to feel that Florence is making a similar compromise between belief and realism. Though she is accepting reality more fully than before, she is also holding onto a sense of the ideal through imagination, and so she can keep at least some belief in that ideal and need not feel reality is all there is. Dickens also hopes that this acceptance of imagination's unreality can enable her to move beyond it to a firmer belief. Accepting reality does not logically strengthen belief, but it provides an emotional support for belief by making us desire it more and making us feel that because we have acknowledged reason's claims, we no longer need worry about its doubts. We feel that Florence has earned belief by accepting reality enough; that reason has been given its say and should let imagination have its turn; that facing reality, necessary though it may be, is not an adequate ending; that Florence has suffered enough to deserve a rescue from despair. After all, Dickens is not constructing an argument for belief (though the weakness of his logic may betray spiritual uncertainty) but rather is trying to take us through an emotional process that he hopes will enable us to overcome our doubts. When Florence runs to the Captain, we feel relief and a pleasure in imagination's ability to rescue her from disillusion. Imagination seems newly strengthened, able to defy the sense of reality.

One factor that reinforces our acceptance of the novel's movement away from disillusionment is Dickens's appeal here again to Oedipal impulses. Dombey strikes Florence for caring about her mother, which suggests the father is punishing the child for its Oedipal desire for the mother. In fleeing from Dombey, she is fleeing from her hatred of him. And by giving up Edith (letting her too flee, out of the novel), Dickens is giving up desire for the mother, purging the guilty aspect of desire (which he has projected onto Edith). It is also at this point that Carker, embodying guilty, masculine, sexual desire, is rejected from the novel. By thus disowning Oedipal desire, Dickens can enable Florence to avoid resenting her father. Though he translates this psychological process into spiritual terms that are more acceptable to the conscious mind, it is the psychological impulses to which it appeals that create a strong motive for accepting it. We want to accept the belief he offers in an ideal father because that belief answers a need to overcome guilt.

Thus when Florence flees from Dombey, Dickens leads her not simply to reality, as he seems to at first, but (with the aid of imagination and the Midshipman) to a higher perception. He wants to make us feel that through reality she can see the divine. She wakes to see the sunlight piercing "loopholes . . . in the spires of city churches, as if with golden arrows that struck through them—and far away athwart the river—, it was gleaming like a path of fire—and out at sea it was irradiating sails of ships—and, looked towards, from quiet churchyards, upon hill-tops in the country, it was steeping distant prospects in a flush and glow that seemed to mingle earth and sky together in one glorious suffusion" (770–71; ch. 49). This positive epiphany follows her negative one, her waking from her dream that Dombey can love her, as the Everlasting Yea follows the Everlasting No. Dickens tries here to combine the sense of reality Florence has learned to acquire with a vision like Paul's deathbed vision of a world of light beyond this one. In other words, he tries to bring the ideal into reality instead of merely locating it beyond this world as at Paul's death.

The light represents the divine, like the "golden" light Paul saw on his deathbed (297; ch. 16), sunset light that hinted that death is what enables us to see the divine. Reinforcing this suggestion, the light is associated with the sea, as at Paul's death, and with churchyards. Dickens uses this light to try to bring the divine into reality by showing the light piercing through (as if from beyond reality) and irradiating this world. Even in "the darker, narrower streets, where the sun . . . is seen through the mist, only . . . in small open spaces," there can still be an "eyelet-hole" (902–3; ch. 57), like the loopholes here, through which the divine light can enter reality. Belief cannot wholly overcome our sense of reality's darkness, but it can do so partly. Dickens is trying to combine idealism and realism, seeing the ideal (light) as coexisting with reality, though in tension with it. Yet though he is trying to make the divine seem immanent, he mainly speaks of it as transcendent; the light comes from beyond reality, as the sea is beyond this world. But if he feels the divine is separate from reality, he hopes that belief in it can irradiate reality. Awareness of reality (of death) can lead us to belief, but that awareness also chastens belief, as sunset dims the bright light of morning. By thus making some concessions to reality's darkness, Dickens makes diminished belief more acceptable. He wants us to feel that one can accept reality yet keep belief, as his vision mingles earth and sky.

The rebirth of Florence's belief is dramatized in the return of Walter as if from the dead; by making him return, Dickens puts a version of the ideal into reality to give Florence fulfillment. It is as if she revives Walter by reviving her belief. But here too Dickens is relying on imagination, as is implied by his making Captain Cuttle a kind of midwife to Walter's rebirth. The Captain, like imagination, helps Florence regain belief in life after death. He tells her of the power of the sea in a way that associates it with death, calling it an "almighty element" that can take people "to the world without end, evermore, amen" and through which people can be "saved by the mercy of God" (781–82; ch. 49). When Captain Cuttle has revived belief in this saving mercy, Walter reappears, acting out that revival.

Once Dickens has shown that belief is strong enough to overcome despair, he can get us to believe that the ideal can be found in this world. As Walter's return overcomes our sense that he is dead, belief in salvation can overcome the sense that death is final. Dickens hopes we will connect Walter's victory over death with belief in a divine mercy able to overcome death. If we still associate Walter with imagination as at the start, his return suggests that imagination has been transformed, made serious because (like Florence) he has faced death and the (apparent) loss of a father figure, experiences that have chastened imagination into belief. This movement from imagination to belief is also shown in an increased seriousness; Florence replaces the Captain with Walter, a more serious character, and both Walter and the Captain become more serious, acting for belief more than imagination. If Dickens still expresses some imaginative playfulness through the Captain, imagination now serves belief, as the Captain serves Florence.

Yet because of its reliance on imagination, this belief is still not wholly satisfying. Both the Captain and Walter seem too weak and not convincingly real enough to provide Florence with a fulfilling ideal that we can completely believe in. Imagination cannot completely overcome our sense of reality, our sense that Dombey not the Captain is Florence's real father and must be dealt with. And because Dickens has emphasized Florence's desire for Dombey much more than her desire for Walter, her marrying Walter does not provide the fulfillment the novel has made us want. What Dickens has presented as reality—Dombey's opposition to Florence's desire for love—continues to demand our attention. Nor has Dickens yet dealt with Dombey's inability to believe; Dombey continues to embody the lack of belief Dickens must overcome to offer us a convincing belief.

Dickens must thus make one last attempt to deal with doubt and the sense of reality. He does this by making Florence confront her father, acting out the vanquishing of despair by faith. She must come to terms with him as the novel seeks to come to terms with rationalist materialism like Dombey's. If Dickens cannot show that Dombey's materialism is rationally wrong, he can instead show that it is loveless and unfulfilling, leading to despair, not only unable to deal with the idea of death but even causing death. Dombey's story has run parallel to Florence's throughout the novel in order to make us compare his rationalism with her idealism; his gradual descent into hopelessness has contrasted with her ability to resist despair. Here at the novel's end, when Florence has completed her victory over despair, Dombey is finally forced to face the emptiness of his beliefs, the admission he earlier tried to evade by marrying Edith. The fact that his final change is explicitly spiritual is one more indication that Dickens's fundamental intention is to offer us a spiritual lesson. Just as Florence has learned that the Dombey she believed in is unworthy of her belief, so Dombey learns that he is unworthy of his own belief. He must reject the pride that led him to worship himself and money and find something else to believe in. He too must reject a false belief in order to replace it with an Everlasting Yea. And to do this, he needs Florence, since she has now gone through that same process herself.

Dombey is in "despair" because he has rejected Florence and the belief in love and forgiveness that she embodies and he needs. His materialism still prevents him from believing in "redemption" (934–36; ch. 59), in any higher being able to forgive him. This despair is still a form of pride. Dombey has fallen like Lucifer, and like Lucifer he is too proud to humble himself and ask forgiveness. But he is now ready to reject "the world" and sees that earthly things do not endure (935; ch. 59). He sees that what he told Paul, that money can replace God, was wrong (957; ch. 61). This insight teaches him the need for something higher than earthly fulfillment, and he sees that Florence embodies that higher value. She has remained constant because she believes in something beyond the temporal. Dickens has frequently emphasized time throughout the novel; it leads to death and is a manifestation of divine power, showing how the things Dombey values are at the mercy of that power. The novel is a search for some belief that can overcome this materialist sense of time.

Once Dombey has given up his false belief, he goes "wandering higher up" toward the nursery (937; ch. 59), as if trying to rise above reality and doubt and return to the childhood self he long ago must have suppressed in himself, thus becoming like his son, seeking belief. When he has become as a child, he is ready for the same kind of redemption that Dickens gave his namesake, Paul. Florence comes to him, bringing the belief she embodies, once more symbolized by the "sunshine" (940; ch. 59) and associated with the sea and rebirth (she has had a baby at sea). Her going to sea is like moving beyond reality to belief in something transcending death; once she has reached that belief, she can return to the land, suggesting that belief enables her to face reality. She can withstand the doubts this world could cause because she has found a basis for belief beyond this world. Her sudden appearance to Dombey may seem unrealistic, but perhaps that is Dickens's point; he is dramatizing his belief that divine grace can be revealed as if miraculously, that it can come from beyond reality. Because Florence has not lost her faith despite her disillusionment, she can finally overcome the sense of reality, converting Dombey into the father she has tried to believe in all along; belief resists realism until realism finally gives up.

It may seem strange that it is Florence who asks Dombey for forgiveness here, but I think Dickens means her to demonstrate her belief in forgiveness to teach Dombey by example to believe in it. He has been "unforgiving" (936; ch. 59) because he cannot believe he can be forgiven. By showing him she believes he can forgive her, she is acting out the process he needs to imitate, teaching him "submission" (940; ch. 59). It is not that Dickens is saying one should submit to people like Dombey; rather, he values the act of submission as an end in itself, as a way to overcome pride. By humbling herself, Florence is trying to create belief in a being to humble oneself to and ask forgiveness from. Thus she finally enables Dombey to say, "Oh my God, forgive me, for I need it very much!" (940; ch. 59). Converting Dombey into a good father is like creating belief in a good father, overcoming her sense that there is no ideal in reality as she overcomes Dombey's own doubts. And by exemplifying belief in a good father, she teaches him to believe in a heavenly father.

At the end, Dombey, like Walter and Florence, seems reborn; he has become like Paul, regaining a childlike belief that can hear the voices in the waves—that is, can accept death, seeing it as redemptive like the sea, not destructive like the train. In its original version, the novel ends with a vision of this power able to overcome death: "The voices in the waves speak low to him of Florence . . . and their ceaseless murmuring to her of love, eternal and illimitable, extending still, beyond the sea, beyond the sky, to the invisible country far away" (975–76; ch. 62). This description suggests that Florence embodies the belief that death teaches; Dombey's being united with Florence is thus like gaining belief. Florence seems to mediate between him and what lies beyond the sea, as belief enables the doubting mind to reach toward the eternal. He has had to give up adult reason, which cannot see beyond this world, to accept this belief, putting himself into a childlike state in which it no longer matters that the ideal is invisible to reason.

Although Florence, like the pure heart capable of complete belief, can find an ideal in reality (that is, can believe it can be real), for Dombey—and I suspect for the adult, doubting side of Dickens himself—the ending is less fulfilling. Dombey has to give up most of what he wanted. Like Emily Brontë, Dickens gives us two endings, one that pictures the ideal in reality (Florence getting fulfillment) and the other (Dombey looking out to sea) making us feel the ideal exists only beyond this life. The novel ends, then, with a typical Victorian compromise, belief mixed with uncertainty.

chapter 6

David Copperfield

David Copperfield continues Dickens's effort to deal seriously with the concerns out of which his fictions rise, especially with the conflict I think lies at the heart of his work, the conflict between his resentment of his parents' neglect and his need to feel loved. *Dombey* faces the parent-child relation more directly than any other Dickens novel, but *Copperfield* comes closest to Dickens's own life. Here as in *Dombey*, however, he tries to get at what he feels to be the reality of his situation not in order to accept reality but in order to give imagination a better chance of dealing with it. Having worked out in *Dombey* the way he wants to transform imagination into belief, he proceeds to make that process the basis of *Copperfield*.[1] Thus, even though *Copperfield* contains a piece of Dickens's autobiography, it surrounds that fragment (like an oyster surrounding sand with a pearl) with layers of fiction that transform the fragment, giving it meaning, making it the basis for a search for a spiritual belief that can deal with the conflicts it arouses.

Although here again Dickens is trying to move from imagination to belief, in this novel he enacts this process in a character who is closer to himself—who is male, and whom he can call "I." It is as if he is trying to enable himself to live up to the ideal embodied by Florence. By using a less idealized protagonist, he is facing his uncertainties more directly; David is not as protected from doubt as Florence is. The character who most resembles Florence, Agnes, is much less central, making us feel that the faith she embodies is beyond the self, difficult to reach. David is more like Paul Dombey and the younger Walter Gay; he too is childish and has difficulty reaching belief. By making such a character his protagonist, Dickens makes the search for belief even more central than in *Dombey*. He locates the difficulties that imagination causes at the novel's center, making their resolution its main process. Though he suggested that Walter could be misled by imagination, he did not pursue that possibility; David acts out a story like that originally intended for Walter, a story based on the dangers of imagination. It seems that the more

Dickens tries to move toward serious belief, the more problematic imagination becomes.

John Forster quotes him as saying at this point in his life that his "early imaginations," in which he once had "guileless belief," have become "worn and torn" because of later disillusion (1:7); the things that raised his "fancy" are gone (1:22).[1] He sounds divided, his reason standing back from his imagination, unable to believe in it. This division between reason and imagination finds expression in *Copperfield;* Dickens creates two representatives of himself, two versions of his "I"—David the character and David the narrator. For the first time he uses a first-person narrator standing back self-consciously from the action, possessing an identity separate from the story. In other words, he locates imagination, seeking wish fulfillment, in David the character, who believes in what he imagines, and locates reason in the narrator, standing apart from and critical of imagination, sympathetic with David's delusions, but recognizing they are delusions. David the character is childish; the narrator is adult, seeing with the disillusioned awareness that Dickens admitted to Forster he himself felt.

Dickens has become more self-critical, creating a voice that enables him to resist imaginative desires, and if he is returning to childhood here, it is to bid it farewell, perhaps wishing he could return to it, but using his adult narrator to distance it and thus to admit he can no longer share the child's belief in the imaginary. Although there is childlike imaginative play here as in earlier novels, the narrator stands apart from it, unable to let it take over consciousness entirely (as, for example, when the maturing David mistrusts Micawber), feeling the need to move on to a more serious purpose, to a kind of fiction where playfulness is subordinated to spiritual purpose. We should not let the modern preference for irony blind us to the fact that Dickens expresses considerable sympathy for David and nostalgia for the childlike. What the child wishes and imagines may not be true, but it would be nice if it were. Though Dickens is critical of imagination, he also wishes he did not have to be, that imagination did not need restraint. But he can no longer fully accept it, and for my purposes here I shall concentrate on his criticism of it.

Dickens begins the novel by asking whether David will be a "hero" (49; ch. 1), warning us that imaginative wish fulfillment is problematic, that we should not simply accept imagination's wish to picture the self as a romance hero (as we could in Dickens's early novels). He also detaches us from David by beginning with David as a child, making us feel his limitations—limitations that are caused largely by imagination. The infant David cannot fully accept and understand reality and has a tendency to "dream" (62; ch. 2) and to use imagination to distort what he sees. Dickens reproduces this tendency by shaping the fictional world to reflect David's desires and fears (Dickens always tends to alter the world like this, but here he is doing so self-consciously, aware that such distortions are childish and unrealistic). The novel begins like this because later David's imagination will continue to mislead his reason, though in less obvious ways, and Dickens is warning us of this tendency.

David's trip to the Peggotty home, like Florence's flight to the Wooden Midshipman, acts out a retreat from reality to imagination, trying to find an ideal home. Like the Midshipman, it is the home a child might imagine, and young David thinks it "the most delicious retreat that the imagination of man could conceive" (82; ch. 3). The "reality" he is retreating from is the home taken over by Murdstone, replacing his mother. Murdstone appears in the novel like a repressive reaction against David's desire for his mother, projecting the Oedipal fear that such a desire will be punished. The Peggotty home is imagination's attempt to reverse this situation, replacing Murdstone with his opposite, Mr. Peggotty, an idealized father figure who will not repress David, as if bringing back to life the real father David has lost (and the belief in a good father he has lost) and rescuing David from his fatherless condition as Mr. Peggotty has rescued Ham and Emily. Emily seems to be imagination's attempt to reverse David's loss of his mother; she is like an (apparently) accessible version of his mother. They seem created by imagination to cancel out their more realistic counterparts. But Dickens makes this episode reflect imagination's limitations. It cannot actually overcome reality; David cannot stay with them but like young Florence at the Midshipman must return to his reality, a world that seems more real because it is not wish-fulfilling like the Peggotty home. The fact that Mr. Peggotty lives at the sea's edge suggests that his home is not quite in reality and makes us feel that this imagined ideal is vulnerable and can be destroyed as a child's belief in the ideal can be destroyed.

But it is mainly through Emily that Dickens implies a criticism of imagination here. Her presence suggests that David's escapism involves physical, potentially guilty desire. Throughout the novel Dickens projects impulses we can infer are David's onto various alter egos, and here he projects the selfish desire David feels for Emily onto Emily. She too is misled by a somewhat selfish imagination and later even acts out a rebellion against and escape from a father figure like what David desires with Murdstone. She imagines "a glorious vision"—but of a merely earthly desire to be a lady (e.g., 85; ch. 3); David similarly uses "fancy" to etherealize her (87; ch. 3). Both are trying to idealize something earthly, to possess the ideal in reality. David must give up such selfish desires as he must give up Emily.

David begins maturing when he returns home to face the reality he has tried to escape, the "blank and strange" world (93; ch. 4) in which he is cut off from the maternal love he had as an infant. But though he needs to accept reality, realism alone (especially in the repressive, utilitarian form in which Murdstone, like Dombey, espouses it) cannot provide a belief that makes reality bearable; instead, it threatens to destroy the childlike imaginative capacity that can enable belief. Murdstone tries to force David "to conform to the ways of the working world" in order to "break" his imaginative tendency (206; ch. 10). In other words, he forces David to face a reality that is the negation of the imagined ideal (especially a loving mother). This negation is clearest when he sends David to work in the warehouse, an experience that threatens to destroy David's "fancy" (210; ch. 11) and make him lose belief in any ideal, as the experience upon which this is based threatened Dickens's belief in his parents. To resist this, David needs to keep "alive" his "fancy" in order to hold onto "hope of something beyond that place and time" (105; ch. 4). Imagination is guilty if it seeks an earthly ideal like Emily, but is valuable (though still imperfect) if it leads toward belief in an otherworldly ideal.

Though realism is shown as inadequate here, imagination is not satisfactory either. Realism is convincing but unattractive; imagination is attractive but unconvincing. It cannot deal with reality; David's retreat into book-reading does not help resolve his conflict with Murdstone. And David's reading is "greedy" because he is imagining himself a "hero" (106; ch. 4). Imagination indulges selfish desires that the novel's opening has hinted we should not accept. Eventually David needs to reconcile his imaginative idealism with an acceptance of reality. At this stage in his development, however, they remain opposed. His imagination is still too unrealistic, seeking escape— for example, in book-reading—and he can only see realism as negative like Murdstone, threatening belief, opposing the heart's need for an ideal.

Because imagination and reason are opposed, David cannot yet move to belief. Thus he is able to conceive of religion only as the "austere and wrathful" faith of the Murdstones (101; ch. 4); that is the only form in which Dickens yet makes religion available to him. By using Murdstone to associate utilitarian realism with repressive evangelicalism, Dickens implies that if one cannot see beyond reality, one cannot conceive of a loving God and (like Dombey on the train) can see the universe only as governed by some negative, unfulfilling power. Here again a secondary character reflects what Dickens wants us to feel is in David's mind; Murdstone's negative religion mirrors David's inability to believe in a loving God, to have a belief that could enable him to accept his mother's death—a belief like that Paul Dombey seeks. As usual, Dickens associates belief in God with belief in a good father.

If David does not believe in a cruel God, he believes in a cruel father, in the absence of paternal love that Murdstone embodies. He has not yet overcome Oedipal desire for his mother, a desire that makes him resent Murdstone for cutting him off from his mother. Insofar as imagination serves Oedipal desire, it will resent fatherlike control and so oppose belief in an ideal father.

David leaves his childhood home, then, leaving childhood and his childish version of the ideal, an Edenic, pre-Oedipal union with the mother. Thus reality seems more "blank" than ever (188; ch. 10); lacking any higher belief, David (like Dombey on the train) can consider death only as a negation of the ideal, can only feel the ideal is absent. But having forced David to face reality here, Dickens then pulls back from it. He confronts reality (which for him, here as usual, primarily means the reality of his parents' neglect when he was a child) not in order to give up imagination but to impel imagination to change so that it can deal more successfully with the doubts, fears, and resentments that reality causes. He confronts what opposes idealism in order to try to overcome that opposition. Dickens's unwillingness to give in to realism is shown here by what happens immediately after David is exiled to the warehouse: Micawber appears. Dickens is using imagination to try to create an antidote to Murdstone—to overcome the sense of a cruel father. Micawber is the opposite of Murdstone, not strong and unloving but weak and affectionate. Imagination is trying to replace what opposes its desires with a version of the father that serves those desires, one through which it attempts to overcome resentment of the father's bad qualities.

As he often does, Dickens projects the imaginative power used in creating a character who is relatively free of realism onto that character, endowing Micawber with an imaginative ability like that needed to create him. Like his creator, Micawber can escape reality through fictions,[2] transforming the bleak world in which David finds himself into "the modern Babylon" (211; ch. 11). Throughout the novel, Micawber seeks "liberty" through his "imaginative powers" (628; ch. 39); he does so by using words, as Dickens does, to turn reality into something he need not take seriously, giving himself the illusion of controlling or at least evading it. Here again a secondary character reflects the phase through which David is passing. Like Micawber, David wants to use imagination to transform his world, as when he tells the Orfling "astonishing fictions" about the world (223; ch. 11). Dickens makes Micawber attractive to reflect David's attraction at this stage to imaginative escape. It is as if David (like Dickens) has imagined the Micawbers in an imperfect attempt to escape the warehouse.

This retreat to the comparative sanctuary of the Micawber home resembles David's earlier retreat to another refuge in which imagination is shielded from too much realism, the Peggotty home. Dickens shows us that David is now more aware of reality and less able to believe in imagination by making the Micawber home less able (like the imagination it expresses) to overcome the pressures of the outer world. The Peggotty home is much more idealized, reproducing the younger David's innocent belief in the imagined ideal. By this point in the novel, however, Dickens is too committed to taking reality seriously to accept Micawber's imaginative freedom uncritically. His awareness that the imagined ideal is not real finds expression by making Micawber imperfect. Imagination tries to see him as an ideal father, but the sense of reality will not let him be one. Just as Dickens's imagination cannot overcome reality, the character representing it cannot; far from being able to defeat reality, Micawber is largely its victim.

Thus Micawber embodies Dickens's sense of imagination's weakness and of the illusory and self-serving nature of its attempts to evade reality. Micawber's attempts to transform reality remain childish, unacceptable to reason, and the ideal he imagines is not spiritual and so cannot prevent him from continually falling into despair. Undisciplined imagination like his, though attractive, cannot fill David's spiritual needs, cannot overcome his sense of the blankness of reality. This tension between an attraction to imagination and a rational mistrust of it is reflected in the way David at this point balances imagination with his sense of reality more than he did as a child, basing his fictions on the surrounding world rather than on books, beginning to reconcile his "imaginative world" with "sordid things" more fully than Micawber can (225; ch. 11).

Dickens is thus using Micawber to show David's growth here. Because he has learned to be more critical of childish imagination, David can see Micawber's limitations and move beyond him (as he moves beyond other characters throughout his development). Earlier Dickens protagonists could find idealized fathers such as the Cheerybles without worrying about whether that ideal was realistic, but now Dickens feels the need to seek a version of the ideal that reason can accept more fully. By leaving Micawber, David is moving beyond a state of mind that can only seek to escape from reality. By going to Aunt Betsey, he is finding a role model embodying a greater acceptance of reality. But here again Dickens is not abandoning imagination; rather, he is trying to salvage it, converting it into a form that he can reconcile more fully with his sense of reality. Aunt Betsey is at least as unrealistic a creation as Micawber is; Dickens is here replacing autobiography (however transformed) with wish fulfillment, giving David a fairy godmother to rescue him from the despair reality could cause.

Like the other relatively idealized parents David finds, Aunt Betsey seems a projection of his imagination. He has a "picture" of her in his "mind," which "might have been altogether . . . fancy, and might have had no foundation whatever in fact" (203; ch. 12), and when he is with her, he feels as if "in a dream" (272; ch. 14). Finding her is thus like making the imaginary come true, convincing reason it is real. And when she defeats Murdstone, it is like imagination overcoming reason and asserting belief in an ideal parent despite reality. Dickens allows David to escape from the urban scene of Dickens's own childhood suffering and retreat to Kent, the setting of Dickens's relatively idyllic childhood,[3] and to find a version of the loving mother David lost in childhood. Imagination is thus seeking to return to a childlike state in which it can believe in ideal parental love.

This retreat comes at the same point in the novel at which, in *Dombey*, Paul escapes to the ideal by dying, and it is as if David is trying to repeat that pattern but cannot fully do so. The chapter in which Aunt Betsey takes him in ends with his looking out to sea like Paul, hoping "to see my mother with her child, coming from Heaven, along that shining path." Unlike Paul, he cannot have this vision. But though he cannot yet reach belief, imagination strives toward it, finding a substitute version of the ideal in "the world of dreams" (255; ch. 13).

By taking him to Aunt Betsey's, then, Dickens is trying to move him toward the ideal, but Dickens's sense of reality is still in conflict with imagination's desire for the ideal, diminishing this version of the ideal. In other words, Dickens is working toward a combination of imagination with realism. Thus, although the trip to Aunt Betsey's seems like another retreat from reality to imagination, imagination here has been considerably chastened by David's exposure to reality. We have seen him beginning to blend realism with his imagination, and there is a similar blending in Dickens's presentation of Aunt Betsey. If she is a version of the ideal parent, she is a less idealized one than Mr. Peggotty; imagination is making concessions to reason's sense that the ideal cannot exist in reality. Dickens projects this sense of reality onto her, giving her a greater ability to accept reality than Micawber has.

Dickens is simultaneously using Aunt Betsey to create a version of the ideal and to express his sense that reality opposes the ideal. He wants to imagine an ideal that (like her with Murdstone) can deal with reality, can survive despite the sense of reality's unidealness. Thus Aunt Betsey embodies a compromise. She has Murdstone's firmness and realism, but unlike him she can accept the childlike, as she accepts David. As a result, she is partly like

Murdstone's opposite, Micawber. Though she is not childlike herself, she gives refuge to Mr. Dick, who resembles Micawber, embodying in extreme form Micawber's childlike use of imagination to escape painful reality. The union of Aunt Betsey and Mr. Dick, then, embodies a union of realism and imagination. Dickens implies that, like Mr. Dick, childlike imagination is valuable when it is under reason's firm control, and reason, like Aunt Betsey, is valuable when it makes room for the childlike heart and imagination. It is Mr. Dick, like the heart, that "sets us all right" (249; ch. 13), telling her to become like a mother to David, as she is to Mr. Dick himself.

Mr Dick's kite-flying suggests imagination attempting to rise above reality. His "belief" in kite-flying as a kind of transcendence comes from "fancy" and inspires David to "fancy . . . that it lifted his mind out of its confusion, and bore it . . . into the skies"; he seems to be acting out imagination's attempt to reach religious belief. But because his attempt is only a "dream," based on imagination, he must "wake" to reality as the kite must come back to earth (273; ch. 15). Only for the moment can imagination rise above the confusion and doubts that reality causes. However, Dickens makes Mr. Dick absurd, implying that, even if he finds childlike imagination attractive, he feels it is inadequate. We can see this in Dick's petition-writing. It is as if Dick (like Mr. Dickens) is trying to be a writer, but unlike his creator he cannot control his imagination. Dickens is implying his own need to bring imagination under the kind of control that Dick lacks.

When David moves in with Aunt Betsey, he has reached a stage that she and Mr. Dick reflect; he has moved beyond Micawber-like escapism to a greater acceptance of reality, but his realism still coexists with a childish imagination like Dick's. Imagination and reason remain separate, as Dick and Betsey are separate, and so he cannot yet reach belief. Aunt Betsey's home is too imaginary, only a diminished, rather playful version of the ideal; Dickens seeks a stronger version, one in which the sense of reality has been more fully reconciled with the desire for an ideal. Aunt Betsey's home is not David's final destination; he must go on by himself and seek a more convincing ideal—that is, seek fuller belief in the ideal. This ideal, and belief in it, are embodied in Agnes, who appears here at the end of the novel's first quarter—the same point at which *Dombey* moves beyond childish uncertainty and Florence takes center stage, embodying a faith like Agnes's. But although Agnes is glimpsed here, it is only as a distant goal toward which David must struggle for the rest of the novel. He has not yet reached the belief that could make the ideal seem attainable for him.

Dickens indicates that David must become worthy of Agnes by disciplining his heart, and the action of the novel shows us that that process also includes disciplining the imagination whose dreams express the heart's wishes. It might seem that by the end of the first quarter, David has already disciplined himself enough to win Agnes; at least he has reached the point where he has earned his first sight of her. But at this point new characters appear as if in reaction against his dawning attraction to Agnes (and belief in an ideal), coming into existence in order to pull David and Agnes away from each other. As the desire for the ideal becomes more serious, the sense of forces resisting it becomes stronger. The characters opposing fulfillment imply that there are potentially guilty elements in David's desire (perhaps because he is reaching puberty). Since Agnes is another of Dickens's mother-like heroines, desire for her could arouse Oedipal guilt. Thus here again Dickens must try to create belief in an ideal by purging imagination of desires that could make it envision an unacceptable ideal.

As Dickens so often does, he objectifies the conflict implied in his protagonist by embodying different aspects of it in different characters, locating guilty impulses in secondary characters so he can keep the protagonist fairly (though not entirely) innocent. David must deal with various characters, then, who embody the forces opposing sublimation. By locating those forces in subordinate characters, Dickens can push them to extremes so we can more easily see what is wrong with them; and because they are outside David, he can reject them more fully.

The first of these characters is Uriah Heep. Uriah embodies, in extreme and repulsive form, one of the selves David must defend against having—one who resents paternal control and indulges in the rebellious, forbidden desires that such control opposes. It is as if Uriah is a projection of David's desire for Agnes in an uncontrolled, frightening form, yet one that nevertheless exercises a certain fascination. Such desires can take over the imagination, a danger Dickens may feel for his own imagination as well as David's. It is as if Uriah objectifies forbidden impulses in David's "distempered fancy" (447; ch. 25). David has a nightmare that Uriah is taking David and Emily off "to be drowned" (293; ch. 16), suggesting that innocent desire like David's for Emily (and now for Agnes) can be taken over by lust like Uriah's, drowning innocence. This nightmare connects Uriah with Steerforth, who, impelled by a lust like Uriah's, does his best to act out this dream. The nightmare, since it is David's, implies that both those characters are his alter egos—that he could be the one who is carried away by lust, abducts Emily, and is drowned.

Like Uriah, Steerforth represents a self David must avoid. I would say Uriah embodies guilty desires and Steerforth represents what David could become like if he gave way to those desires. Like Uriah, Steerforth is related to David's imagination, again implying that imagination can be taken over by such desires. The particular desire Steerforth is associated with is the desire to be a romance hero, which is a guilty desire because it is selfish. David's imagination has indulged in "daydreams" of becoming "like the hero in a story" (188; ch. 10), and Steerforth reflects this side of David by acting out the desire to be a hero, showing us what David could have become if he had tried to seek the kind of wish fulfillment romance heroes seek. Steerforth also corresponds, of course, to the side of David that was attracted to Emily. Dickens connects these two desires when he shows David imagining himself becoming a hero who can win Emily (203; ch. 10); that is, he imagines becoming like Steerforth. Such fantasies are selfish and indulge desires that can get out of control, as Steerforth's example teaches David.

Dickens connects the desire Steerforth represents with David's imagination by having Steerforth encourage David to indulge in imaginative escapism, telling stories. His exploiting of David shows how selfish desires can put imagination to their own uses, and how imagination is susceptible to them. David tells us, "Whatever I had within me that was romantic and dreamy, was encouraged by so much story-telling in the dark" (146; ch. 7). His being in the dark suggests that he is being encouraged to avoid facing reality, and perhaps being led away from the light of a higher belief by using imagination in a merely escapist way.

When Steerforth reappears in the novel, he is again associated with David's imagination. David has again begun indulging "visionary considerations," making him think life is "like a great fairy story" (330; ch. 19). He daydreams of being grown-up and free, and Steerforth appears as if to make his dreams come true (and thus show him what is wrong with them). To gratify his imaginative desires, David has just gone to the theater, where he can identify (as in childhood) with "noble" heroes and feel as if he is "leading a romantic life" (344; ch. 19). At this point Steerforth appears, so that David's dream of playing the hero seems to have brought him back into existence. Now that David is with Steerforth again, he feels as if he is "in a dream" (349; ch. 20), and under Steerforth's influence he builds "castles in the air" (378; ch. 22). Dickens clearly shares David's attraction to Steerforth (and to Romantic imagination) to a considerable extent, but he also uses Steerforth's influence on David to show that imagination can seek the selfish gratification of escape from reality rather than some spiritual belief—a sin of which the Victorians accuse the Romantics. Steerforth functions like imagination when he gets David drunk, leaving him "in a feverish dream" that ends in "remorse and shame" (423; ch. 24). Imagination becomes selfish, guilty, and even destructive when it allows too much desire. Not only does Steerforth cause this state in David, he is also a "nightmare" to himself (381; ch. 22).

Steerforth also cannot convert imagination into belief because he does not take it seriously, as we can see when he mocks David's belief in the play. Since he is too cynical to try to turn imagination into belief, he only uses it as an excuse for indulging desires, making it selfish and destructive, "pursuing" his "fancy" in a "desperate way," trying to overcome "all obstacles" and find earthly fulfillment rather than accepting that the ideal can only lie beyond this world (488; ch. 28). His failure to find an earthly ideal makes him fall into self-pity and resentment of reality, attitudes that prevent belief. Without belief in a higher control, he cannot restrain imagination from giving way to selfish desires. Whereas David learns to accept that he cannot return to a childhood paradise, Steerforth tries to act out imagination's desire to reenter childhood by becoming a guest at the Peggotty home. That desire evidently arouses Oedipal guilt; Steerforth's crime wounds Mr. Peggotty, the idealized father. Steerforth first appears at the point in the novel at which David has just rebelled against Murdstone, another version of Oedipal rebellion; Steerforth appears in the next chapter as if to embody this rebellious side of David. His example, then, exists to show David how uncontrolled imagination can give way to guilty desires of this sort, and thus needs to be disciplined (as Steerforth needs a father's guidance).

Led by the imaginative impulses in himself that correspond to Steerforth, David too tries to make a wish-fantasy come true. Since Steerforth reflects David's childish desire for Emily, it is at this point in the novel, when Steerforth's influence is strongest, that David acts out his own (carefully restrained) version of Steerforth's passion by falling in love with Dora. Dickens keeps David innocent and sympathizes with his infatuation, but David here shares some of Steerforth's lack of discipline, allowing desire to run away with his imagination and seeking a merely earthly ideal. Like Steerforth, he is attracted to a childlike woman, implying that there is something childlike about their lack of self-control. The story of David and Dora is like love stories in early Dickens novels, seeking wish fulfillment by killing off a heavy father and marrying a child bride, retreating from the adult world. But Dickens sees this now as only "a dream," not "real" (548, 546; ch. 33); he can no longer accept such unrestrained imagination.

As he was with Emily, David is misled by "fancy" (457–58; ch. 26), seeing Dora as a "Fairy" (450; ch. 26) in a sentimental "reverie," imagining himself "in a garden of Eden" (452; ch. 26), trying to escape reality and find a selfish version of the ideal. And here again the character he is attracted to reflects his own state; Dora embodies the same childlike imagination, unable to face reality, that Dickens implies in David. Because David has reverted to a childlike state, seeking to return to the sort of relationship he had with his mother and that he dreamt of having with Emily, some of the characters from his childhood now reappear in the novel. The fact that Dora's companion is Miss Murdstone suggests that Dora is as childlike now as David was when he lived with the Murdstones, and that rather than helping David to grow up, she is causing him to regress to a similar condition. Also at this point in the novel, Micawber returns, reflecting David's tendency to indulge imagination somewhat the way Micawber himself does; under Dora's influence David even expresses himself rather "in the style of Mr. Micawber" (618; ch. 38).

More important to Dickens than the way selfish imagination prevents David from accepting reality is the fact that it prevents him from reaching belief in an ideal beyond reality. By attracting him to Dora, it pulls him away from Agnes, who represents that higher belief. As David tells her at the novel's end, his "heedless fancy . . . wandered from" her (936; ch. 62), as uncontrolled imagination of the kind Dora represents wanders away from serious belief. David's education requires that he move beyond Dora and Steerforth and the uncontrolled, selfish use of imagination that corresponds to them, rejecting false ideals as with Carlyle's Everlasting No. Losing Steerforth is like giving up his vision of himself as a Romantic hero, and losing Dora is like giving up the childish belief that he can find a paradise on earth. In both cases he learns that the ideal he believed in was only a figment of his imagination, that reality is unlike what he imagined.

Once the characters associated with rebellious desires have been removed from the novel, David can move on to his final conversion, his Everlasting Yea, the true belief to replace the false one he has rejected. He gives up Dora and turns to Agnes, thus replacing imagination with belief. The fact that Dora must die before David can have Agnes implies that Dickens feels imagination and belief are opposed. It is only by giving up the desire associated with Dora, desire to possess the ideal in an earthly form, that imagination can be purified into belief. But Dickens wants to make us feel a continuity between the two; he wants belief to grow out of imagination so that he need not reject imagination too much. Thus Agnes too is partly associated with and appeals to David's "imagination" (279; ch. 15). In addition, Dickens has Dora anoint Agnes as her successor. It is as if he is transforming Dora into Agnes, acting out a transformation of desire by transforming its imagined object; he wants to keep the childlike desire expressed through Dora but to purify it by combining it with the acceptance of a higher control that Agnes exemplifies. Dora herself at last moves beyond "foolish fancy" (835; ch. 53) and learns to value Agnes, reflecting what David will do.

By giving up Dora, David has given up his illusion that he can be a hero and win a romance heroine; thus it is appropriate that Dora's death is followed by the death of Steerforth, the character who tries to play the hero.

Steerforth's death is like a nightmarish "dream" (854; ch. 55), making us feel that imagination is dangerous and unfulfilling so that we will move beyond it, or at least making us feel that this final evocation of the violent, rebellious forces in imagination has exorcised them, purging imagination of the desires that resist spiritual belief.

Once Dickens has rejected uncontrolled imagination, he can move David on toward belief, which has been connected with Agnes throughout the novel. The first time David sees her, he associates her with "a stained glass window in a church" (280; ch. 15), and Dickens continues to use language that both makes her seem holy and links her with belief in what is holy. Agnes, as David finally realizes, is "like a Heavenly light by which I see all other objects" (950; ch. 64). She represents a belief that enables one to accept reality by seeing the divine through it (not, evidently, in it). Agnes is especially associated with belief when Dora dies and Agnes appears in her place, pointing "upward towards Heaven" (839; ch. 53). The message she (like faith) is bringing David is that the ideal he has sought to possess in this world can exist only in heaven—but that he should not despair at having failed to attain it, since it does exist in heaven. Here as in *Dombey*, then, Dickens uses death to force imagination to accept that it cannot possess the ideal in this world. One must give up desire for an earthly ideal in order to reach belief, as David must give up Dora and the desires she represents before he can see Agnes pointing to heaven and understand the belief she embodies. This sacrifice enables belief by removing its object beyond the reach of reason's reality-testing.

Agnes is another embodiment of the mother figure David keeps seeking; when she first appears, she seems like her own mother reborn. But unlike other mother substitutes in the novel, she is not only an object of belief but also an embodiment of what belief should be like, providing David with the model he must imitate in order to overcome Oedipal guilt; she submits to her father and forgives his weakness (as Dickens evidently wished to forgive his own father). By imitating her submission, David can make his desire acceptable, canceling the Oedipal elements Dickens has implied in it. (In contrast, his desire for Dora, like Steerforth's for Emily, involves opposing her father.) Dickens, however, largely rationalizes these Oedipal elements, as usual, by associating submission to a father with belief in a heavenly father. Agnes exemplifies belief in both earthly and divine fathers, but it is mainly her spiritual example that Dickens emphasizes, perhaps because it is easier to accept a divine father than a real and imperfect earthly one.

David completes his conversion in the novel's climactic scene in Switzerland. The scene begins by making explicit David's disavowal of undisciplined imagination. He sees that "the whole airy castle"—the imagined ideal he has believed in—has been "shattered," leaving him feeling that reality is a "ruined blank and waste." Since imagination alone cannot overcome his sense of the unidealness of reality, he must "look up" above the "abiding places of . . . Fancy" to something higher, to a "dawn" for which he thanks "Heaven," implying that a spiritual belief dawns in him. Although there is a rather conventional Romantic appeal to nature here, Dickens, unlike the Romantics, cannot fully base belief on nature—that is, cannot locate the divine in reality. David "could almost have believed" that the music he hears here is "not earthly"—but only almost; nature cannot quite inspire belief in the divine.

After nature has done all it can, David needs Agnes and the belief she embodies in an ideal beyond this world to take him the rest of the way to faith; he receives letters from her that commend him to God and guide him toward "a firmer and a higher tendency." The belief she represents is higher than imagination, "far removed from my wild fancies." By holding Agnes "sacred," David is able to become "self-denying" and give up earthly desire (since he thinks he cannot marry Agnes), accepting an otherworldly ideal instead; Dickens's language asks us to associate this with religious belief. David uses his belief in this sacred ideal, which he sees as existing beyond his world, to enable himself to accept the loss of an ideal in his world—associated with the loss of Steerforth, who seeks an earthly ideal, and Dora, who seems to David to represent an earthly ideal. He says he "endeavored to convert what might have been between myself and Agnes, into a means of making me more self-denying" (886–91; ch. 58); believing that the ideal exists beyond reality makes bearable its absence in reality.

But although Dickens tries to move beyond imagination here, he cannot give it up entirely, since he cannot base his belief on a sense of reality. Instead of abandoning imagination, David reconciles it with belief by winning Agnes's sanction for his "imaginative world" (931; ch. 62). He is "inspired" by her to have a "new fancy," writing a novel (888–89; ch. 58). In other words, he does what Dickens is trying to do here, write a more serious kind of fiction by making imagination serve belief.

One way Dickens implies this combination is through his use of Micawber. Micawber embodies childish, unrealistic imagination, and yet he (like imagination) still has a role to play in saving Agnes. When Uriah gets power over him, that implies that imagination can be taken over by selfish passions, that it needs some higher control to resist such passions. Like David, Micawber is inspired and thus transformed by Agnes. She gives him the belief in an ideal to serve that enables him to defeat Uriah. In other words, if imagination serves a higher belief, it can overcome selfish passions.

And the climax of the Uriah-Wickfield plot suggests that imagination is necessary. Agnes alone cannot defeat Uriah; she needs Micawber.

Similarly, Dickens evidently feels that he needs both a spiritual purpose and imaginative play in his work. If one is to reject guilty passions, one needs an alternative outlet for their energies; imagination offers such an alternative, an outlet that is playful enough to avoid guilt, not taking desire too seriously. If Dickens's imaginative play did not offer a safe way to get rebellious impulses out of his system, submission to a higher power might seem too repressive, denying those impulses expression rather than diminishing them to an acceptable form. It is because Uriah is denied a playful outlet that he (and the impulses he embodies) finds submission unbearable and rebels against it; and it is because Micawber, like imagination, can express himself playfully that he doesn't mind serving Agnes and being rather submissive (and we don't mind it for him). Nevertheless, once Micawber has served his purpose, he is sent into exile. Once Dickens has reached serious belief, he apparently feels he should set aside merely playful imagination.

The novel's last sentence is a prayer that the belief Agnes represents will enable David to accept death; he asks that Agnes be "pointing upward" (950; ch. 64), toward the afterlife. The ideal can exist only beyond reality; unlike his Romantic predecessors, Dickens can find no real-seeming embodiment, no objective correlative, for the divine. He locates the ideal in the "soul," which he equates with Agnes (950; ch. 64). Unable to find an object of belief, he instead offers us the mind seeking belief as an end in itself, without finding any object. He can only hope that when he dies, he (like Paul Dombey) will reach certainty. As with many other Victorian idealists—Tennyson in *In Memoriam* and "Ulysses," for example—belief remains something to strive for, not to possess.

chapter 7

Bleak House and *Hard Times*[1]

Having worked out the way he wants to move from imagination to belief in *Dombey* and *Copperfield*, Dickens proceeds in *Bleak House* to the question of how that belief should be related to reality. Esther Summerson has already reached a fairly satisfactory faith, and the novel mainly focuses on what comes after that, on the way she defends her belief against reality and realism as Florence Dombey does in the later part of her novel. For Florence, that defense is a personal matter that she can resolve by changing her relationship with her father. For Esther, however, the problem is more intractable; although it involves her relationship with her mother, Dickens also sets her in opposition to the entire world her mother inhabits, the world that centers on Chancery and that represents social reality in general. As he does in his other late novels, Dickens transforms the parent-child relation into a symbol of the social situation; the way people in society are cut off from each other is represented by the way children are cut off from parents. By adding this social half to the novel, he pits Esther against all of society, and idealism against all of reality. The question the novel poses is whether an idealist like Esther can hold onto her belief in the face of a reality as unideal as the Chancery world.

The dual narrative emphasizes the opposition of idealism to realism.[2] The side of Dickens that seeks to believe in an ideal speaks through Esther's narrative, which is concerned with the search for an ideal (for perfect parentlike love, for a perfect home, and for a society based on those things); the other half of the novel expresses the side of him that remains aware of how reality opposes this desire for an ideal. The impersonal narrative shows us the external, perceived world of objects; Esther's narrative expresses the self that perceives and tries to deal with that reality, the mind capable of belief and therefore able to move beyond a view of the world as mere separate, physical objects. This division of the novel evidently reflects a tension between idealism and realism like that in other Victorian writers, since, as I have already mentioned, there are similar divisions in other Victorian novels, including *Wuthering Heights* and *Vanity Fair*. But *Bleak House* is more deeply divided; idealism and realism are given separate narrators.

The Chancery world is not just "reality," however, but "reality" as seen by idealism and thus seen as negative, opposing the desire for an ideal. It is caught in a timeless stasis, its inhabitants hardly able to change or escape and unable to see beyond the materialist goals society has taught them to believe in. Dickens tells us at the start that this world opposes idealism: it causes "a loose belief that if the world go wrong, it was, in some off-hand manner, never meant to go right" (9; ch. 1). Because there is no evidence of any benign control in society, we are likely to lose belief in the possibility of a benign control in the universe, of anything that can mean and purpose; if there is any God, he is merely off-hand and indifferent. Chancery has replaced God in people's minds; it seems to have godlike power, but it is a god of law and punishment, not a forgiving god one can believe in fulfillingly. Dickens uses Richard Carstone's story to show how Chancery destroys belief and purpose, and he uses Lady Dedlock's to show how society causes despair.

By using the impersonal narrator, Dickens gives us a sense of the absence of a mind (like Esther's) able to find meaning and anything to believe in in this world; he withholds a sense of meaning through that narrator to make us wish for the qualities Esther expresses. In contrast, Esther's narrative presents an individual trying to hold onto belief in an ideal in a world that offers no basis for such a belief. In her narrative characters can get away from Chancery's influence, find something better to believe in, and become good. By allowing Esther to exist in a separate narrative, Dickens makes us feel she is in the world but not of it; he can insulate her from the disillusion Chancery could cause. But at the same time he is implicitly admitting that he cannot wholly reconcile idealism and realism, that he must protect belief from the sense of reality, and that belief cannot fully overcome reality. The ideal he wants to believe in cannot exist in the reality he perceives, and so idealism must retreat to a separate narrative where it can be protected from reason's doubts. Esther's segregation prevents her from acting on the Chancery world very much, suggesting the inadequacy of an idealism cut off from reality.

The novel, however, is an attempt to overcome this weakness. Dickens breaks the novel in halves in order to make us feel something is wrong and want to reunite what has become separated. The novel is concerned with finding a way for idealism not only to resist realism but to enter into reality and act on it. Dickens hopes that Esther's idealism can change reality, as Jarndyce defends against becoming jaundiced (by keeping his faith in human goodness) and overcomes the bleakness of Bleak House. Thus Dickens is especially concerned here with charity—with the way idealism can act on reality. Nevertheless, he has conceded so much to reality that he has made charity's task almost impossible. He does show some ways true charity can help those caught in social reality (for example, Charley), but his sense of the unidealness of that reality and the way it is largely beyond the reach of an idealist like Esther undercuts his hopes for charity. Woodcourt cannot save Jo; Esther cannot save Richard. Society corrupts most charity into mere Jellybyism, one more way of evading an acceptance of how unideal reality is.

As a result of this pessimism, for the first time in Dickens's career we have a novel that is unable to offer an ending that is completely fulfilling. The central plot action involves Esther's relation to her mother, and she is unable to rescue Lady Dedlock from the Chancery world and the despair to which it drives her. After these failures, the nominal happy ending seems rather weak; in contrast, Florence ends up with both Walter and her father, not just a rather drab mate as Esther does. Furthermore, Esther's happy ending can only take place outside the novel's world; Dickens seems to have given up hope that Esther can make a difference and concluded that the only way to save her idealism is to allow her to escape from reality altogether. That escape may be meant to show us that one should give up material concerns, but since the rest of the novel is about trying to save people from the Chancery world, the ending seems more of an evasion than a solution. A happy ending can take place only in Esther's half of the novel; the half of Dickens that faces reality more fully no longer seems able to believe in happy endings.

Since Dickens's idealism cannot overcome his sense of reality, *Bleak House* seeks some way to hold onto belief even though it must coexist with a realistic awareness that opposes it. In the preceding novels he felt imagination could create a bridge between these two; here, however, realism and idealism are more irreconcilable, impossible to bring together in one narrative, and this opposition makes imagination's job almost impossible. Dickens no longer appeals to imagination as a basis for belief but rather sees it as almost completely disabled by reality,[3] unable to overcome the world's unidealness. It is almost as if one must be born into the right narrative to have a chance of being saved; if one has the misfortune to live in the Chancery world, belief is impossible, and imagination can only grope for it in vain. If one is like Esther, one already has belief and doesn't need imagination to obtain it.

The extreme example of the way the Chancery world opposes imagination is the Smallweed family. They are against "all story books, fairy tales, fictions, and fables," and Dickens makes it clear that this materialist denial of imagination prevents them from reaching any spiritual belief. Grandfather Smallweed's concern with "the hardest facts" makes him incapable of "ideality, reverence, wonder" (257–58; ch. 21). The Chancery world does its best to turn other characters into Smallweeds, suppressing or deforming imagination by denying them anything they can idealize. For example, the servant Guster has "a susceptible something that possibly might have been imagination" if reality would allow her to develop it (136; ch. 11). Characters who try to use imagination—for example, Snagsby, who "solaces his imagination" by seeking something better than the Chancery world (118; ch. 10), and Miss Flite—are weak, unable (like imagination) to overcome reality.

In this anti-ideal world, when imagination is not defeated by reality, it goes to the opposite extreme, trying to escape reality, as Harold Skimpole's example shows. Skimpole is rather like sentimental poseurs in Dickens's early fiction, but where Dickens once merely laughed at sentimental Romanticism, he now takes it seriously, seeing Skimpole and the attitude he embodies as a real threat. Skimpole uses his pose to escape having to deal with reality and to indulge his own selfish desires.[4] His "imagination" is not "regulated" by being "adjusted" to a sense of reality and so it cannot be "serious" but merely seeks "amusement" (522; ch. 43); that is, it cannot lead to belief as Dickens wants imagination to. Its "brightest visions" are admittedly "imaginary," merely selfish efforts to escape "the darkness of Chancery" as he encourages Richard to do (460; ch. 37).

Dickens here seems to be rejecting the playfulness of his early fiction, the ability to escape from seriousness that we value in Sam Weller and that he still finds somewhat attractive in Micawber; he now feels that imagination needs to be balanced with the serious concerns Esther represents. If Dickens is so critical of Skimpole, it may be because he fears his own imaginative playfulness may work against his serious purpose. Skimpole's attitude is as much a product of the Chancery world as the Smallweeds'. He agrees with them that reality is unideal and there is no point seeking any belief with which to deal with it. Where they give up idealism entirely, he gives up realism, rejecting "Common Sense" as "painful" and "disagreeable" (468; ch. 37)—as opposing his desires. He has given up attempting to convince reason to accept imagination's visions; thus he is not trying to use imagination to reach belief. Instead, he is acquiescing in the novel's polarization of realism and idealism, accepting that one can have only one or the other, that there is no middle ground between "poetry" and "prose" (726; ch. 61). It is that polarization that Dickens wishes to overcome.

The main character whose imagination falls victim to Chancery is Richard Carstone. Here again I would guess that Dickens is describing a state that he fears he himself could fall into, his idealism destroyed by reality—a state he creates Esther to try to counteract. Richard resembles Steerforth in going bad for want of belief in fatherly guidance, but he also resembles Copperfield in being misled by imagination into seeking an ideal in this world. The comparison indicates that Dickens is more pessimistic here than in *Copperfield* about whether imagination can find an ideal to believe in. Perhaps this is because he now sees imagination as more influenced by society. It is Chancery that arouses Richard's hopes and thus makes him susceptible to Skimpole's influence, implying that it is society that leads him to indulge in the kind of selfish imagination Skimpole embodies.

Richard convinces himself that his "dream" (609; ch. 51) of an "imaginary" fulfillment (464; ch.37) can be realized through Chancery. Because he cannot restrain his desire for an earthly ideal, he is unwilling to accept that the ideal must be beyond this world. He replaces God with a social idol, thinking he can get "truth and justice" (464; ch. 37) not from God but from Chancery. But since he cannot get these, his imagination has led him not toward but away from belief, leaving him "purposeless" (489; ch.39), infected with "uncertainty" (151; ch. 13). Dickens uses the Chancery suit to symbolize the search for earthly fulfillment; like Chancery suitors, those who seek material, social success are doomed to despair, since, like Richard, they seek fulfillment from a world that offers only one ending—death. As in Lady Dedlock's case (and Dombey's), materialism ends in despair.

Only by freeing oneself of earthly desires—symbolized by giving up the desire to win in Chancery, as Jarndyce does—can one escape the disillusion those desires cause. Once one has done this, one can move on to belief in an ideal beyond this world, as Richard finally does. He "wakes" from his "troubled dream" and realizes that the ideal can exist not in this world but only in "The world that sets this right" (763; ch. 65). Thus Dickens now feels one must reject imagination—wake from its dream—to find true belief. But if he can find no basis for belief either in reality or in imagination, belief is more precarious than ever.

Esther is Dickens's attempt to solve this problem, and the solution she offers is not based on imagination. Rather, she is a character who tries to face up to reality. She is not, however, simply a realist. The main realist in the novel is Inspector Bucket. By making Bucket a sympathetic character, Dickens shows that he is more willing to accept realism now (just as he is more critical of imagination), but Bucket, like realism, has limitations. He begins by working for the novel's other main realist, Tulkinghorn, and thus working against the forgiveness and charity Esther values. Realism alone, like Bucket, cannot provide a higher belief able to overcome social selfishness. Only when Bucket works with Esther can he work toward fulfillment, implying that realism needs to be subservient to belief.

We can say, then, that Esther embodies a belief that can accept and work with realism, that can face reality without losing idealism. Esther is more of a realist than Jarndyce, seeing through people like Skimpole (and thus rejecting the imagination he represents), whereas Jarndyce's Pickwickian belief in human goodness makes him unaware of what Skimpole is really like. Here again Dickens betrays a sense that realism and idealism are opposed, that idealism prevents one from perceiving reality. However, he tries to use Esther to overcome this opposition. She is aware of the reality that Jarndyce cannot face, of the way natural human goodness can be perverted in society, but at the same time she values and serves Jarndyce's idealism and does not give way to despair or retreat into imagination as Richard does. Thus she can combine Bucket's realism with Jarndyce's idealism. Unlike Jarndyce she can enter the Chancery world, though like Jarndyce she cannot stay there; she faces reality but returns to idealism instead of giving way to the despairing sense that reality is all there is. Thus she can act on reality in behalf of idealism, rather as Dickens wants his fiction to accept reality yet lead to belief in something more.

Because she must accept reality so completely, Esther must largely do without imagination. As a child she accepts that she cannot be like "the princesses in the fairy stories" (17; ch. 3), giving up desire for an earthly ideal as Copperfield must give up his desire to play the hero. She acts out this giving up of childish imagination that seeks selfish gratification by burying her doll. The doll has a beautiful complexion (17; ch. 3), and when Esther later gives up her complexion as she has given up the doll, it is another surrender of imagination's desire for earthly wish fulfillment. Though she cannot wholly resist the "dreams" of "fancy," she sees they are "idle" and not "unselfish" and forces herself to oppose them (75–76; ch. 6). Nevertheless, she does not entirely reject imagination; like her creator, she converts it into an unselfish form, using it, for example, when she tells the Jellyby children fairy tales to counteract their mother's utilitarianism. But unlike characters in Dickens's earlier fiction, she mainly rejects selfishness not by transforming imagination but by giving up the desires which imagination would indulge. For example, she accepts that the ideal she wishes for (a loving mother) cannot exist in reality.

Esther acts out this self-abnegation when she becomes ill. Her going blind is like facing the darkness of reality, and her illness is like giving up earthly desires (especially the desire for Woodcourt), accepting that she can find the ideal only beyond this world: "I might aspire to meet him, unselfishly, innocently, better far . . . at the journey's end" (443; ch. 35). Attaining this belief is symbolized by her regaining her eyesight. But what she sees is reality, which suggests that her newly strengthened conviction enables her to accept reality without giving in to the despairing sense that its darkness is all there is. Her recovery is immediately followed by her discovery that Lady Dedlock is her mother; in accepting this, she puts to use her new ability to accept that she cannot obtain the ideal (a loving mother) in this world. She makes a similar act of self-abnegation when she accepts Jarndyce's proposal; she is accepting dutiful submission to a father-like control as a substitute for ideal fulfillment (Woodcourt). That submission is a way of overcoming rebellious-ness like Richard's, a resentment of reality's unidealness that could lead to despair; thus submission is a way of salvaging idealism, so that she can finally be rewarded with a version of the ideal, marrying Woodcourt.

The novel's ending, then, offers a mixture of realism with idealism. Dickens's endings (like those of many writers) typically offer a compromise in which we seem both to find an ideal in this world and at the same time to go beyond this world, especially since the fulfillment is located in the time after the novel is finished. Thus his endings half admit that the ideal they present is unattainable. In Dickens's later fiction, the sense that the ideal exists only beyond reality becomes stronger, and reality limits his characters more. We can see him moving in that direction here, allowing greater expres-sion to the attitude that opposes a happy ending. The ending is not, however, meant to be an unhappy one; rather, it seems to be an attempt to resolve the conflict between idealism and realism.

Jarndyce gives up the ideal he desires (marriage to Esther), his attempt to make the imagined ideal—his "old dream" (751; ch. 64)—become real. But the novel tries to make us see this not as a surrender to an unideal reality but rather as a victory for idealism. Jarndyce can give up Esther because he be-lieves in a higher, unselfish ideal, a belief that enables him to feel that giving her to Woodcourt is fulfilling. By making this sacrifice, he inspires Esther with a similar belief, in the ideal of unselfish submission that he embodies, so that she sees him as godlike, irradiated with a light like "the brightness of the Angels" (752; ch. 64). Like Agnes Wickfield, Jarndyce is both an example and an object of belief; what Dickens sees as godlike is the act of unselfish belief as an end in itself, as embodied in Jarndyce and Agnes. Dickens wants us to feel that Jarndyce is not giving up fulfillment but rather trading earthly ful-fillment for a higher fulfillment, beyond this world; he shows Jarndyce's sac-rifice as a kind of religious fulfillment.

As a result of Jarndyce's sacrifice, Esther receives not only a fulfillment like his—a stronger conviction that the angelic is possible in this world—but also what we are meant to feel is an earthly version of the ideal in Woodcourt. But that fulfillment involves an acceptance that the ideal is not fully attainable in this world, since he embodies that acceptance. He is "a man whose hopes and aims may sometimes lie . . . above the ordinary level, but to whom the ordinary level will be high enough after all, if it should prove to be a way of usefulness and good service"; he accepts the necessity of working within the limitations of "commonplace" reality "instead of spasmodically trying to fly over it" (717; ch. 60). Esther's diminished fulfillment, resembling the ending of *Middlemarch* (and both seem like the ending of *Paradise Lost*), seems to be an attempt to keep the ending from seeming like a mere escape from the Chancery world, to leave us with belief that charity is worth practicing in this world and thus a hope that we can work gradually toward the ideal (as Tennyson hopes at the end of *In Memoriam*).

Dickens tells us that belief in something higher than reality can be reconciled with an acceptance of reality; one can reconcile realism and idealism by rejecting the excessively Romantic wish to escape reality, which imagination (Richard's, for instance) can lead to. By giving up imagination's insistence on finding the ideal in reality or else rejecting reality, one can accept reality without losing belief. In marrying Woodcourt, then, Esther is accepting this compromise rather than winning a romance hero who will seem to take her beyond the confines of reality. And though Dickens evidently wants us to feel that Woodcourt is a more fulfilling mate than Jarndyce, I cannot help feeling some letdown here, not only because Woodcourt is so marginal and conventional but also because, here as usual in Dickens, the main focus has been on the desire for parental love, and it is Jarndyce who is the parentlike character. I feel that Esther too has had to make a sacrifice, as I have mentioned—that she has been unable to find an ideal father in this world just as she has been unable to find an ideal mother. Thus there is a combination of an idealized happy ending with a sense that the ideal is not fully possible in this world.

Although Dickens probably intends the ending as a satisfying compromise between the spiritual and the realistic, tensions remain largely unresolved here. Most importantly, although Esther's narrative can still reach a happy ending, though a considerably diminished one, there is no such ending in the Chancery world. Because that world remains dark, I feel that the novel has given up on reality rather than overcoming it, and Esther's fulfillment seems rather to exist beyond reality than in it. Perhaps her retreat from London shows that she can now distance reality because she believes in something beyond it. She can move to an area that, though it partly seems real, partly seems otherworldly, exemplifying the way Dickens is mixing his sense of reality with belief in an ideal.

The novel's last paragraph shows the uncertainty involved in this mixture. It simultaneously tries to make us feel that Esther has entirely overcome the way reality scarred her and has regained an ideal purity, and at the same time it admits that it is impossible, at least in this world, to be certain that such an ideal is possible. Esther says, "I am not certain that I know" (770; ch. 67), suggesting spiritual doubt. Dickens tries to accept this uncertainty, ending with a partial belief that is in unresolved tension with doubt so that he cannot finish the final sentence; the ending (and certainty) are possible only beyond the book, and presumably beyond this world. As long as she is in this world, Esther can only suppose the ideal may be possible; she cannot be certain.

Other aspects of the novel reinforce this sense of the way reality opposes the ideal. One of these is the darkness of the Chancery world; its fog keeps out the light as social materialism keeps people from having a sense that there is a God. At Jo's death, for example, the world remains "dark," and the only "light" he can find is after death (571–72; ch. 47). It is not, I think, that Dickens cannot come up with any convincing social way to save Jo; rather, he is making the point that salvation cannot be merely social (as Mrs. Jellyby thinks it can). He wants Jo's death to teach us that we too need to look beyond this world. To make this point, Dickens often shows that, though this world is dark, light can come into it, as idealism can survive despite reality. Esther can see "a distant prospect made so radiant by its contrast with" the "shade" in which she stands "that it was like a glimpse of a better land" (228; ch. 18). Instead of destroying belief, reality's darkness can give us a stronger sense of an ideal beyond this world, as Browning seeks in a poem like "Abt Vogler" to make the imperfection of reality create belief in a transcendent ideal. Despite our sense that reality is unideal, we can hold onto belief that there is an ideal beyond it. Light can break through into this world (e.g., 544; ch. 45), as belief can partly overcome realism. Nevertheless, the way Dickens repeatedly mingles light and shadows also implies that idealism cannot wholly overcome reality's darkness.

Because of Dickens's increased awareness of the pressures of reality, imagination is forced to accommodate the claims of reality more here than in his early fiction. Yet imagination still has its place in the novel. If it finds less expression in his characters, it is perhaps more important than ever in his way of narrating. He tells us in his preface that he is showing "the romantic side of familiar things" (4),[5] and I take this to mean he is using imagination to color perception of reality. This implies that imagination must coexist with realism, as the two halves of *Bleak House* must coexist. Imagination cannot overcome reality; it can only modify our way of seeing it. As Dickens put it in a letter, he modifies "literal" realism through "fanciful treatment"; "The exact truth must be there," but art lies not in simply reproducing it but in "the manner of stating the truth" (Forster, 2:279). If imagination's job is to modify reality, Dickens is conceding that realism is more basic, subordinating imagination to it. If imagination tries to transcend reality, it becomes delusory, as in Richard's case, or selfishly escapist, as in Skimpole's.

The fact that imagination mainly finds expression in the impersonal narrative means that it is largely cut off from the idealism Esther represents, unable to share her seriousness and reach the ideal and therefore forced to find imperfect outlets, merely trying to make reality bearable. Perhaps imagination finds more expression in the impersonal narrative because it is more needed there; since there is no voice to speak for idealism, imagination is all that is left to try to deal with reality. In addition, the seriousness of the first-person narrative largely precludes imaginative playfulness. In the Chancery world, on the other hand, imaginative play is a valuable defense against reality; it prevents us from taking the social world seriously, as Richard does, and thus yielding to its values.

The main way Dickens uses imagination in the impersonal narrative is through characters trying to envision an ideal but failing; his narrator, however, uses it not to picture an ideal but rather to see reality as a denial of the ideal. By doing so, he smuggles in the idealist values that the narrative's impersonality and insistence on reality do not allow him to express more directly. We can see this use of imagination in the light and dark imagery I have mentioned. Dickens describes the fog, for example, in a way that makes us desire the light it obscures, which means he is describing reality in a way that makes us desire the ideal it cuts us off from. Imagination enables this vision; the narrator tells us in the opening paragraph that "one might imagine" the sun is dead (5; ch. 1), and this whole description presents a world transformed by imagination, a world seen as opposing imagination's desires, an embodiment of the absence of divine control and its replacement by a false social idol.

In other words, Dickens is using symbols. In his earlier fiction he usually relies on metaphors, which are less serious than symbols because they admit that the imaginary is separate from reality. Though to some extent Dickens of course still values the playfulness of his early fiction and still uses metaphors often, as he becomes more concerned with finding serious belief, he tends to rely more on symbols. Whereas metaphors enable imagination partly to evade the sense of reality by supplementing the "real" image with an alternative, symbols try to transform reality, accepting it more fully, yet giving it meaning. Symbols are an attempt to locate the imagined ideal (or its absence) in the work's reality. They are not set apart from that reality as metaphors are and so do not admit they are imaginary; thus they ask us for more belief than metaphors do. Dickens is using them to try to induce belief in the imagined ideal. He wants us to see the light that shines into the Chancery world, for example, as something real but also as a manifestation of something higher than reality. And he wants the darkness to make us feel that society has shut out that higher illumination. This use of symbols attempts to reconcile imagination with his sense of reality, making the ideal seem real so that reason can accept it.

Hard Times is more directly concerned with imagination than is *Bleak House*. Despite his assertion in *Bleak House* that one must face up to reality, Dickens does not want to abandon imagination, and he uses *Hard Times* to try to overcome the difficulties he encountered in *Bleak House*. In *Bleak House* realism and idealism threaten to split apart, and by returning to an emphasis on imagination, Dickens hopes to heal that division. *Hard Times* is an attempt (and I think a fairly self-conscious one) to find a role for imagination to play in this more pessimistic kind of fiction. Dickens has been making increasing concessions to realism and growing more critical of imagination; now he needs to redefine imagination's function in order to defend it from his own doubts. One sign that he feels the unidealness of reality more is the fact that this is his first novel without a happy ending, suggesting that his imagination can no longer overcome his sense that there is no ideal in this world. If imagination cannot create an ideal, he must find a new job for it.

Dickens shows his concern with imagination by representing it in one of the novel's main symbols, the circus.[6] When we look at how he describes the circus, however, we find him emphasizing its shortcomings, implying that he feels imagination has analogous limitations. Here is our first glimpse of the circus: "He had reached the neutral ground upon the outskirts of the town, which was neither town nor country, and yet was either spoiled, when his ears were invaded by the sound of music. The clashing and banging band attached to the horse-riding establishment . . . was in full bray" (8–9; pt. 1, ch. 3). Probably one reason he makes this scene ugly is that he is showing us how it appears to Gradgrind, the observer here. It is Gradgrind, presumably, who feels the music is an invasion of his world and therefore ugly, as society opposes the circus and imagination. But Dickens has deliberately given us a negative first impression of the circus. I think we should not conclude (as some critics have)[7] that he is trying to make the circus (and imagination) impressive and failing, but rather that he is trying to make us feel the weaknesses of both. In a world as hostile to imagination as Gradgrind's, it can find no more adequate expression than this weak one. An imagination that is expressed only in braying cannot create a beautiful ideal we can believe in.

The fact that the circus cannot overcome reality suggests that imagination has the same weakness. Unlike similar places in his earlier fiction—the

Crummles theater, the Wooden Midshipman—the circus cannot offer a sanctuary from the outer world, not even an imperfect, temporary one. Similarly, imagination can no longer create an ideal refuge from reality; it cannot envision a believable version of paradise within which characters can be protected by an idealized parent from the pressures of reality, like David Copperfield at Aunt Betsey's. Sleary cannot replace Gradgrind and offer anyone a home. The circus and its denizens cannot enter Coketown and act on its world, as imagination must be segregated from the sense of reality. Because the circus, like imagination, is relegated to this marginal role, it cannot offer much fulfillment; Sissy cannot return to it or regain her father through it, and Louisa is even more cut off from it. Unlike earlier Dickens protagonists, Louisa is shown as enclosed within a reality that places her beyond imagination's help. Dickens's imagination cannot overcome her reality, and he reflects this in her. She lacks the imagination to conceive of any fulfillment beyond the merely social, and so cannot find fulfillment.

Unlike similar institutions in Dickens's earlier novels, the circus has a consistent, serious, evidently intentional symbolic and thematic function of a sort which there is no evidence to make us believe Dickens intended in such earlier counterparts as Crummles's theater and Mrs. Jarley's waxworks. Those earlier outlets for imaginative playfulness are quite marginal to the plot, unlike the circus at the climax of *Hard Times*. Nor does Dickens try to invest them with significance. They are expressions of imagination, but not symbols of it. Crummles and his troupe exist not to serve some external purpose but for their own sake, as a comic outlet for Dickens's energy, independent of any moral concern. Where Sleary preaches (though with a lisp), Crummles plays parts. In *Nickleby* Dickens still values the play of imagination as an end in itself, but in *Hard Times* he is self-conscious about such playfulness and must give it a thematic significance, as if trying to understand and justify it.

We can see Dickens's awareness of imagination's limits in the novel's comparative sobriety. There is less play of fancy, less exuberant elaboration of detail, than in other Dickens novels; the fact that he was willing to write such a short work indicates that he now feels imaginative play is expendable. When he does make characters imaginative, their imagination is not playful, not an end in itself as in many earlier characters, but is used to show how the world around them (as in *Bleak House*) suppresses or perverts imagination.[8] In a society based on Gradgrindian materialism, Dickens must have felt that imagination was doomed, like the circus, to a marginal, ineffectual existence. Perhaps he felt rather like a circus performer himself, unable to transform society as he wished, seen as a mere entertainer, not taken seriously.

Instead of relying on the circus as his main agent of salvation, then, Dickens uses Sissy, who (like Esther Summerson) acts not for imagination but for belief. She has a "faith" analogous to religious belief (42; pt. 1, ch. 9); she believes in a father who, like God, is absent from this world but may return, and she believes he is sacrificing himself for her sake, as a Christian believes in Christ's love and sacrifice. This faith enables her to become Christlike; she has been sent into this world to redeem people. She represents faith in giving Louisa something to live for and in defeating Harthouse, who embodies the lack of "faith" that Louisa could fall into (91; pt. 2, ch. 1). Sissy's "simple confidence" in a higher love overcomes his lack of "belief" (177; pt. 3, ch. 2), as Dickens wants us to believe faith can vanquish doubt.

Here again Dickens shows spiritual faith replacing belief in a social idol and connects spiritual attitudes to parent-child relationships. He makes us see social control as analogous to the control of unloving parents by paralleling Gradgrind's treatment of his children with Bounderby's treatment of his workers. Both of them impose an unloving control that can cause a loss of belief in an ideal control like God's; Gradgrind drives Louisa nearly to despair and Bounderby does the same with Stephen Blackpool. The novel's central conflict is mainly within Louisa. She is half like Sissy, with a natural "disposition to believe" (127; pt. 2, ch. 7), but half "doubtful" (10; pt. 1, ch. 3), too rational (like her father) to believe. The whole novel is concerned with this same tension, seeking a way to overcome the unbelief caused by reality—the reality of an unloving father and an unloving society. To overcome Louisa's "doubts and resentments" (127; pt. 2, ch. 7), Dickens relies on the faith embodied in Sissy. She has even more reason to resent an inadequate father than the Gradgrind children have, but she suppresses that resentment by believing in an ideal father. She helps Louisa to overcome resentment like Tom's, who corresponds to the resentful side of Louisa, and to forgive Gradgrind as Sissy has forgiven her father. Similarly, Stephen could be driven into rebellion by Bounderby and join the strikers (who are resentful like Tom), but instead he learns to become like Rachel (who corresponds to Sissy in his plot) and to believe in forgiveness. Both protagonists learn to forgive a repressive father figure by believing in a higher, ideal control.

Like Esther Summerson, Sissy embodies a belief that has little relation to imagination. She cannot stay in the circus, suggesting that to reach belief, one needs to leave imagination behind, giving up its desire for an earthly ideal and, like Sissy, facing reality. Reason cannot believe in an idealism that does not take this world into account. However, though Dickens expresses reservations about imagination, he also (in contrast to what he does in *Bleak House*) shows that faith has its own shortcomings. Like the circus, Sissy seems deliberately limited. Dickens does not make her the protagonist as he does Esther; she does not act in the novel's plot much more than the circus does. Her role remains defensive, as in defying Harthouse, which implies that Dickens feels that the best faith can do is ward off doubt. She never fulfills the main desire associated with her; she cannot regain her father (as Esther cannot regain her mother), nor can she find some idealized parent figure to replace him with. This failure suggests that although Dickens values belief, he no longer feels it can overcome reality; its ideal cannot exist in this world. That Sissy's belief in her father is shown as a delusion also implies a criticism of faith, a sense that (though valuable) it is unrealistic.

Instead of putting Sissy and belief at the novel's center, Dickens places his main emphasis on Louisa, who embodies the absence of belief, the awareness of reality that Dickens seeks to reconcile with faith. He is making doubt more central than in earlier novels. Gradgrind's rationalism has left Louisa "doubting, misbelieving," yet she feels the need for belief, sensing that Gradgrind has robbed her of any "belief" that could be a "refuge from what is sordid and bad in the real things around" her. All she (like reason) can see is reality, but its unidealness makes her wish to believe in something beyond it, giving her "an ardent impulse towards some region" where Gradgrind's rationalism would no longer prevent belief (165–66; pt. 2, ch. 12).

By the novel's end, Dickens can partly reconcile Gradgrindian reason with belief; Louisa can value what Sissy stands for. But Sissy's faith cannot overcome the reality Louisa must come to terms with; reason, like Louisa, cannot find any ideal in the reality it perceives and so remains unable to find a happy ending like the one faith earns for Sissy. Reason remains separate from belief as Louisa remains separate from Sissy. Sissy's happy ending does not seem to exist within Louisa's reality; we do not even know who Sissy's mate is. The ideal that faith believes in remains separate from the reality that reason must accept; as at the end of *Villette*, the ideal is possible for belief (Sissy) but not reason (Louisa). Similarly, Stephen's star remains distant, and the faith it represents seems attainable only beyond this life. Since belief cannot fully convince reason, Dickens is forced to let the two coexist, as in *Bleak House*. By admitting the ideal is separate from reality, he can protect belief from the sense of reality, removing it to a level where reason cannot attack it. Sissy's fulfillment is like a glimpse of an ideal beyond Louisa's reality, and Stephen's vision of the star is a similar glimpse. Dickens hopes that belief in an ideal beyond reality can enable us, like Louisa, to bear the absence of any ideal in this world, to keep belief despite our sense of reality.

Because belief is limited in this way, Dickens does not abandon imagination entirely. In *Bleak House* he seemed to feel that belief could largely replace imagination, but here he shows that he feels the need for imagination after all. He accepts that imagination's role must be diminished, but he wants to redeem and justify it. Though he shows how reality opposes it, he does so to make us wish it could deal more adequately with reality. Here again, then, he has shown what opposes idealism in order to try to overcome that opposition. As in earlier works, though now in a weaker form, he hopes to transform imagination so that it will serve belief. He wants, as he says at the end, to keep the "heart of infancy," with its capacity for imagining, from dying (226; pt. 3, ch. 9), as the circus, though reduced to a "skeleton," can be revived (221; pt. 3, ch. 7).

Dickens implies the connection between imagination and belief in several ways.[9] For one thing, the fact that Sissy comes from the circus suggests that belief comes from imagination. And Louisa implies to Gradgrind that it is because he has not developed her "fancy" that she has not been able to reach "belief" (165; pt. 2, ch. 12). At one point the narrator tells how imagi-nation can grow into belief. He is discussing the way Louisa should have been brought up:

> The dreams of childhood—its airy fables; its graceful, beautiful, hu-mane, impossible adornments of the world beyond; so good to be be-lieved in once, so good to be remembered when outgrown, for then the least among them rises to the stature of a great Charity in the heart, suffering little children to come into the midst of it, and to keep with their pure hands a garden in the stony ways of this world, wherein it were better for all the children of Adam that they should oftener sun themselves, simple and trustful, and not worldly-wise—what had she to do with these? Remembrances of how she had journeyed to the little that she knew, by the enchanted roads of what she and millions of inno-cent creatures had hoped and imagined; of how first coming upon Rea-son through the tender light of Fancy, she had seen it a beneficent god, deferring to gods as great as itself; not a grim idol, cruel and cold, . . . never to be moved by anything but so many calculated tons of lever-age—what had she to do with these? (150–51; pt. 2, ch. 9)

We start out, then, with imagination—"The dreams of childhood," "the ten-der light of Fancy"—but we outgrow our ability to believe in them. Yet we should still keep imagination in memory, somehow converting it into spiri-tual belief, creating a "Charity in the heart." Awareness that reality is "stony" makes us value the child's ability to believe in an Edenic garden even if it prevents us from fully sharing that belief. The ideal, though partly lost (seen as only imaginary), is partly shifted from reality to a place where it can still survive—the childlike heart (the same source of belief Tennyson turns to at the end of *In Memoriam*). This is a way of partly holding onto belief despite adult awareness of reality.

Dickens concedes that we must acquire reason, but we can keep this partial version of belief despite reason if we come to reason "by the enchanted roads" of imagination, seeing reason through the "light of Fancy." Imagination can soften reason, making it defer to belief in "gods" that are beyond its ken, objects of belief that only imagination can conceive of. By admitting these gods are only imaginary, we can get reason to accept them, not subject them to reality-testing. Imagination can create a diminished version of the ideal, which reason need not directly oppose, so that reason need not be "cruel and cold" like Gradgrind, rejecting belief. Thus rational awareness of an unideal reality can coexist with belief in some ideal beyond reality, though this involves an admission that belief is separate from reason, based only on imagination.

Dickens's fiction is making a similar journey, from a relatively childlike belief in imagined paradises (at least at the end of his earlier novels) toward a greater awareness of how stony reality is and thus of how much we need some serious, chastened belief that can enable us to deal with that awareness. By giving up the childish illusion that one can reach the ideal in this world, Dickens can move to an unselfish, spiritual belief in an otherworldly ideal. As in *Bleak House*, he is using realism to try to teach "Charity in the heart," to make us feel compassion for those with a childlike desire for an ideal who are caught in a reality that opposes their desire. He hopes to arouse our imaginative desires and then use his realism to convert those desires into an unselfish form, teaching us to believe in an ideal beyond this world by showing its absence in this world.

This movement beyond imagination is reproduced in Sissy's story. Though she comes from the circus, she must leave it and (like Esther Summerson) face the outer world. The fact that she cannot return to it may reflect Dickens's sense that he cannot return to childlike belief in imagination's visions. By facing reality, Sissy can go beyond the childishness of the circus (and of imagination), giving up imagination's desire for an earthly ideal, and develop a serious belief. Gradgrind's taking her from the circus is like rationalism trying to destroy childlike belief in an ideal (an ideal father), trying to make her become like Louisa. However, instead of reason's converting faith, faith ultimately converts reason. By accepting Gradgrind, Sissy faces up to rationalism and reality, but this awareness does not destroy her belief. Instead, she combines the two, seeing how reality is unlike the ideal—how Gradgrind is unlike an ideal father—and learning from this to pity him. Her faith in an ideal father makes her believe Gradgrind can be converted. Her final victory over him acts out the process whereby faith convinces reason to defer to "gods as great as itself."

Since neither imagination nor belief alone is very strong, Dickens combines the two. Neither Sissy nor the circus alone resolves the novel's conflict; rather, the two combine to do so, as Micawber helps Agnes defeat Heep and as Dickens feels imagination should serve belief. Given its weakness, the circus cannot enable a very happy ending, only a diminished version of one—the rescue of Tom. If Tom embodies resentment against Gradgrind (and on a more general level, resentment against the failure of society to give the individual anything to love and believe in), then Louisa's saving him from resentment and the punishment it could cause is like overcoming her own resentment and lack of belief. The fact that the circus contributes to this substitute fulfillment implies that, even if imagination cannot create belief in an ideal (as the circus cannot provide a happy ending), it can enable us to overcome the resentment and loss of hope that an unideal reality can cause.

This defense against realism is acted out when the circus performers keep Bitzer at bay so that Tom can escape (220; pt. 3, ch. 8). Bitzer represents rationalism pushed to its logical extreme, an inability to believe in anything beyond reality, leaving the individual with only material self-interest. This materialism is the opposite of spiritual faith, as Dickens suggests by setting Bitzer and Sissy in opposition to each other at the novel's start. If the circus can thwart Bitzer, then this implies that imagination can fend off the loss of faith that rationalism could cause. The circus people cannot punish or reform Bitzer, just as imagination cannot fully overcome rationalism. But imagination can prevent rational skepticism from gaining complete control and leaving us, like Bitzer, with nothing but materialism, as the circus prevents Bitzer from triumphing. Presumably, imagination fends off doubt by enabling us to envision an ideal beyond reality. Thus it can lead to something like salvation; Tom is "saved" by the circus (210; pt. 3, ch. 7).

Imagination's role here, then, seems mainly negative. If it can no longer create happy endings and the belief in an ideal that they enact, it can at least enable Dickens to keep realism at bay and thus prevent reason from destroying belief. Dickens is trying to heal the split between realism and idealism we saw in *Bleak House*; he wants to overcome what he sees as the intransigence not so much of reality as of the realist view of it. What he dislikes about rational materialism of the kind embodied in Gradgrind is its intolerance of the imaginative ability to envision an ideal—its insistence that there is nothing but reality. The mind can become "chained . . . down to material realities," which can cause it to lose "faith in anything else" (127; pt. 2, ch. 7), as

Gradgrind's rationalism has left Louisa with no belief enabling her to resist Harthouse and passion.

Dickens feels rationalism is threatening because it demands belief in nothing but reality; Forster quotes him as saying that literature was entering a "dark age," becoming too realistic—"frightfully literal and catalogue-like" (2:279). As Dickens puts it in "Frauds on the Fairies," in this "utilitarian age" there is a danger the nation will become "without fancy" because of people's concern with reality. Dickens sees utilitarianism as an "iron binding of the mind to grim realities"; if we can see reality only as a "moody, brutal fact," it is because we have cut it off from the "sympathies and graces of imagination."[10] Thus realism can destroy religious belief, replacing it with an infidel creed that replaces God with Fact (125; pt. 2, ch. 6), an attitude summed up by the Gradgrindian exclamation "Fact forbid!" (7; pt. 1, ch. 3).

Whereas Dickens sees God as forgiving, he sees fact as forbidding; Gradgrind's rationalist creed refuses to allow for heart or fancy. If one can conceive of nothing beyond reality, like the people lost in the Chancery fog, one is liable to lose faith, like Harthouse, and become resentful, like Tom. Dickens does not simply see imagination as escapist, then, but rather sees its escape from realism as a means toward an end; by using imagination to loosen reason's hold on the mind, we can move toward belief. At the novel's end, he tells us Louisa has learned to accept "fancy," which beautifies "lives of machinery and reality with . . . imaginative graces and delights," not just for decoration but to prevent the "heart of infancy" from withering—to prevent us from entirely losing the child's belief and becoming "morally" dead, unable to believe. He adds that we need this belief based on imagination in order to accept mortality—to be able to watch "the ashes of our fires turn gray and cold" (226–27; pt. 3, ch. 9).

Perhaps imagination can perform this function because it lacks the seriousness of belief. Faith and realism are too uncompromising, each demanding complete belief, and so irreconcilable. But by not insisting on serious belief, imagination can disarm reason. We needn't worry about whether a vision of the ideal is real if we know it is only imaginary. If reason could accept faith, imagination might not be necessary, but since reason remains skeptical, Dickens needs imagination to replace serious belief. Similarly, the circus can deal with Tom because no one takes it too seriously; it is not very demanding (like imagination) and thus doesn't arouse Tom's resentment as Gradgrind does.

This process involves not a victory over realism but a compromise with it. As Dickens puts it in a passage I have already quoted, imagination teaches reason to defer to other gods, as Gradgrind ultimately learns to bend his "inflexible theories," "making his facts and figures subservient to Faith, Hope and Charity" (225; pt. 3, ch. 9). Reason needs to accept coexistence with belief, not trying to subject belief to rational tests. But this means that belief also has to accept coexistence with reason. Dickens is willing to concede at this point in his career that he cannot entirely convince reason and therefore that imagination must remain in unresolved conflict with reason's sense of reality. He calls imagination "Another Thing Needful" (167; pt. 3, ch. 1), not the only one, and when he speaks of its adorning reality (226; pt. 3, ch. 9), he implicitly accepts that it must coexist with that reality, not replace it. Elsewhere Dickens talks of a "fusion of the imagination with the realities of life," an "interweaving of truth and fiction." He wants to "meet" Gradgrind "at some halfway house where there are flowers on the carpets, and a little standing room for Queen Mab's chariot among the steam engines." And he sees this "blending" of "the understanding and the imagination" exemplified in Christ,[11] which implies again that imagination can lead reason to religious belief. Dickens evidently hopes that by thus making concessions to rationalism, he can win its acceptance of the imagined ideal, even though he has had to admit the ideal is only imaginary in order to convince reason. And he evidently feels that imagination is unconvincing if it is too unrealistic, just as realism is unsatisfactory if it is unimaginative. Thus he wants to present a convincingly unideal reality yet retain imagination's ability to alter it, to project feeling and meaning onto objects.

This idea of a compromise between imagination and realism may be implied by the way the circus lies between town and country.[12] Though it cannot enter Coketown, it does not flee to the country either. Dickens may feel that imagination too cannot or should not wholly escape reality and retreat to the "natural," childlike state in which one could wholly believe in the ideal. As the circus lies between social reality and idealized nature, so the imagination is caught between realism and belief in an ideal, trying to combine these. Imagination acts as a go-between, as the circus stands in for Sissy in enabling the happy ending. Imagination is a representative of belief, but one that has been diminished so that it can do business with the realm of reality and can get reason to defer to its viewpoint.

Imagination has a double nature, forced to accept realistic limitations while still trying to envision the ideal. This double attitude is like Sleary's eyes, one "fixed" and one "loose" (27; pt. 1, ch. 6). Like Sleary, imagination keeps one eye fixed on reality but also remains partly free of it, able to conceive of something beyond. This double attitude enables it to act as a mediator, leading from realism toward a sense of the ideal. As the circus retreats to neutral ground between town and country, then, Dickens retreats to the neutral ground of imagination, where he can partly accept reality because he distances it, does not take it too seriously, and so can balance realism with belief in something else. He does this, for example, at the novel's end; Louisa's unhappy ending expresses reason's sense of reality's unidealness, while Sissy's ending expresses belief in an ideal. Neither attitude prevails; they are forced to coexist, each accepting the other as Louisa and Sissy do.

Here again Dickens's concern with reconciling reality with belief finds expression in his use of symbols. To deal with his sense of reality, he puts imagination to a serious use, just as he makes the circus, which seems only playful and childish at first, serve a serious purpose and have a serious meaning—that is, transforms it into a symbol. Symbols give imagination a serious function because they involve an effort to convince reason to believe in the imagined ideal by representing that ideal (or its absence) through objects reason can accept as real. Almost every character and object in *Hard Times* carries symbolic meaning. Bounderby is associated with repressive, unforgiving social control, Stephen with the natural virtue that society victimizes, and I have already mentioned the qualities I think Louisa, Sissy, and others represent. As the circus offers children a "loophole" (7; pt. 1, ch. 3), these symbols offer us a glimpse of something beyond the novel's reality. Imagination creates a kind of loophole in reason, an area partly exempt from our concern with reality, enabling us to glimpse something other than what is "real."

Stephen finds this kind of loophole when he looks up out of the pit into which this world has caused him to fall (as it causes people to fall into a hell-like despair) and sees something beyond the world, a star. What he is seeing here is not "reality" but a symbol, an object with a spiritual meaning; thus it is as if he is looking beyond reason, seeing imaginatively. He sees the ideal through the medium of reality, since the ideal is symbolized by an image in the novel's reality, but he is moving beyond a rationalist mode of perception, using imagination to give the object meaning.

Dickens uses symbols, then, to make us work against realism. To rationalism like Gradgrind's, a thing can be only a thing, but imagination can give that thing another, symbolic, meaning. In doing so, it makes an implicit criticism of a rationalism that cannot understand symbols, making us feel Gradgrind's shortcomings, the inability of reason to do what imagination can do; we feel superior to him, able to see more. And our judgment is given a spiritual significance; we see that Gradgrind represents reason's inability to attain spiritual belief. Dickens thus makes us read in a way that shows us that rationalism is not enough and moves us toward belief. His symbols make us value imagination by making us use it, giving us a sense of its powers. In this way the circus is an example of what it symbolizes; it both represents imagination and calls upon us to use imagination in reading it as a symbol.

chapter 8

Little Dorrit

Little Dorrit, like *Bleak House* and *Hard Times*, seeks a version of idealism that can deal with a bleak view of reality. All three novels begin by presenting a strongly negative view of the reality in which their characters must live. As in *Bleak House*, that reality is represented by a symbol—in this case, the prison. Once more Dickens is using the symbol because, although all three novels are undeniably concerned with social reality, he wants us to see that reality from a spiritual perspective, to see reality as signifying something beyond itself. From a social perspective the prison symbolizes a society that encloses and corrupts people, warping them so they worship money instead of God, but from a spiritual perspective it symbolizes reality as seen by despairing weariness, "the prison of this lower world" (831; pt. 1, ch. 30)—a world in which there is no sign of the divine, no object worthy of belief.[1]

To a despairing mind—a mind like Dombey's when he sees death as like a train—this world seems merely a prison because it denies our desire for the ideal, making us feel as if there is a wall preventing us from reaching anything beyond reality. Perhaps Dickens has in mind Wordsworth's description in the "Intimations" ode of reality as a "prison-house" whose "Shades" prevent us from seeing divine light (line 68). He must also associate prison with inability to believe in an ideal because his own father's imprisonment must have made him lose belief in his father. The prison represents the world of "fact," the world as seen by Gradgrindian realism, a world that "has no knowledge of the brightness outside" (40–41; pt. 1, ch. 1) as realism has no knowledge of the divine. Being imprisoned is like being caught in this materialism, unable to believe in anything beyond reality. It is this sense that there is no ideal in reality that Dickens must deal with if he is to offer us belief.

The weary mind that tends to see the world as a prison Dickens embodies in Arthur Clennam; the prison is a projection of the state of mind into which Arthur is in danger of falling and which he must overcome. Thus here as with Louisa Gradgrind it is doubting reason, struggling for a belief that seems far off, that Dickens makes central to the novel, locating it in his protagonist. Perhaps because Arthur is closer to Dickens's sense of what he himself is like, doubt seems more pervasive and personal here than in *Hard Times*. Arthur's story is rather similar to David Copperfield's, but the comparison shows how much greater Dickens's doubt has become, how much farther away from belief he must now begin. Arthur is like a David who has already left behind his Dora (a Flora, in this case) and seems caught in a permanent Center of Indifference, a state of mental paralysis in which it seems he will never reach his Agnes (Little Dorrit), his Everlasting Yea.

It is this in-between state, after the childish belief in imagination's visions has been lost and before any higher belief has been found to replace it, that Dickens is centrally concerned with here. The novel drops Arthur into a world that reflects his hopelessness, like an Esther Summerson lost in the Chancery world without any Jarndyce to rescue her, in order to show a process by which reason can deal with this despairing sense of reality and work its way to belief. We see Arthur facing this prison-like reality at the novel's beginning: "Nothing to see but streets, streets, streets." It is a world that offers no basis for belief, "Nothing to change the brooding mind, or raise it up" to a sense of the ideal. Dickens makes us see reality's emptiness (which is reflected by the "void" in Arthur's heart) as the absence of any sign of God by emphasizing that it is Sunday, a day on which God should be especially evident, so that his absence—his replacement by a repressive, prison-like social religion that prevents belief—is especially apparent, causing "despair" (67–69; pt. 1, ch. 3; and 59; pt. 1, ch. 2). This despair is the obstacle that the novel seeks to overcome.

The hopelessness results from the fact that God has been replaced by society, represented here mainly by the Circumlocution Office, which, like Chancery, demands submission and even worship (e.g., 148; pt. 1, ch. 10) but fails to provide any spiritual fulfillment and so can lead to "total infidelity" (148; pt. 1, ch. 10), a sense that there is nothing worth believing in. Arthur must be "saved" from the "selfishness of holding that because such a happiness . . . had not come into his little path, . . . therefore it was not in the great scheme" (207; pt. 1, ch. 13)—that because one cannot find the ideal in reality, one should give up belief in it entirely. Characters who give in to this cynicism include Blandois, Gowan, and Miss Wade, who rejects "belief" because society has taught her to see virtue only as pretense (61; pt. 1, ch. 2). These unbelievers represent the void in the heart that Arthur must beware, the state we see him verging on when the novel begins. Like Miss Wade and Tattycoram, he has had an unloved childhood, has been denied any object of belief, and so could conclude that since the ideal (especially maternal love) does not exist in reality, there is nothing worth believing in. This conclusion could lead to despair, as Merdle's materialism and consequent inability to believe in anything higher than reality drive Merdle to despair.

The characters who resist this cynical rationalism tend to retreat to imagination to make reality bearable. These alternatives seem to express a division in Dickens's mind, a difficulty in reconciling reason and imagination[2]. His rationalists reject imagination, and the characters who embrace imagination tend to reject reason. Thus despite his attraction to imagination, Dickens partly accepts reason's criticism of it; as in *Bleak House*, he often depicts imaginative characters as deluded, and shows that imagination can be corrupted into pursuing false, worldly ideals—for example, worshiping Merdle and the Circumlocution Office. The Dorrits, the chief worshipers at the social shrine, have been warped by their imprisonment into imagining (like Richard Carstone) that society offers true fulfillment—that their wealth can raise them up out of reality into a paradise (467; pt. 1, ch. 35). They have become spiritually imprisoned in materialism, unable to believe in anything beyond the walls of reality, and so they can only imagine selfish versions of the ideal. Mr. Dorrit's "castle-building" (695; pt. 2, ch. 18) is wrong because he is seeking a false, selfish ideal in this world, and Mrs. Clennam's "imagination" also draws false, selfish "pictures" (865; pt. 2, ch. 31). Both characters need to face reality in order to learn that a true ideal can exist only beyond this world.

In addition to characters who corrupt imagination, there are those who use it in a more harmless but equally self-deluding way. Chief among these is Flora Finching.[3] The tension in her between imaginative escapism and reluctant realism is like the tension in Dickens's earlier comic characters, but it is now more conscious and exacerbated. Dickens realizes that the conflict between reason and imagination threatens the belief he seeks, and he therefore takes that conflict quite seriously. As much as he evidently enjoys Flora's use of imagination, the way she tries to break free of reason, he is also forced to be critical of her (as Arthur feels forced to reject her) because he sees that this escapism arouses an unresolvable conflict with reason, that using imagination as she does cannot overcome reason's sense of reality and so cannot produce belief. This failure to adapt imagination to reality shows the need for a belief that can take reality into account. Dickens is thus reacting against the kind of playfulness he valued in his early fiction.

The imaginative characters, like the unbelieving materialists, exemplify a danger Arthur must defend against. His mother's retreat from reality has infected him, and her failure to provide him with a loving God (and a loving parent) to believe in has made him retreat from reality into imagination. This escapist side of his character is reflected in Flora. Like Copperfield with

Dora, he has idealized Flora in his imagination, becoming a "dreamer" who sees her in "the bright glories of fancy" (80; pt. 1, ch. 3). This tendency is dangerous because it can lead him to seek a false, selfish version of the ideal. Because it is based on a delusion (that the ideal can exist in this world—for example, that a creature of this world like Flora can be ideal), it can also lead to disillusion when he finds what reality is really like—when he sees the real Flora. When they meet, the "reality" destroys "the old fancy" created by "his affection and imagination," which he has tried to hold "sacred" (191; pt. 1, ch. 13)—that is, to believe in. Imagination cannot create belief because it cannot overcome his sense of reality. Thus Arthur now realizes the ideal he tried to believe in was only "foolish dreams" (194; pt. 1, ch. 13), "while all that was hard and stern in his recollection, remained Reality on being proved— was obdurate to the sight and touch," unlike his dream, which will "not bear the test" of reason (206; pt. 1, ch. 13). It is because Arthur has indulged in imaginative escapism that reality seems so negative to him, opposing imagination's selfish desires. Dickens uses Flora to reflect this escapist tendency in Arthur and thus show him how unsatisfactory it is; in rejecting Flora, he is also rejecting his childish dreams and learning to face reality in a way Flora refuses to.

Because Arthur lacks a firm belief that the ideal exists beyond reality, he continues to desire other versions of a merely earthly ideal, and he must give those up too. He must relinquish Pet, perhaps because her childishness (which resembles Dora Spenlow's) reflects his lack of realism. Her attraction to Gowan, like Arthur's youthful infatuation with Flora, is another mistaken attempt to possess an earthly ideal. And Arthur's attraction to her is merely "fancied," "forgetting" reality (430; pt. 1, ch. 32). He also seeks earthly fulfill- ment when he helps the Dorrits retrieve their fortune and when (like Richard Carstone seeking fulfillment from Chancery) he invests in Merdle's enter- prises. In each case, the resultant failure is meant to teach him that he should look beyond this world for true fulfillment.

Arthur must thus avoid overvaluing both reason, which refuses to accept imagination's need for an ideal and (like Gowan) denies all belief, and also imagination, which refuses to accept reason's awareness that there is no ideal in reality and (like Flora) persists in seeking one. Yet though Dickens is criti- cal of imagination, he also sympathizes with it—more than in *Bleak House*. For example, he tells us the inhabitants of Bleeding Heart Yard need to be "imaginative" because their "hour-glass . . . was filled with the earthiest and coarsest sand," so that they don't want "to be despoiled of the one little golden grain of poetry that sparkled in it" (176–77; pt. 1, ch. 12). Though the narrator cannot share their belief in the imaginary, he sees that the unidealness of reality impels them to picture some ideal, even if an irrational one. We see this mainly in Mrs. Plornish, who rejoices in the "little fiction" that turns her shop into a pastoral cottage: "No Poetry and no Art ever charmed the imagination more than . . . in this counterfeit" in which the "Golden Age" is "revived" (630; pt. 2, ch. 13). Such unrealistic, idealizing art resembles what Dickens does in his early fiction (for example, at Dingley Dell), but reason can no longer believe in it. The narrator sees it as only imaginary, counterfeit. Yet Dickens also values imagination's ability to enable Mrs. Plornish to believe in an ideal—a Golden Age.

Because he values imagination, Dickens wants to modify it so that it can provide a more satisfactory alternative to rational disbelief than this escapism can. He replaces escapist imagination with an imagination that can come to terms with reality and thus give up selfishness. Daniel Doyce, for example, has a factory that has "at once a fanciful and practical air" (313; pt. 1, ch. 23). I think Dickens is offering Doyce as an example of what he feels a creator should be like, accepting and working in reality (like Esther Summerson) and yet able to imagine something better, so that his imagination inspires him to try to improve reality. Dickens seems to be trying to unite realism and imagination in his own work, as Doyce does, incorporating reality into his fiction more successfully than the painter of Mrs. Plornish's cottage by not making fictions that, like Flora's, seek to defy reality.

The main example of this higher use of imagination is Little Dorrit. She embodies Dickens's defense against the prison and all it represents. She lives in the prison but does not fall into either the cynicism or the escapism it could cause. She accepts it without giving up belief in something higher. Thus she combines realism (accepting that we are imprisoned in an unfulfilling world, that reality offers no ideal but rather is a prison cutting us off from the transcendent) with idealism, belief that an ideal lies beyond the prison walls of reality, even though as long as we remain imprisoned in this world we can only envision that ideal through imagination. Dorrit is a realist in that she has "no belief" her father is what she wishes and she cannot share the "delusions" of those like her family who believe in an earthly ideal (209; pt. 1, ch. 14). But though she is enclosed by the prison's "blank walls," she can look up through the bars at the sky (109–10; pt. 1, ch. 7), suggesting that she can see beyond blank reality even though she is imprisoned in this world. Because she can hold onto belief in a higher ideal despite reality, she can accept the prison— and reality—more completely than others can.

Even Arthur when he is first locked inside the prison wants to "escape" and so indulges his "fancy" (129; pt. 1, ch. 8), retreating into imagination rather than accepting reality. He indulges in a "dream" of rescuing Little

Dorrit from prison, whereas she recognizes it is "hopeless" (139; pt. 1, ch. 9) to seek any such escape from reality and fears Arthur may "fancy too much" (306; pt. 1, ch. 22). In a letter, Dickens makes a similar criticism of himself, saying he seeks his "realities in unrealities" and adding that such an "escape from the disappointment of heart" is "dangerous" (Forster 2:196). A sense that reality does not live up to the heart's desire for an ideal—the feeling Arthur has at the start—can lead imagination into escapism, a tendency Dickens wants to counteract through Little Dorrit.

When Dorrit uses imagination, she does so in a way that largely accepts reality. Dickens seems to be pulling back from the distrust of imagination he expressed through Esther and Sissy, no longer seeing imagination as mainly opposed to belief but trying to reconcile the two, evidently because he can find no basis for belief except in imagination. Dorrit holds onto belief despite her awareness of reality by accepting that her belief comes from imagination, is make-believe; she says she couldn't have "been of any use if [she] hadn't pretended a little" (211; pt. 1, ch. 14). She sees her father's failings but can put aside that awareness through this make-believe, as when she imagines a party, seeing a "vista of wonder" that enables her to forget for the moment the reality around her (217; pt. 1, ch. 14).

Like Dickens, however, she combines imagination with her awareness of reality, as we can see in the fairy tale she tells Maggy. The story is sad; imagination cannot keep out reality. Instead of centering it on the idealized, wish-fulfilling princess—the kind of character imagination prefers—Dorrit chooses as protagonist a "tiny woman" whose size (like Dorrit's) suggests an acceptance of the way reality diminishes our fulfillment and who is cut off from the idealized fairy-tale world. Yet the tiny woman, like Dorrit, though she accepts that the ideal she wishes for has "gone far away, quite out of reach, never, never to come back," still keeps a "bright" shadow of it (341; pt. 1, ch. 24). Similarly, imagination can create an image of the ideal that we can keep in our minds even though we cannot believe it can exist in reality; by holding onto that image, we can believe that the ideal can exist beyond reality. Thus Dorrit (like Dickens) converts imagination from the wish-fulfilling form it takes in fairy tales to this chastened form that allows a sense of reality yet retains a shadow of belief in the ideal. As before, Dickens purifies imagination of selfish desire for an earthly ideal, but his sense of reality's darkness is stronger here than before, and imagination is less able to overcome it; the tiny woman dies alone.

Dickens imprisons Dorrit in this world to test her, to prove that she (and the faith she represents) will not give in to disillusion. Her liberation is another test, to prove that her faith can also resist the attraction of escapism.

The other members of her family believe they can not only get out of prison but can escape reality itself, can find a paradise on earth. But since prison has taught Little Dorrit that the ideal she imagines cannot exist in reality, she does not share the family delusion. Only prison is "a reality" to her (517; pt. 2, ch. 3), as reality is only a prison, not a realm in which one should seek the ideal. Thus she sees that an earthly ideal is illusory and feels that the Dorrits' false paradise is only "a dream" (516; pt. 2, ch. 3). By holding onto her belief in an otherworldly ideal, she can overcome her father's false, worldly belief, converting him as Florence Dombey converts her father (though less fulfillingly). Mr. Dorrit has to give up his castles in the air, his belief in an earthly ideal, in order to replace that vision with a spiritual one. His "dream" is cancelled (700; pt. 2, ch. 19), and he accepts that prison is the true reality—and thus that reality is a prison cutting us off from the transcendent. Then he is ready to turn to his daughter, realizing he needs the belief in an otherworldly ideal she embodies. His conversion thus acts out a movement from selfish, escapist imagination to belief. Little Dorrit's faith, because it can accept reality, vanquishes his illusion.

Her partial conversion of her father is the prelude to her conversion of Arthur; to him too she brings belief. Like Mr. Dorrit, Arthur has desired an earthly ideal, and when that search fails (with the loss of Pet and then of his investment), he is in danger of falling completely into despair, of seeing nothing but prison-like reality and feeling cut off from the ideal (a state Dickens dramatizes by locking him in prison). I think his movement from near despair to belief is the novel's central action, and Dorrit's main function is to inspire that movement. Dickens puts her faith to the test to prove to Arthur (and through him, to us and himself) that belief can withstand reality. Dorrit's situation is similar to Arthur's; both have been denied love and been virtually imprisoned by a parent. By holding onto her faith despite this deprivation, Dorrit shows Arthur that he should do so too (as Sissy shows Louisa, but in a less fulfilling way).

Like other Dickens heroines, then, Dorrit is both the object of belief and an example of it—something for Arthur to believe in and also to believe *like*, so that believing in her is like believing in belief. Like belief she is both of this world and not of it, starting from reality but aiming beyond it, accepting it but believing in something above. She can pass unscathed through reality as Dickens hopes belief can resist the pressures of this world. When she enters Arthur's dark world, it is as if she is coming from beyond the world, to lead Arthur beyond it. But at the same time her belief in something beyond this world enables her (and ultimately Arthur) to accept reality's "miserable muddy streets" (140, 144; pt. 1, ch. 9). Dickens seems to be trying to discipline his own imagination, marrying it to an acceptance of reality by embodying that acceptance in a positive form, not as something that will destroy imagination but as something (like Dorrit) that can lift it to belief.

To win Dorrit and acquire belief like hers, Arthur must overcome his tendency to see the ideal as merely imaginary by combining idealism with a greater acceptance of reality as Dorrit does. Thus he "must begin . . . with looking well to his feet on earth," accepting his "Duty on earth" even if he feels he cannot "mount on wings of words to Heaven"; he must make do without spiritual certainty, hoping that an acceptance of reality will be "the first steep steps upward" toward eventual belief (368; pt. 1, ch. 27). This intermediate phase follows an Everlasting No, a rejection of belief in a false, imaginary ideal in hopes that this will lead to an Everlasting Yea, a new belief. Such a belief cannot be convincing unless it has taken reality into account, though Dickens is admitting that the sense of reality is hard to reconcile with belief. But here again he balances the two by teaching Arthur to believe in an ideal yet accept that it cannot be found in this world. He acts out the renunciation of an earthly ideal when he gives up Pet, an act that parallels Dorrit's acceptance that she cannot have Arthur.

Arthur's final acceptance of reality is represented by his acceptance of prison. Early in the novel he fears the prison, just as he finds reality too bleak to accept. But at the story's climax he learns to accept imprisonment as Dorrit does (and as Dickens wants to accept his father's imprisonment); that acceptance makes belief possible, symbolized by Dorrit's coming to him to answer his need. Only after he realizes that reality is like a prison, is not the realm in which one can find true fulfillment, does he realize he needs Dorrit and the belief she embodies—belief in an otherworldly ideal in order to live at peace with reality's prison. He sees that without Dorrit and belief, reality is "mere waste and darkened sky" (802; pt. 2, ch. 27), suggesting that it is only through an act of belief that God is put in heaven.

Dorrit's appearing like an angel to Arthur in prison is prefigured early in the novel, but at that stage Arthur is not yet able to accord her a full acceptance like that involved in religious belief. He feels caught in a "dark" world, but his mind is trying to "rise into the light," like Dorrit looking up at the sky from her prison. This movement toward belief in an ideal beyond this world is dramatized by the appearance at that moment of Little Dorrit, "as if" in "answer" to Arthur's need for belief (207; pt. 1, ch. 13). At this early stage of the novel, Arthur cannot yet understand what Dorrit signifies and so remains cut off from her and from belief; this preliminary revelation is to show him (and us) what he needs to move toward, leading him toward the later revelation prefigured here. Dorrit seems too imaginary here, appearing "as if" in answer, and Dickens wants to overcome this sense that the ideal is only imaginary. Though Arthur has valued Dorrit (as he has desired belief) from the start, she seems distant and not quite real to him. His "fancy" tends to see her as a "fairy" with an "ethereal appearance" that is "not in unison" with the reality around her (305; pt. 1, ch. 22). He cannot see the ideal as something he can possess, and so he cannot possess Dorrit. He needs some belief that can overcome this sense that the ideal and reality are opposed, not in unison; he needs to convince reason the ideal can be more than imaginary.

At the climax, Dickens tries to enable Arthur to reach belief by combining his acceptance of reality with a chastened, higher form of imagination that can be reconciled with realism. Arthur's acceptance of reality impels imagination to shift from envisioning a selfish earthly ideal to picturing something higher; by doing this, it can overcome reason's sense that the ideal cannot be real. Arthur is at his window (like Catherine in *Wuthering Heights*), "yearning to be beyond the blind blank wall," seeking something beyond reality because reality is blank, offering no ideal. And he does see beyond the wall, but through imagination, "dreaming" that Dorrit has come to him. Dickens is implying that we need imagination to reach the ideal, but he then tries to strengthen belief by making the imaginary seem real, making the vision come true (like Adam's dream). First we are told that Dorrit "seemed" to come in, but then she is seen as "a living presence"; Dickens is trying to make the fictional (the "as if" of Dorrit's earlier appearance to Arthur) into the factual. He does this by merging the admittedly imaginary and the apparently real in a higher "reality," which he exempts from reality-testing: Dorrit comes as if from "Heaven" (823–25; pt. 2, ch. 29). Dickens has raised imagination to a spiritual form that reason cannot oppose.

This moment, which the entire novel leads up to, acts out what Dickens wants his art to accomplish—to make the imagined ideal seem real, to make us feel imagination can create the ideal. Making Dorrit suddenly appear here (as Florence appears to Dombey) is a way to give us the sense of a revelation, the sense that we are seeing the ideal incarnate in reality. He apparently feels that merely hoping one can find the ideal after death is too weak a basis for belief; he wants to support that hope by giving us Dorrit as a manifestation of the ideal, a pledge that it does in fact exist, even if Dorrit does not seem to be really of this world. Dorrit is a projection of Arthur's need for belief, embodying what he needs to overcome his weariness, and by making her "become real" here, Dickens wants to make us feel that the need for belief can create belief, can call the ideal into being. He creates an embodiment of the ideal to make us believe in the existence of the ideal; he is using imagination to try to induce belief, offering us Dorrit as proof that imagination can picture the ideal.

However, if we compare this moment with similar epiphanies in Dickens's earlier novels, his sense of the difficulty of overcoming reality seems stronger. Arthur has had to go through a long period of wandering in the wilderness, a chastening exposure to a very unfulfilling reality, and when his revelation finally comes, it is diminished by being located in the prison. Arthur imagines a "garden" like Eden, but all he can actually have are some flowers (824; pt. 2, ch. 29); within the prison of reality, we can find only a very limited version of the imagined ideal. Dickens is admitting how unfulfilling reality is, but he also makes this scene take place in prison in order to try to locate the ideal (and belief in it, embodied in Dorrit) in reality, showing that belief can face reality and not be extinguished. Nevertheless, he has had to diminish belief in order to reconcile it with reason's sense of reality.

This reconciliation with reason makes belief possible. Dorrit enables Arthur "to believe" in her "devotion" and thus to feel a similar devotion, belief in the divine forgiveness of which she is a manifestation. Thus even though he is "in the shadow of the wall" of the prison, "the shadow fell like light upon him" (827; pt. 2, ch. 29). Transforming darkness into light suggests that it is the acceptance of dark reality that makes possible this belief in an ideal beyond reality, turning darkness into a source of illumination. Dickens seems to feel, as Browning does, that the unidealness of reality can be seen as implying that there must be an ideal beyond reality. Arthur says it is only when the "light . . . has passed far away" that he can "see" it "brightly" (828; pt. 2, ch. 29); he can only believe once he has given up seeking the ideal in this world. Moving it beyond reality evades reason's demand that it be real. Yet this admission that the ideal exists only beyond reality can undermine belief, and so, although Dickens moves the ideal beyond this world in order to keep it, he also tries to make it seem real. This is an example of the tendency I have mentioned to combine idealism and realism even though they are logically opposed. Having made Dorrit seem too good for this world, a glimpse of something beyond it and thus an embodiment of the ideal, Dickens now wants to locate her in reality—bringing her back into the prison. By winning her hand, Arthur acts out this attempt to make her seem real—that is, capable of being possessed.

Here again Dickens also tries to strengthen belief by making the process of reaching it resemble, in a disguised form, the process of overcoming Oedipal guilt. Arthur's possession of Dorrit acts out a displaced version of the Oedipal fantasy. By occupying old Dorrit's prison room, Arthur is replacing the father; winning Little Dorrit is a version of winning the mother's love, since she is maternal, though idealized in an innocent—even childlike—form that removes the guilt that could otherwise be caused by desiring her. Translating the relationship to a spiritual level also helps free it of unconscious guilt. But the doubt that remains about whether Arthur can actually possess Dorrit can be seen as a rationalized version of a submerged Oedipal guilt that Dickens has not wholly overcome. He makes Dorrit more attainable by having Arthur go through the process of giving up earthly desires (represented by his investment in the Merdle enterprises) and his resentment of parental inadequacy (though that resentment is shifted from a father to a mother, leaving Dorrit with the inadequate father). As in other Dickens novels, the overcoming of filial resentment is dramatized as the parent's transformation, though in a weaker form than earlier. Both old Dorrit and Mrs. Clennam are humbled so that they can be pitied rather than hated. And here again Dickens gives this process a spiritual meaning. Replacing Mrs. Clennam with Little Dorrit (the ideal mother figure replacing the resented one) acts out a replacement of unforgiving Old Testament religion, which sees God as "the hater of the unrighteous," with a New Testament belief in "the patient Master who shed tears of compassion for our infirmities" (861; pt. 2, ch. 31).

The novel's last chapter shows how Dickens is trying to balance this idealism with his sense of reality. He tries to locate the divine in reality but at the same time admits that it lies beyond this world, visible but not attainable. Though Arthur is still in reality, with Dorrit's help he can envision the ideal; Dickens implies he does this through imagination, saying that Nature encourages "playful fancies" and childhood "imagination," which (as he also said in *Hard Times*) ultimately germinate into "tenderness and humility," leading to belief. That belief offers a "retreat" from "blighting" reality, unlike the prison of materialist realism, which looks "ignorantly," unable to see any ideal. But though Dickens here tries to deny the sense of reality, to replace the prison with a vision of the ideal, reality remains present; Arthur is still in prison. Dickens cannot escape his sense of reality's unidealness even in his description of idealized Nature.

As in Keats's ode "To Autumn," the vision of an ideal in nature coexists with a sense of reality's darkness, but unlike Keats, Dickens accepts that sense so that he can try to counteract it. It is "autumn" but "healthy"; winter will come but it is "hardy." Similarly, Arthur is "weak but otherwise restored," as his belief is restored so that winter (and reality) no longer seems bleak. Dickens balances realism and idealism by suggesting that we can see the ideal from reality, as "from the seashore" we see "the ocean" full of "joyful animation." Like Wordsworth at the end of the "Intimations" ode, Dickens suggests we can see beyond the prisonhouse of this world as one sees beyond the land, getting a glimpse of the divine. We presumably get this glimpse through imagination, since we are seeing beyond reality. It is because winter is coming that the "prospect" of the sea is so "clear," which hints that it is the awareness of death (making us accept that there is no ideal in reality) that enables us to believe in an ideal beyond this life. As in *Dombey* the sea is associated with what is beyond this life; it is a place where sails are "drifting away like autumn-tinted leaves"—that is, like the dead passing beyond this world, as in Shelley's "Ode to the West Wind." To the idealist imagination, death is transformed into the harvest that comes after life, the wakening that follows the drowsiness of summer (and life).

In this passage, then, Dickens combines imagination with an acceptance of reality (death). He also implies that these two coexist by describing the prison, unable to reveal any manifestation of the ideal, showing only deadness, and then saying that Arthur can nevertheless picture Nature; imagination envisions life surviving despite blank reality. We can conclude Arthur's vision is imagined because it is induced by Dorrit's reading to him (883–84; pt. 2, ch. 34)—presumably reading a work like the novel they are in, one that inspires imagination to envision the ideal. Her reading to him resembles faith guiding imagination.

Dickens, however, is admitting more than in earlier novels that the ideal is imaginary and that reality is prison-like and cannot fully be reconciled with the imagined ideal. Before *Hard Times* he was able to believe that the ideal could finally be brought into reality. Now he is trying to offer a happy ending like his earlier ones, but he can no longer wholly overcome the sense of reality's unidealness, which became so strong in *Hard Times*. Thus this ending combines the sad "realism" of that novel with the idealized endings of earlier novels, creating tension that Dickens does not entirely resolve.

Dickens seems to feel here that, like Arthur, he is in the autumn of life, far from his childhood belief in imagination. But he tries to use his intimations of mortality to transform the merely "playful fancies" of childhood, to reap a harvest by getting imagination to look beyond this world and see the afterlife, enabling imagination to attain a higher belief. Thus Arthur's experience of reality has not destroyed his belief but has restored him, as Wordsworth's imagination is restored in *The Prelude*, raised to a higher perception. And since Dickens implicitly compares this maturation to autumnal ripening, he suggests that it is by leaving behind childhood and facing mortality that imagination can be transformed. The harvest that the seeds of childhood imagination produce in the autumn of life, then, is the belief in an afterlife, which enables one to accept the coming of winter and death.

This combination of an acceptance of unideal reality with belief in the transcendent informs the novel's final page. Arthur finally wins Little Dorrit, so it seems that he can possess the ideal in reality; by winning her, he has also acquired the faith she represents, faith that is implied by "the sun shining on them through the painted figure of Our Saviour" when they are married (894; pt. 8, ch. 34). If reality is like a prison, there are windows in it—windows through which imagination can see beyond it to the divine. But Dickens's sense of the world's darkness remains in tension with his belief in the transcendent. The light comes from beyond this world. Though Arthur and Dorrit are upheld by their belief in the divine source of that light, they cannot escape reality but must go "down into the roaring streets," the city that Arthur viewed with despair at the novel's beginning but that belief now enables him to accept. It is a world whose "shade" is mixed with "sunshine" (895; pt. 2, ch. 34), as awareness of reality is mixed with belief in the ideal. Though he and Dorrit can keep their belief despite the darkness of reality, that belief is autumnal and chastened, accepting that the ideal does not exist in the world around them, but able to accept that world because of a sense that the ideal still exists and that its light can penetrate into reality.

chapter 9

Great Expectations and *Our Mutual Friend*

In *Great Expectations* Dickens reverts to his more pessimistic view of imagination, seeing it as mainly delusive. The novel tells a story like David Copperfield's but in a more negative, self-critical version. Like David, Pip is misled by imagination into pursuing a false, earthly ideal.[1] But where David can move on from Dora to Agnes, Pip cannot replace Estella with Biddy. No ideal is available; he can only give up imagination's false visions and accept a reality from which almost any manifestation of the ideal has been eliminated (especially in the original version). And Dickens is more critical of Pip's delusion than of David's. Whereas Dora is treated fairly sympathetically and can give David some fulfillment, the false ideal envisioned by Pip's "fancy" (253; ch. 29; and 378; ch. 44), Estella, is much more negative. She represents the loss of belief caused by pursuing imagination's vision of a merely earthly ideal. She has been denied the ability to believe in anything beyond physical reality, and (like Edith Dombey, Steerforth, and similar characters) she shows the disillusionment this materialism can lead to. Thus if Pip possessed her (at least before her final conversion), he would end up not with fulfillment but with the emptiness and despair she embodies. As with Arthur Clennam, there is a danger that the alternative to believing in imagination's visions will be hopelessness, an alternative Dickens tries to defend against by finding some belief with which to replace imagination (though in this novel that belief is weaker, its object more remote, than in any other Dickens novel).

Another sign that Dickens is more critical of Pip's retreat into imagination than he is of David's is the fact that he shows Pip using imagination to avoid accepting his home (as I think Dickens himself did). Dickens uses Magwitch to symbolize the shame that Pip is trying to escape (a shame that reflects Dickens's own shame at his father's having been a prisoner too); Pip's ultimate acceptance of Magwitch acts out a forgiveness of the father that I think expresses Dickens's wish to forgive his own father. Initially, however, Pip's response to his home and to the sense of shame associated with Magwitch is his attempt to escape to a dream world, an idealized home, by going to Miss Havisham's. Here again, Dickens is much more critical of Pip's delusion than of David's. When David retreats to an alternative home like Mr. Peggotty's or Aunt Betsey's, it is quite idealized; in *Copperfield* Dickens largely sympathizes with imagination's search for an ideal. But here the substitute home Pip finds is the opposite of ideal, a nightmarish world that closes out reality and, by indulging imagination's selfish desires, cuts the self off from belief as Miss Havisham cuts herself off from the light. Such a retreat into imagination leads not to belief but to eventual disillusionment and hopelessness (the state Estella embodies) when one finds that the imagined ideal does not exist in reality after all.

In *Great Expectations*, then, Dickens sees imagination as mainly opposed to belief, as perverted and selfish. Infected by Miss Havisham's "sick fancy" (88; ch. 8), Pip too becomes unwilling to accept "reality" (135; ch. 14), wanting to escape his home and create an imaginary world. Miss Havisham seems like a "fairy godmother" to him (184; ch. 19), an embodiment of the imagined ideal. He sees himself as a "Knight of Romance" and Estella as "the Princess" on whom his "fancy" is set (253; ch. 29). She seems "the embodiment of every graceful fancy" his mind has known (378; ch. 44). He wishes he "devoutly believed" in her, but because his ideal is merely imagined, it goes "against reason" (253–54; ch. 29) and so cannot lead to true belief. Dickens teaches him to reject selfish imagination by first making his dream come true—his "wild fancy" seem to become a "reality" (165; ch. 18), as with the Dorrits. Dickens allows Pip to become the gentleman he has dreamed of being in order to show that this is not fulfilling as Pip imagines, that it is a false ideal. Pip is ultimately forced to see that it has all been a "mere dream" (341; ch. 39), that there is no ideal in this world, and that the best one can manage is to give up imagination's delusions and accept one's duty in an unfulfilling reality. He can overcome the resentment that Magwitch and Miss Havisham arouse in him and thus fend off unbelief, but he can find no ideal that seems real and attainable. Like Louisa Gradgrind, he can see the ideal only from a distance, without sharing in it; the happy ending is not for him.

Yet although Dickens seems more willing to give up imagination here than in any of his other novels, he does not want to surrender it completely. He offers us one suggestion of how it may be able to survive despite the need to accept reality. If imagination cannot overcome realism, at least it can coexist with it, as Wemmick's example shows. In Wemmick, Dickens accepts that the conflict between imagination and realism is irreconcilable, that the split he has tried to overcome since *Bleak House* cannot be overcome. Wemmick is half like his employer, Jaggers, a realist who must "take everything on evidence" (351; ch. 40), but the other half of him reacts against that materialism. His imagination separates itself from this realism, since it cannot find such an attitude fulfilling, and retreats from reality, creating its own world, an island surrounded by a reality to which Wemmick accepts he must return, but from which imagination can temporarily escape.[2] His imaginary world is like a fortress, a defense against the outer world, a way of resisting its realism. But by partly accepting that world, Wemmick keeps his imagination from becoming selfish like Pip's; he does not try to find the ideal in reality but rather tacitly admits that the ideal is only imaginary. Thus Dickens seems to be saying that the only way he can hold onto imagination is by letting it be merely playful, giving up the Romantic attempt to convert it into serious belief. Imagination's ability to deal with reality is weaker here than in any previous Dickens novel.

We can read *Our Mutual Friend* as a reaction against the growing pessimism in Dickens's preceding novels, especially *Great Expectations*. Perhaps Dickens feared he was losing his imaginative ability and wanted to revive it. The novel is divided into two rather different halves, one with Bella Wilfer as protagonist, the other with Eugene Wrayburn. The two halves present parallel stories, each leading its protagonist from unbelieving materialism to idealist belief, but the story centered on Bella and Noddy Boffin treats this situation in a much more playful way. Seriousness and imaginative play, which Dickens's mature novels have tried to integrate with each other, are here once more relatively separated. In Eugene's story despair is almost as serious and hard to overcome as in *Great Expectations*, and perhaps Dickens feels the need to use the playfulness of Bella's story as a defense against that seriousness, to keep it from becoming too threatening. Perhaps too he feels the need to remove most seriousness from Bella's story in order to keep it safely playful, so that he can allow imaginative play to survive. The novel is thus rather like Wemmick, allowing imagination and a sense of reality's unidealness to coexist by protecting imagination from that realistic sense. Especially in Bella's area of the novel, Dickens returns to the highly idealist, wish-fulfilling kind of story we find in his early novels, but—especially in Eugene's half—he also expresses a much stronger sense of the difficulty of reaching the ideal.

In both parts of the novel, Dickens gives imagination a more important role than ever. He seems to be reacting against the sense of imagination's marginality we saw in Wemmick by seeking a more satisfying outlet for imagination, trying to recapture the comic playfulness of his early works— though his attempt is rather tired and self-conscious—and also trying to make it serve his idealism more fully. It is rather as if the novel (especially Bella's half) is written by a Wemmick, trying to hold onto imagination despite his sense of how much reality opposes it, segregating it, finding a place for it by accepting outlets that are admittedly unserious. This part of the novel has a fairy-tale quality, as if Dickens, like late Shakespeare, is no longer so concerned with trying to make his work seem realistic and is seeing the work of art as an end in itself, a kind of ritual to be enjoyed for the illusion of fulfillment it creates, even while we remain aware that what it offers is only illusion. Perhaps this is because Dickens has failed to replace imagination with belief and has been unable to overcome his sense of reality, so that he must fall back on imagination instead. He remarks at one point, for example, that it is better for Twemlow to "believe in" a "Fancy" than to be aware of the unideal reality that opposes any "capacity of imagining" (467; pt. 2, ch. 16); it is better to hold onto imagination than to give way to the hopelessness reality could cause, even though what Dickens says here shows he cannot escape the awareness of reality, as Twemlow can, and so cannot take imagination too seriously.

However, Dickens reacts against this tendency to lose seriousness (a tendency he locates especially in Eugene) by trying more consciously than before to integrate imaginative play with his serious purpose. He allows more playfulness than in the preceding novels but tries to counteract the centrifugal pull of that playfulness by imposing a strong structural control on it. Thus he makes his comic characters serve his serious plot, giving them greater importance in the novel's central action than in any other of his novels. There are two main stories, one leading up to Eugene's conversion and the other to Bella's. Jenny Wren has a major role to play in the former and Noddy Boffin in the latter. These are characters of the sort Dickens usually employs for comedy, but here they are mainly agents of imagination and thus are made subservient to the search for belief. In Jenny, Dickens is trying to revive imaginative idealism, to use imagination once more to provide a vision of the divine. In Noddy, he is trying to revive the kind of imaginative playfulness he earlier used in playing tricks on his characters—tricks like the pious frauds practiced by old Martin Chuzzlewit.[3]

Dickens uses Noddy to convert Bella the way he uses ghosts to convert Scrooge, Micawber to confound Heep, and the circus to thwart Bitzer, acting out the defeat of materialism by imagination. But I cannot help feeling that he is rather trying to recreate his earlier playfulness than actually doing so; Noddy lacks Micawber's imaginative ability to keep things from becoming serious, and his role-playing seems more forced than amusing. In Jenny Wren too Dickens's serious purpose tends to outweigh his imaginative play, so that she ends up sounding more like a Little Dorrit than like a Flora Finching. As in Wemmick's case, Dickens's playfulness has become too self-conscious to remain very playful. He has succeeded in rescuing imagination only by binding it so tightly to his serious purpose that it has lost its freedom.

But if he seems less successful here in finding playful comic outlets for imagination, he is more successful than in any previous novel in bringing imaginative play into his main characters, in giving Bella and especially Eugene some of the ability to make their world comic that we find in earlier characters like Sam Weller and Dick Swiveller. Thus here again imagination is combined more fully with his serious, spiritual purpose,[4] not only entering the main plot more than before but also entering the main characters more. In his early fiction the characters with the greatest implied inner conflicts are comic secondary characters; by locating such conflict mainly within Eugene and Bella, Dickens makes us take that conflict more seriously and wish for a more complete resolution to it. And by locating imagination in those characters, he enables it to deal with that conflict. Although he has sacrificed imagination's playful freedom, then, he has gained an ability to integrate it more fully with his serious concerns.

Because he is placing considerable emphasis on imagination here, Dickens must deal with its dangers. He uses Silas Wegg to show how it can be abused. Boffin (and to a lesser extent Mr. Venus) are childlike characters who wish to believe in imagination's visions, and Wegg takes advantage of that wish, showing how it can lead one to value false ideals. Venus is an "artist" who can "fancy" things (852; pt. 4, ch. 14), though a diminished one, suggesting the weakness of imagination—its inability to overcome death, for example. He finds his "art" cannot bring fulfillment; imagination cannot make the world "flowery" (126, 128–29; pt. 1, ch. 7), cannot create an Eden and overcome the sense of reality. Perhaps Dickens felt the danger of a similar disillusion with his own art and needed to find a way for it to overcome deadness (so that Jenny Wren could be his attempt to counteract this sense of the artist as weakling). The failure of Venus's imagination makes him vulnerable to Wegg, who seems to offer the ideal Venus cannot find. But it is a false, earthly ideal, and far from overcoming death, it leads to death, represented by dust.

Boffin too is in danger of having his imagination taken over by Wegg's selfishness. Boffin's problem is "What to believe" (538; pt. 3, ch. 6), and he hopes to find a basis for belief in imagination by getting Wegg to read to him. But Wegg perverts imagination—for example, by quoting songs in a way that distorts them for his selfish purposes. He is rather like Skimpole, not seriously believing in imagination's visions and so putting it to selfish, materialistic uses. His poetic flights are mere pretense, false idealizations undercut by the intrusion of unpoetic words. He does exercise "imaginary power" (88; pt. 1, ch. 5), but selfishly, seeking to control reality in order to make it gratify his vanity. The danger of a childlike belief in imagination like Boffin's is that it may be led to accept a false, selfish version of the ideal, like Wegg's, as Pip is led astray by Miss Havisham and Copperfield by Steerforth. Dickens induces us to think Wegg has infected both Venus and Boffin with his materialism, but only so that he can reject that possibility more dramatically.

Here as in *Little Dorrit*, one alternative to naive acceptance of imagination, like Boffin's, is a total rejection of imagination, and Dickens shows this to be even worse than a deluded imagination. The character who exemplifies this lack is Bradley Headstone, and Dickens reveals his inability to envision anything beyond reality to be a grave handicap. A materialistic, Gradgrindian education has taught him to value only reason, giving him a "habit of questioning" (267; pt. 2, ch. 1) that prevents belief. His protégé Charlie Hexam shares this rationalism, condemning Lizzie as a "dreamer" who is not concerned with "the real world" (278; pt. 2, ch. 1). Bradley's inability to believe in an ideal renders him incapable of idealizing Lizzie, and thus his desire for her remains physical, unsublimated, not converted into a higher form as desire must be for Dickens to allow it. Bradley is thus left in despair and guilt, without any belief that could enable him to overcome death as Eugene is ultimately enabled to.

Once again, Dickens seeks a middle ground between these extremes, naive belief and unbelieving materialism. We have seen how difficult it was for Arthur Clennam to find a belief he could reconcile with his sense of reality, and in *Great Expectations* Dickens no longer seemed able to believe in any ideal that could exist in reality. In this novel he tries to regain that belief, but he can no longer do it in as serious and convincing a way as in *Dorrit*. He still describes a conversion to belief, but it seems more fictional and forced. There is the same sense that the imaginary is unreal that we saw in Wemmick. This lack of seriousness is mainly evident, as I have mentioned, in Bella's and Boffin's half of the novel; her conversion has much of the fairy-tale quality of Dickens's Christmas stories, in which he feels less need to take into account our sense of reality.

Bella is pulled between the two extremes I have mentioned, half believing in an imagined ideal but half rejecting any serious belief. We are told she "imagined" voyaging to some sort of paradise (373; pt. 2, ch. 8), using imagination selfishly to seek an earthly ideal. But because she cannot find the ideal in this world, she is in danger of losing belief in any ideal at all. She asserts that she doesn't believe in imaginary things but is only concerned with "realities" like "wealth" (376; pt. 2, ch. 8). However, she has enough imagination so that she is not satisfied with mere materialism and seeks something higher to believe in. She learns from Lizzie's example to convert desire into an "unselfish" form (591; pt. 3, ch. 9). Lizzie uses imagination (expressed through her fire-gazing) to find some ideal she can believe in unselfishly, and Bella too uses imagination when she is converted.

Bella rejects materialism by rejecting the "bad" Boffin, replacing the materialist ideal she has tried to believe in with an unselfish one that exists in imagination. She says she will keep Mrs. Boffin in her "fancy" (665; pt. 3, ch. 15), using imagination to keep belief in an ideal parent (as she used it earlier to pretend her father was a good parent). Mrs. Boffin also embodies the belief Bella is learning to emulate, a belief in which "fancy" is "guided . . . by a religious sense" (146; pt. 1, ch. 9). Under these influences, Bella learns to replace her false golden idol with "images" of a higher ideal (667; pt. 3, ch. 16), an unselfish love. Once he has taught her to imagine such an ideal, Dickens makes it come true, giving her a fulfillment as complete as those in his early novels—an idealized mate and an idealized home, complete with perfect parent substitutes to replace her inadequate real parents. It is as if Dickens is trying to make us believe in such an ideal, to make us "overcome" our "doubts," like John Harmon, and reach "firm belief" that the ideal can be real (843; pt. 4, ch. 13).

But where Dickens's early fiction tried to make this kind of fulfillment seem real, here he is evidently unable to do that. Although he still wants to believe in an ideal, he can no longer fully overcome reason's sense that it is merely imaginary. If full belief is impossible, a playful make-believe like Bella's is what he has to offer us instead. He seems to feel that a "fairy vision" can have "complete realization" (380; pt. 2, ch. 9) only if, like Sloppy's, it is childlike and reason need not take it too seriously. What he offers us in Bella's story, then, is a merely playful version of the ideal happy ending, implying an admission that it is only imaginary. In this way, like Wemmick, he uses imagination to evade reason's skepticism, an evasion we can see taking place, for example, at the moment of fulfillment, Bella's wedding. Dickens deals with reason by embodying it in a diminished, comic form that he can overcome, the "Gruff and Glum" pensioner who observes the wedding. Like reason, this observer stands apart, unable to share in the ideal (that is, unable to feel the imaginary is real). However, because Dickens has segregated reason in a form that does not demand to enter into the ideal and make certain it is real, reason can accept it from a distance. Thus reason can allow imagination to create a semblance of belief; the vision of the "ethereal" ideal Dickens offers here makes the old man "spread" the "wings of his mind" and be "wafted up from the earth" as if rising above realism (731–32; pt. 4, ch. 4), and Dickens hopes to induce us to take a similar flight into imagination.

Dickens also tries to disarm reason by presenting the scene in a more self-consciously imaginative way than in his earlier fiction, telling us what "might have been fancied" and "might be imagined" (731; pt. 4, ch. 4), comparing it to "a dream" and to the Arabian Nights (732, 735; pt. 4, ch. 4). He is playing at idealization, letting imagination replace belief, hoping that if he concedes the ideal is only imaginary, reason will not reject it. We can see Bella doing this when she tells John, "your wishes are as real to me as the wishes in the Fairy story, that were all fulfilled as soon as spoken"; if he wishes her something, she has "better than got it" (748; pt. 4, ch. 5). She asserts that imagining fulfills desire because she can believe in the imagined ideal as well as if it were real—perhaps better, since imagination does not demand reason's acceptance as belief does. The imaginary can coexist with a sense of reality's "muddy streets" (748; pt. 4, ch. 5), whereas the sense of reality cannot coexist with serious belief.

Dickens tacitly admits Bella's happy ending is based on imagination by making the main agent of it Boffin, who seems to act for imagination, using "make-believe" (like Dickens) to repudiate the "unbelieving" state he has seemed to be in (847; pt. 4, ch. 13). He is doing what Dickens uses imagination to do: using make-believe to make something seem real. But he is too playful and childlike to make his belief seem very serious. Dickens wants to make the ideal seem real by showing it overcoming an anti-ideal reality, transforming Boffin into an ideal father, but since this transformation is enacted only in play, it seems only imaginary.

Though giving up seriousness in this way weakens belief, it also makes possible at least a simulacrum of belief. By giving up her desire to find the ideal in reality and accepting that it can exist only in imagination, Bella can overcome her selfishness, her desire for earthly fulfillment. By purging imagination of selfishness, she can reconcile it with a version of belief. Her "playful" quality can now serve a "graver reason" than before (753; pt. 4, ch. 5), and she can acquire a "deeper and quieter sort of seriousness" (756; pt. 4, ch. 5). She says that she needs "believing" (755; pt. 4, ch. 5), though this is a self-conscious, willed kind of belief. She is using imagination seriously to try to create belief, so that she can finally show her "perfect faith" in John (815; pt. 4, ch. 11)—a faith we can see as analogous to religious faith, especially since for Dickens the act of belief is more important than its object. Belief is similarly based on imagination in the case of the Reverend Milvey, who does not let blighted reality make him become "savagely wise" and give in to disillusion but rather is able to "distantly imagine" God as something beyond reality (386; pt. 2, ch. 10). If realism prevents complete belief, imagination can offer a version of belief that admits the ideal is unreal and so prevents reality from disillusioning us.

Dickens treats Eugene's conversion with more seriousness than Bella's, perhaps because he feels that Eugene, as a male, is more like himself and expresses doubts closer to his own. Eugene represents the doubting reason that Dickens has been making central in his novels since Louisa Gradgrind, the side of the mind that sees how unideal reality is. Reason on its own cannot fully resist passion, as we see when Louisa almost gives in to Harthouse and when Bradley Headstone does give in to his lust. Reason thus needs to be led to belief in order to resist that passion, as Eugene's conversion enables him to transform his feeling for Lizzie into unselfish love. Eugene's conversion also enables him to overcome spiritual doubt. I think Dickens is using Eugene to try to overcome his own uncertainty, but making Eugene so disillusioned— and so central in the novel—implies that Dickens feels doubt is stronger and more inescapable than ever. It is thus more difficult to overcome; whereas Bella's conversion is fairly easy and playful, Eugene's is painful and barely possible. It is hard to convince reason (as embodied in Eugene) that the ideal can exist in reality; he almost has to leave reality behind to attain the ideal, virtually dying. By going through a process like death, he can be purged of the guilty, potentially rebellious masculine side of himself—the passions that resist submissive belief and that Dickens embodies in Headstone so that they can be shifted away from Eugene and rejected from the novel through Headstone's death.

Eugene is led beyond doubt by Lizzie, who embodies the belief he needs to emulate. Lizzie too reaches belief through imagination; she is "a dreamer" (278; pt. 2, ch. 1) who sees visions in the fire, which has "nursed" her "fancies" (589; pt. 3, ch. 9). And like Bella, she could be misled by imagination; she feels Eugene offers her "glimpses of an enchanted world" whose "brightness" seems an escape from "the dark common street" (465; pt. 2, ch. 15), the reality she inhabits. Imagination's wish for "escape" (589; pt. 3, ch. 9) could lead her to indulge selfish desires and fail to accept reality. Like Bella, she must purify the ideal she envisions before Dickens can allow her to attain it. She too does this by replacing desire for an earthly ideal with belief in an admittedly imaginary ideal, replacing Eugene with "a kind of picture of him—or of what he might have been," an idealized picture in which she can have a "belief" that is unselfish because it does not seek possession "on this earth," and that she can thus use to protect herself from doing "wrong" (590–91; pt. 3, ch. 9). She transforms imagination into belief (though a belief that seems only imaginary) by freeing it of selfishness, and thus she can lead Bella and Eugene to do the same. Similarly, she helps old Betty Higden move from "fancies" (567; pt. 3, ch. 8) that enable her to see beyond reality to an ultimate certainty, belief in the imagined ideal, even if that belief can be reached only through death; Lizzie, like the belief she embodies, lifts Betty (as she later will Eugene) "as high as Heaven" (577; pt. 3, ch. 8).

But here as in Bella's story, belief alone is not enough; Eugene and reason need the help of imagination also. In other words, Eugene needs not only Lizzie's help but Jenny Wren's, who embodies the visionary imagination that leads to belief like Lizzie's.[5] This suggests that, as in Bella's story, Dickens is admitting more openly than earlier that he must base belief upon imagination, that he can reach some version of belief only with imagination's help. We might see Jenny as embodying the imaginative side of Lizzie; she urges Lizzie to indulge her "fancy" (404; pt. 2, ch. 11). Jenny uses imagination to transform reality so she can avoid resenting it, so she will not take its unidealness (which again here means a father's inadequacy) too seriously. Despite her unhappy home life, she can find a "compensation for her losses" in "Pleasant fancies" of Edenic "flowers"—fancies that Eugene's "commonplace," realist mind cannot share (289; pt. 2, ch. 2). She also uses imagination (as Dickens often does) to replace the father she cannot respect with a "father" she can believe in, Mr. Riah.

Yet despite the fact that Dickens here feels a need for imagination, he is not willing to allow it much comic play of the sort he allows in earlier characters such as Micawber; he wants it to serve his spiritual purpose more completely, as Jenny serves Lizzie. Jenny thus uses imagination not simply for escape but to create a vision of the divine, of "blessed children" like angels, who can take her to someplace like heaven (290; pt. 2, ch. 2; and see 334; pt. 2, ch. 5). Riah's connection with Judaism, with the roof garden where Jenny sees angels, and with a "godmother" makes us associate him with a divine father. It is as if Jenny—and Dickens—are trying to replace an earthly father with God. Dickens retains some sense here that imagination is escapist, rising above reality, and not wholly serious, since the imaginary children take Jenny to "play." But he evidently hopes he can lead us, like Eugene, to take this vision seriously, to believe in the ideal it shows us. He needs imagination to deal with reality's unidealness, as Jenny needs it to accept the "pain" of this life (290; pt. 2, ch. 2). This need is too strong for him to allow imagination the freedom to be merely playful.

When Jenny is up on the roof, it is as if she has risen above reality to a state where imagination can envision heaven and so accept death. She can "see the golden arrows pointing at the mountains in the sky" and thus imagine herself dead, picturing death as a higher state. And she has "fancied" resurrection for

Riah too, imagining that he has come "out of his grave" to a higher existence than "life down in the dark." Imagination cannot wholly overcome reason's awareness; she remains conscious of "the close dark streets" down below. But that awareness enables her to feel "pity" (334; pt. 2, ch. 5); by imagining heaven, she can keep from resenting reality and can instead pity those whom it cuts off from higher awareness. I think Dickens wants the same combination of an awareness of reality with an ability to envision something higher, enabling us to supplement our sense of reality, which could otherwise make us cynical or despairing, with a belief that is set apart and protected from realism (as Jenny is separate from reality, up on the roof) and able to counteract that realism. Like imagination, Jenny is in a halfway position, seeing both the real below and the ideal above.

Dickens's use of Jenny, however, implies a recognition of imagination's limitations. She is a cripple, suggesting that the imagination she represents (like the circus in *Hard Times*) is unable to overcome reality and is weakened by awareness of reality. Though Jenny can envision the ideal, she cannot attain it (cannot reach a highly idealized happy ending), implying that imagination cannot create belief that the ideal is entirely real and attainable. She is also childlike, not entirely serious, like imagination; we find in her the same inability to take imagination wholly seriously that I have described in Bella's half of the novel. The ideal she imagines is too childlike to compel very serious belief; Riah is "like the fairy godmother in the bright little books." The modifiers surrounding the word "god" here diminish it to the imaginary. Jenny says, "Let's believe so," trying to turn imagination into belief but in a self-conscious way that implicitly admits she is only playing at belief, that all this is only a "fancy" (493; pt. 3, ch. 2). Dickens suggests Jenny is forced to rely on imagination because the reality she lives in prevents complete belief; her world makes her lose "her way on the eternal road"—her belief in heaven—and makes her partly "of the earth, earthy" (294; pt. 2, ch. 2). Imagination is weaker than belief because it cannot fully overcome the sense of reality and remains in tension with it.

Making Jenny a dolls' dressmaker not only suggests she is childish but also implies she is a kind of artist and thus an imaginer. Like Dickens, Jenny bases her art on reality, observing fine ladies, but she can also use imagination for a higher vision, as Dickens wants to. Yet Jenny (like Mr. Venus) reveals the artist's shortcomings. Like dolls, imagination's creations are not something we can take completely seriously. But by making the imaginary admittedly less than real, Dickens can keep it from becoming selfish. Jenny makes dolls that are images of the self she would like to have, as when she imagines herself Cinderella (493; pt. 3, ch. 2), but by acknowledging that this is only imaginary, she can keep from taking seriously the desires she expresses. She does not try to attain the ideal in reality; she merely lets her dolls (and imagination) attain it. She recognizes those desires are "selfish" and should be expressed only in play (494; pt. 3, ch. 2). Perhaps because she accepts that imagination cannot wholly replace belief and does not demand total certainty, she can manage a compromise between idealism and realism. Here again she may represent the attitude Dickens himself wants to have.

Dickens's sense that he must allow belief to rest on imagination is expressed by his having Jenny bring about Eugene's salvation. As I have said, Eugene represents the doubting reason that Dickens seeks to lead to belief; if Jenny enables him to end up with Lizzie, that represents imagination leading reason to belief. And it is Jenny rather than Lizzie who mainly accomplishes this, in contrast to *Hard Times*, where Sissy (belief) seems stronger than the circus (imagination). I think Dickens has tried to move from imagination to belief but has finally concluded that he cannot do so, that a partial belief admittedly based on imagination is the best he can hope for. Lizzie alone cannot convince Eugene, suggesting that belief cannot wholly overcome doubt. He asks himself if he can "even believe" in Lizzie's power over him, and he cannot answer. He can only feel "almost as if" Lizzie is "sanctified" (764; pt. 4, ch. 6); he cannot quite believe in the divine, in an ideal that can be real to him. He can give up the selfish, earthly ideal he has sought, but he cannot believe in the existence of a higher ideal with which to replace it.

In other words, Eugene has reached an Everlasting No, a rejection of his earlier values; his near-death acts out the death of his earthly desires. But to reach an Everlasting Yea, a vision of something better than the earthly, with which to replace what he has rejected, he needs Jenny and the imagination she embodies. He can be saved, unlike Bradley Headstone, because he has (despite his doubts) the capacity to allow imagination, which Bradley lacks, a capacity shown in Eugene's playfulness earlier in the novel. Thus he can appreciate Jenny's "pretty fancy" and wish for a vision like hers of something "most beautiful and most Divine" (807; pt. 4, ch. 10), and it is Jenny who can guess Eugene's feeling and thus enable him to marry Lizzie.

However, Jenny can no longer see the angelic children she once saw, suggesting a partial loss of the childlike belief in the imagined ideal. Dickens can overcome the doubt Eugene has embodied only by partly giving in to that doubt, giving up some belief and thus admitting more fully than in his earlier fiction that the ideal is only imaginary. But by accepting this diminished version of belief, he can reconcile imagination and reason, like Jenny and Eugene. If he admits that the ideal is imaginary, he can get reason to accept it more fully than if he demanded serious belief. Basing belief on imagination like this resembles what Bella does in her half of the novel.

Since Dickens is accepting imagination more fully in this novel, he places greater emphasis on the act of writing for its own sake. His narrative persona here is especially self-conscious, willing to admit that what he presents is imaginary. He tells us what a scene would suggest "to the fanciful observer" (89; pt. 1, ch. 5) or "to an imaginative mind" (677; pt. 3, ch. 16). He introduces a metaphor by saying it may be something "fanciful to suppose" (717; pt. 4, ch. 2). He seems to be accepting that (as for Wemmick) reality remains apart from and untransformed by imagination, that imagination cannot really convince reason and so must be used less seriously.

We can see this attitude more clearly in a minor piece written shortly after *Our Mutual Friend*, "A Holiday Romance." As the title suggests, the work is a kind of holiday from seriousness. The story is narrated by children, as if Dickens feels he must take on a childlike identity to allow imagination expression, giving up his adult self, which cannot believe in imagination's visions. But even these child personae cannot escape the feeling that the imaginative play they are trying to believe in is only "pretending" (695; pt. 1) and that belief is problematic. The narrator begins by telling us we "must believe" him (691; pt. 1), while at the same time admitting that some belief is less complete (more imagination) than other kinds. The fact that it is a child narrator asking for belief undercuts our belief. Adults prevent the children's play from coming true, as adult reason prevents belief in the imaginary. Thus it is the adults' fault that there are no "fairies" any more (696; pt. 1)—that the imaginary cannot seem real.

In reaction, the children decide (as Dickens himself seems to have decided by the time of *Our Mutual Friend*) that they "must pretend in a new manner." Like Dickens, they "will pretend" they "are children," will "veil [their] meaning under a mask of romance," and thus "educate" adults who no longer accept imagination, hoping they can thus make "the fairies . . . come back" (697; pt. 1). That is, by not taking imagination too seriously, admitting that it is childlike and its visions merely romance, Dickens hopes to convince adult reason to accept it, thus regaining a childlike version of belief. He too veils his serious point under a childlike disguise, hoping to circumvent skeptical reason by evading its reality-testing and to educate it (and us) into accepting imagination.

To win this acceptance, however, imagination here again must give up selfish desire, its demand to overcome reason, as Eugene gives up his desires. Dickens tries in "A Holiday Romance" to overcome this threat to imagination by having Alice, representing the submissive, female side of imagination, overcome Robin, expressing its male, rebellious side, which would resent reality for opposing imagination's desires. Alice tells him they must not directly rebel against the adults, implying that imagination should not oppose reason too directly but rather must accommodate the adult sense of reality, conceding that the imaginary is not real. But by conceding in this way that one cannot take imagination too seriously, setting it apart from concerns with reality as Wemmick does, Dickens prevents us from taking this imagined happy ending seriously; the stories have happy endings, but their openly imaginary nature prevents us from fully believing in those endings. Thus, although a return to the childlike imagination begins as an attempt to hold onto belief, the appeal to imagination undermines belief.

At the end of his career, then, Dickens (like late-nineteenth-century writers of fantasy) is less confident than earlier that the ideal he imagines can be anything more than imaginary. If we look at passages in *Our Mutual Friend* where he tries to rise above realism, like the churches struggling "to get their heads above" the city fog (479; pt. 3, ch. 1), the sense of struggle and of not being able to go beyond reality seems stronger than ever. He describes "the great serene mirror of the river," reflecting the sky as a "mirror" reflects "images," and says it "seemed as if it might have" reflected none of the "horror or distress" of this world but only "what was peaceful" (585; pt. 3, ch. 9). In a related passage he moves from the river's reflecting the sky to a view "beyond" reality, "away to where the sky appeared to meet the earth, as if there were no immensity of space between mankind and Heaven" (757; pt. 4, ch. 6). Both these passages try to bring the ideal into reality, to reach a vision of the ideal through reality. But in both the sense of reality's unidealness is at least as strong as the glimpse of something beyond it, and the second passage admits that the divine is far from reality. Both passages introduce their vision of the ideal with the phrase "as if," tacitly admitting that the ideal is only a supposition of the imagination. The image of a mirror reflecting heaven sounds like a description of imagination; in this world the ideal can exist only indirectly, as reflected in imagination. As long as the divine remains this distant from reality, and the wish for belief remains so opposed to the sense of reality, imagining the ideal is the best one can hope for.

chapter 10

How Dickens Uses Imagination

In describing ways in which imagination fails to create belief, I have probably sounded as if I assume that the job of literature is to induce belief. But although Dickens and many other Victorian writers evidently wanted literature to do that, literature is not religion and we should not expect it to be. On the contrary, what we most value in it these days is likely to be its very failure to create certainty, the ways in which even those writers who seek to make us believe undermine their own ostensible purpose and express conflict. What we value is not the ideal goal imagination seeks but never quite reaches, but rather the by-products of that search. We do not read a Dickens novel for its last page but rather for the process by which it moves toward that page. We probably care less about what literature teaches us than how it acts upon us, causing tensions in us. When a writer seeks to force imagination into belief, he creates conflicts, arouses resistance to that attempt, and those conflicts, far from weakening his work, can be very productive, can be what give birth to the work's complexity. It is imagination's failure to reach the ideal and the tensions and doubts that accompany that failure that make the work of a writer like Dickens exciting and interesting.

What I want to do here is to look at the way Dickens's imagination actually finds expression. So far we have mostly examined the way imagination acts in a work's structure, a structure based on the movement toward belief, but we should also pay attention to the way it acts in the work's verbal details. Dickens wants to use imagination to contribute to a spiritual process his serious characters go through, but how is that process related to the constant imaginative play in his novels? I think much of this play comes from imagination's attempt to overcome what opposes it. His very effort to use imagination to reach the ideal causes him to feel reality as an entity resisting imagination. The more imagination seeks to convince reason to believe in an ideal, the more it forces reason to resist it, arousing a sense of the way reality is unlike the imagined ideal.

Nevertheless, imagination keeps trying to transform what it feels to be reality, if not to idealize reality at least to reduce it to forms that do not seem to oppose desire so seriously. The versions of the ideal that Dickens imagines seem to be versions of a return to a paradisal childhood world in which his parents had not failed him, and to a pre-Oedipal infantile union with a mother whom he could still see as loving and totally wish-fulfilling. Because the versions of fulfillment he imagines are so close to primal fantasy, the desires he expresses through imagination are especially intense; and because he allows desires such a strong outlet, his sense that there is a force opposing them (which he thinks of as reality) is also especially intense. As a result, he presents a "reality" that he sees as highly unideal, actively opposing the desire for the ideal, grotesque, even frightening. The more one desires to see the world as a paradise, the more likely it is to seem a hell. There is presumably an element of guilt reaction in this, punishing imagination for having desired too much.

When we look at the ways in which Dickens's imagination actually finds expression, then, we discover that although it is striving to create belief in an ideal as we would expect from Dickens's concept of it, that idealization is mixed with elements that express doubts and conflicts, impulses that prevent the desire for an ideal from finding a pure, complete form of expression.[1] In his treatment of setting, for example, we can often see the effort to find an ideal arousing a sense of the way reality opposes the desire for an ideal.

I think that when Dickens imagines his fictional worlds, he usually does something like what he explicitly does at the start of *Copperfield;* he activates imagination by putting himself into a relatively childlike state of mind in which he is partly freed from rational restraint. Early in *Copperfield* he largely suspends adult awareness of the significance and interrelationship of objects, seeing each thing for itself alone. Similarly, during the tempest in that novel, he heightens the intensity of his description by putting his narrator in a state where he has "lost the clear arrangement of time and distance" (859; ch. 55). By suspending reason in this way, he gets a dreamlike effect, letting his mind work more in the mode of what Freud calls the primary process that dominates dreams. Insofar as he suspends reason, imagination can control perception as it does in dreams (and as it probably tends to in children), altering perception in obedience to the desires that dominate imagination (and to the reflex of those desires, the fear of what opposes desire).

Imagination (like a child) desires such things as unity, softness, warmth, light, openness, freedom, order—a world in harmony with our wishes. Thus it tends to see the reality that opposes it as the negation of these qualities—as fragmented, hard, cold, dark, enclosed, disordered. In describing reality in these terms, Dickens is not merely expressing a rational sense of what the world is like (though that sense enters into his description); he is also allowing covert expression to imagination, since these negations imply the desire they deny. If a writer cannot show us the ideal as convincingly as he wants, he can create images of its opposite, an anti-ideal "reality," to make us believe in, or at least wish for, what that reality denies. Dickens thus often describes a world whose solid, obdurate thingness can be felt as a resistance to desire, a refusal to be transformed into the idyllic as imagination wishes to transform it.

Dickens's imaginative desire is so strong that he also projects it onto the world he describes, endowing objects with a force that sometimes acts for and sometimes actively resists desire, making objects seem animate. To imagination, what opposes desire seems to have power—the power of desire, projected onto the object in a negative reflection; the more one pushes against an object, the more it seems to push back. We transfer our energy to the object and see that energy as transformed into a negative energy, actively opposing us. Since idealism wants not simply to push against reality but to transform it, reality's very realness, its simple existence, can seem negative and hostile. I would guess that realism in general is a result of idealism; realists see the world as negative because it opposes the idealist wishes they have inherited from Romanticism. Dickens's presentation of reality as so hostile that it takes on an imaginative life of its own may be a result of his especially strong desire, his being less willing to give up idealism than a realist would be.

Early in *Copperfield* there is a clear example of the way Dickens uses "realistic" details not simply to give us a picture of reality (if such a thing can be done) but mainly to give us a sense of reality's unidealness, of reality seen as an opponent by the childlike vision of imagination. David has come home to find Murdstone in power and his childhood paradise lost. He sits alone and thinks "of the oddest things. Of the shape of the room, of the cracks in the ceiling, of the paper on the walls, of the flaws in the window-glass making ripples and dimples on the prospect, of the washing-stand being rickety on its three legs, and having a discontented something about it, which reminded me of Mrs. Gummidge." This passage is here not just to enable us to picture David's room but mainly to help us feel his feelings, the "desolation" that makes his world seem "blank and strange," meaningless and unsympathetic (93–94; ch. 4). At first the details seem neutral, apparently merely reproductions of reality, but gradually Dickens gives us a sense of the way reality is opposing desire. It seems enclosing, cracked, flawed; it reflects the fact that David's prospects are not hopeful and that he is discontented. Imagination projects its discontent onto objects because those objects oppose its desires. It is forced to accept images imposed upon it by the mind's awareness of reality, but it tries to transform those images; if it cannot make them seem ideal, it seeks revenge by turning them into negative, ugly, villainous versions of reality. Thus "reality" is gradually transformed here; imagination brings it to life, finally turning a washing-stand into a character like Mrs. Gummidge. And imagination gives objects meaning: their meaning is that they oppose its desire, they embody discontent.

If we examine a much more complex example of Dickens's description—the description in *Chuzzlewit* of the world around Todgers's, a passage that Dorothy Van Ghent takes as describing Dickens's typical world[2]—we can read it as a product of imagination's attempt to find some ideal:

> Surely there never was, in any other borough, city, or hamlet in the world, such a singular sort of place as Todgers's. And surely London—to judge from that part of it which hemmed Todgers's round, and hustled it, and crushed it, and stuck its brick-and-mortar elbow into it, and kept the air from it, and stood perpetually between it and the light—was worthy of Todgers's, and qualified to be on terms of close relationship and alliance with hundreds and thousands of the old family to which Todgers's belonged.
>
> You couldn't walk about in Todgers's neighbourhood as you could in any other neighbourhood. You groped your way for an hour through lanes and by-ways, and courtyards, and passages, and never once emerged upon anything that might be called a street. A kind of resigned distraction came over the stranger as he trod those devious mazes, and, giving himself up for lost, went in and out and round about, and quietly turned back again when he came to a dead wall or was stopped by an iron railing, and felt that the means of escape might possibly present themselves in their own good time, but that to anticipate them was hopeless. (185; ch. 9)

This stranger could be imagination itself, a stranger to reality, seeking to escape from it and find the paradise it desires, but continually brought up short by reality. In other words, there is a desire implicit in this description—a desire not to be hemmed in, a desire for air and light, a desire to find some meaningful destination, or at least to escape. And it is imagination that sees the world in terms of desire, giving images meaning and value by seeing them as serving or opposing desire. The more imagination desires an ideal, the more it sees a reality that opposes that desire as negative. "Reality" reflects the observer as London is "worthy of" Todgers's; subject and object are parts of one whole, reacting to each other. The world here is like a maze or prison because of the desire to find a way out and escape; it pushes in because of imagination's desire to push out of it. And here as elsewhere in Dickens the way reality opposes imagination threatens to undermine spiritual belief. People are groping, as if seeking something in which to believe, in a reality that offers them no ideal and thus renders them hopeless, causing "irreligion" and a loss of "belief" in "virtue" (187; ch. 9), as at the beginning of *Bleak House*, where people are also groping and have lost belief. Imagination sees reality as preventing belief in an ideal because that belief is what imagination seeks.

Imagination is active. It not only contemplates an object; it creates that object so it can act on it, trying to make the object fulfill its desires. Imagination can simply create images, as in a lyric, but it often sets them in motion as well, causing them to act out conflicts as in narrative. In the Todgers world things are not merely objects imagination seeks to act on and transform; they also become subjects. Imagination creates agents to act for it in the world it describes, animating them with its desires so that they seek to fulfill those desires for it. Thus, enclosed in the Todgers world are things, much like the stranger in the passage I have just quoted, that are trying to get out of that world. For example, there are "trees, still putting forth their leaves in each succeeding year, with such a languishing remembrance of their kind (so one might fancy, looking on their sickly boughs) as birds in cages have of theirs" (186; ch. 9). Fancy here transfers its desire to the trees. We can compare their putting forth leaves to imagination's seeking some outlet, some way to express its desires; as the trees struggle against the reality that makes them sickly and prevents their fully leafing out, so imagination struggles against the awareness of reality's unidealness, which opposes and distorts its self-expression. Again here the world is cagelike because it opposes the desire for escape and transcendence. Yet imagination is not wholly defeated; it can put some of its energy into that world so that reality does not seem entirely negative.

Dickens also transfers some of imagination's energy to negative objects, seeing them also as subjects animated by a force. These objects oppose desire, and so the force that imagination sees animating them, rather than serving desire, is its reflex—an active tendency to oppose desire. In the first paragraph I quoted above, London is not simply a passive object on which imagination tries to act; it becomes active, hustling, crushing, and elbowing. This activity is the negative reflection of the desire not to be enclosed and to escape. But often energy is so blocked in such a prison-like world that activity cannot even be negative. In the following passage it becomes mere action for its own sake:

> vast bags and packs of goods, upward or downward bound, were for ever dangling between heaven and earth from lofty cranes. There were more trucks near Todgers's than you would suppose a whole city could ever need; not active trucks, but a vagabond race, for ever lounging in the narrow lanes before their masters' doors, and stopping up the pass; so that when a stray hackney-coach or lumbering wagon came that way, they were the cause of such an uproar as enlivened the whole neighbourhood, and made the very bells in the next church vibrate again. (186–87; ch. 9)

This activity is going nowhere, serving no purpose, caught in a state of perpetual repetition. We can see it as expressing imaginative energy that can find no fulfilling outlet, yet keeps seeking expression, however unsatisfying, for the mere sake of having some outlet. Imagination seems to be reacting against the sense of reality or of repression opposing it, and that reaction is projected onto these objects, which seem to be reacting against the way the world encloses them. The more the world denies them a fulfilling outlet, the more fiercely they (and imagination) seek any outlet at all, no matter how unfulfilling. It is as if the way to any fulfilling outlet, like the street, is stopped up, and so imagination can only make an uproar, its energy pushing against reality without being able to overcome it. Like the cranes, imagination here would like to rise up to heaven but cannot escape earth, so that it must get its unfulfilled energy out of its system any way it can. Dickens often uses it in this way, to fill his world with as much clutter and bustle as possible, creating as many objects as he can squeeze in, each one bursting with energy as if trying to overcome what holds it in—very like the characters who also crowd his pages.

Imagination can thus partially compensate itself for frustration by finding substitute outlets for its energy, even though Dickens's sense of the way reality opposes desire makes it take such indirect, unfulfilling outlets. It can partly make up for the recalcitrance of the images reality forces upon it by transforming those images, giving us the feeling that reality is something it can control or at least play with, that we are not wholly at the mercy of physical objects and need not take them too seriously. If imagination cannot create belief in the ideal, it can at least free us from the grip of reality, making us feel reality is not all there is so that idealism can remain possible.

Imagination can also project its energy onto its version of reality in a way that is exhilarating enough to overcome much of our dislike of reality. As a result, Dickens's imagination, like young Bailey, can make itself at home in the Todgers world, coexisting with reality. It can do so because, like Bailey, it can use reality as something to play with, an opponent to outwit, an obstacle to surmount, at least using metaphors to transform it halfway. In Dickens's later novels there is less exhilaration and a much greater sense of the need to rise up toward heaven and of the grimness of the reality which prevents that. But when, in the first paragraph of *Bleak House*, Dickens puts a dinosaur in the streets of London, he is still showing imagination's power to move beyond realism, to find playful outlets despite its awareness of reality.

In passages like the description of Todgers's, Dickens is using compromise formations, partly accepting that there is a reality that opposes desire and partly allowing imagination to overcome that sense of reality. Like Sleary, Dickens sees with a double vision. As J. Hillis Miller puts it, Dickens combines an adult and a childlike view of the world.[3] We can see compromise formations of this sort as the result of a process whereby imagination tries to transform reality and fails. But it has at least succeeded in preventing reason from making us wholly accept reality. Reason and imagination remain in unresolved tension.

We can also see imagination and the sense of reality interacting in this passage describing Florence Dombey's world:

> Florence lived alone in the great dreary house, and day succeeded day, and still she lived alone; and the blank walls looked down upon her with a vacant stare, as if they had a Gorgonlike mind to stare her youth and beauty into stone.
>
> No magic dwelling-place in magic story, shut up in the heart of a thick wood, was ever more solitary and deserted to the fancy than was her father's mansion in its grim reality, as it stood lowering on the street . . ., a frown upon its never-smiling face.
>
> There were not two dragon sentries keeping ward before the gate of this abode, as in magic legend are usually found on duty over wronged innocence imprisoned; but besides a glowering visage, with its thin lips parted wickedly, that surveyed all comers from the archway of the door, there was a monstrous fantasy of rusty iron, curling and twisting like a petrifaction of an arbour over the threshold, budding in spikes and corkscrew points. . . . There were no talismanic characters engraven on the portal, but the house was so neglected in appearance, that boys chalked the railings . . . and drew ghosts on the stable door. (393; ch. 23)

Here again Dickens wants things both ways; he says this is no imaginary place in a magic story but rather is grim reality, but he simultaneously says this is not just reality but a monstrous fantasy. Having first made concessions to reality, he then feels free to let imagination transform reality. The walls seem blank, opposing the desire for escape as at Todgers's, but then they become alive, having a mind to stare at Florence and turn her into an inanimate object, as if they have taken her energy. That is, imagination's energy, unable to find a satisfying outlet in positive, virtuous form, finds expression in a form that opposes imagination's desire (though it is imagination that has given them that energy). The house is not a story-book house, but then it has a face. There are no dragons, but then reality comes to life, acquires a glowering visage like a dragon's, and begins curling and twisting, as if the energy imagination has transferred into it is forcing its way out even though it can do so only in this twisted way. There are no talismanic characters, but imagination (like a playful child) can inscribe its own images on reality, as if replacing the talismanic significance religion once gave to reality with its own less serious meaning.

In each of these cases, it is as if the eye of realism (or anti-idealism) looks at the world and finds no meaning, only blankness. But though Dickens half accepts that vision, he simultaneously lets imagination turn reality into something onto which it can project its images, as the children do, even though his adult self sees this is merely something he is imposing on the perceptual. He makes this coexistence possible mainly through metaphors, which admit that the imaginary is not real. He describes objects that "seemed to say" something (393; ch. 23), half admits his image is only imaginary, but half allows it to seem real.

What Dickens does with his characters is quite similar to what he does with physical objects. Just as he often sees inanimate objects as animate subjects, he often turns characters into subjects.[4] We see characters primarily as objects if they exist for desire to act upon, if they exist to fulfill or oppose desire. But even though most Dickens characters function in this way, they usually also function as subjects of desire, expressing it in various (often highly distorted) ways. Characters are more amenable to this treatment than physical objects, since they have a greater ability to act and express themselves and thus allow imagination a more satisfying outlet.

We can see the same conflict I have been discussing in many Dickens characters, then; they too express both imagination's attempt to find an ideal and the forces opposing its wishes. This conflict is especially clear in Flora Finching in *Little Dorrit*. Flora functions primarily as a negative object, an embodiment of the way reality fails to fulfill Arthur Clennam's desire, an obstacle to overcome. However, Dickens also gives her desires of her own; he has so much imaginative energy that it keeps seeking expression through the objects that oppose it. But just as she exists in opposition to Arthur's desire, so she opposes the desire Dickens expresses within her, acting as an obstacle to herself. This tension creates a strong conflict in her speech—a conflict I think is typical of those that usually accompany imagination in Dickens, though here it occurs in a particularly clear, exaggerated form. Dickens is giving freer expression than usual in her speech both to imagination and to the forces opposing it, perhaps because he is more conscious of their conflict than in his earlier fiction.

Flora's speech simultaneously expresses desire (mainly for Arthur) and impulses that oppose that desire:

"My goodness Arthur!" cried Flora . . . "Doyce and Clennam what a start and a surprise for though not far from the machinery and foundry business and surely might be taken sometimes if at no other time about mid-day when a glass of sherry and a humble sandwich of whatever cold meat in the larder might not come amiss nor taste the worse for being friendly you know you buy it somewhere and wherever bought a profit must be made or they would never keep the place it stands to reason without a motive still never seen and learnt now not to be expected, for as Mr. F. himself said if seeing is believing not seeing is believing too and when you don't see you may fully believe you're not remembered not that I expect you Arthur Doyce and Clennam to remember me why should I for the days are gone but bring another teacup here directly and tell her fresh toast and pray sit near the fire."

. . .

"And now pray tell me something all you know . . . about the good quiet little thing and all the changes of her fortunes carriage people now no doubt and horses without number most romantic, a coat of arms of course and wild beasts on their hind legs showing it as if it was a copy they had done with mouths from ear to ear good gracious, and has she her health which is the first consideration after all for what is wealth without it Mr. F. himself so often saying when his twinges came that sixpence a day and find yourself and no gout so much preferable, not that he could have lived on anything like it being the last man or that the precious little thing though far too familiar an expression now had any tendency of that sort much too slight and small but looked so fragile bless her?"

· · ·

"In Italy is she really? . . . with the grapes growing everywhere and lava necklaces and bracelets too that land of poetry with burning mountains picturesque beyond belief though if the organ-boys come away from the neighbourhood not to be scorched nobody can wonder being so young and bringing their white mice with them most humane, and is she really in that favoured land with nothing but blue about her and dying gladiators and Belvederes though Mr. F. himself did not believe for his objection when in spirits was that the images could not be true there being no medium between expensive quantities of linen badly got up and all in creases and none whatever, which certainly does not seem probable though perhaps in consequence of the extremes of rich and poor which may account for it." (589–90; pt. 2, ch. 9)

Flora is a hopelessly divided character, like a mermaid—half rational and aware of prosaic, unideal reality, but half incurably romantic, constantly re-treating from the unfulfilling reality that imprisons her into an imaginary world she cannot reconcile with her rational awareness. She is aware that "Romance has fled" and "stern reality usurped the throne" (329; pt. 1, ch. 24), but she works herself up into a state in which "she did actually believe whatever she said" (332; pt. 1, ch. 24), using imagination to try to create belief. Her conflict is one Dickens is continually concerned with, usually in more serious forms—for example, in Clennam's search for some idealist be-lief he can reconcile with his sense of reality. But through Flora, Dickens can take a vacation from that seriousness and reduce the conflict to something comic, giving up any attempt to resolve it and instead enjoying the way the two viewpoints undercut each other, the realistic making the romantic ri-diculous, and desire for the ideal preventing complete acceptance of reality. Dickens can deal with the anxiety this conflict could cause by locating the conflict in Flora and thus distancing it from the serious rational self that would feel the need to resolve it.

Flora's romantic desires are often expressed in her wish to see herself as a romance heroine and Arthur as her hero, a wish she continually hints at by calling him Arthur and using sentimental language. But her desires are also expressed in her use of poetic language to try to make reality romantic, a tendency shown here in her description of Italy. However, she always ex-presses these desires in ways that undermine them, as if reacting guiltily against them. She often expresses them in clichés; we do not take them seri-ously because she seems to be repeating what she has read rather than ex-pressing her own desires. And because the bits of poetry she quotes are taken out of context, the desire expressed through them does not seem related to a serious sense of reality with which it would be in conflict. (This practice resembles the way Victorian comic writers such as Calverley and Gilbert reduce the Romantic to the merely conventional.)

Flora's romanticism is also constantly undercut by her (and Dickens's) awareness of a reality that cannot be reconciled with the imagined ideal, an awareness that prevents belief in that ideal. No sooner does she take off on one of her poetic flights than realism brings her down to earth with a thump, interrupting "Fancy's fair dreams" with an awareness of how "deficient" reality is (887; pt. 2, ch. 34). The words and images that interrupt her poetic language are unpoetic, comically incongruous, resisting idealization; they are not the images Romantics prefer, images that can be seen as ideal because they belong to nature or some such realm beyond ordinary experience.

In addition, Dickens expresses Flora's conflict in a way that implies that desire is opposed not only by realistic awareness but also by irrational guilt. The moment she uses the name *Arthur*, trying to see him as her lover and let desire control perception, she feels the impropriety of that word and feels compelled to try to cancel it, as if in a guilt reaction against desire. She tries to invite him to come see her, but gets hopelessly bogged down in prosaic details, not just humble sandwiches but, branching out from that (the way Dickens's novels keep branching out), her awareness of the whole profit-making society surrounding her, a reality as hard to escape in her language as it is in actuality.

Flora tries to turn her loss of romance into something romantic ("the days are gone"), seeing herself sentimentally as a victim, but again the unpoetic details of teacups and toast immediately undercut her attempt. Even when she tries to talk of Little Dorrit, she is unable to use the idealizing language one would expect from Dickens but ends up talking about Mr. F.'s gout instead, a subject so incongruous it risks making Dorrit too ridiculous. And when she tries to see Italy as a land of poetry, a place like heaven in which one is surrounded by blue, this vision is undermined by her sense of what is "probable." It is as if Flora, like the Italians she imagines, can find "no medium," no way to compromise between a wholly idealized and thus unrealistic imaginary vision and a wholly unpoetic, unideal reality.

Because Flora cannot reconcile imaginative desire with realism, she can never fully accept her own sense of reality, and her desire, still unfulfilled, keeps seeking new objects. (This is a parodic version of what happens in Dickens novels; the sense of reality keeps balking the desire for an ideal, but that desire keeps finding new outlets, gradually moving toward a final victory over the sense of reality—a kind of victory that is denied to Flora.) Each time

Flora cancels one poetic vision, she seeks a new one. She "cannot overcome" calling Arthur by his first name (887; pt. 2, ch. 34), as she cannot overcome her desire for him, and, similarly, she cannot stop indulging in romantic escapism. Like her creator, she has desires too strong and irrational to give in to realism. But because her desire cannot accept rational restraint, her reason cannot accept her desire and keeps opposing imagination. She wants to believe in the imaginary, to feel that seeing is believing—that she can actually see the ideal—but she cannot help admitting that not seeing is believing too—that she cannot see any ideal and therefore that she must believe it does not exist. She cannot help feeling it is "beyond belief," or at least telling us that Mr. F. "did not believe" in the imagined ideal. Mr. F. expresses the realistic side of Flora, which mocks the poetic (he is thus the opposite of Mrs. Gamp's Mrs. Harris, who exists to provide an outlet for desires that seek to overcome the sense of reality).

This tension between reason and imagination finds expression not only when the two alternate but also when they combine in compromise formations in which both realism and idealism are implicit, each modifying the other. For example, when Flora describes a land of nothing but blue, she not only expresses a desire for a paradise but also implies a realistic awareness that such a paradise is impossible by making the description unbelievable and ridiculous, as if to disarm reason's skepticism. She describes their youthful love as a time "when one bright idea gilded the what's-his-name horizon of et cetera" (591; pt. 2, ch. 9), reducing the Romantic desire for imagination to transform reality (gild it) to mere words as in Lear and Carroll, tacitly admitting that this talk has no signified in reality. Doing this can keep desire from becoming serious—that is, from looking for an object in reality—so that, like Micawber, she can enjoy even its disappointment. Transferring rational disbelief to Mr. F. and expressing it in a joking form—as what he says "when in spirits"—is one of many ways Flora uses imagination to modify reason, reducing it too to a less serious form whose criticism imagination need not fear. Throughout Dickens there are similar compromise formations; we can probably consider all his comic expressions of imagination as simultaneously expressing the desire for the ideal of Romantic imagination and expressing the anti-Romantic awareness that reality is unideal, combining these two conflicting views in ways that diminish the ideal or make it seem unreal or incongruous.

Flora's example, then, shows the conflicts imagination can cause and the way those conflicts generate characterization. In addition, the strong imaginative desire Dickens expresses through characters like Flora creates conflicts within the novels' structure; the characters' energy tends to conflict with Dickens's serious purpose, as Flora's comic expression of imagination undercuts the serious feeling we are asked to have about Arthur and Dorrit. Especially in comic parts of a novel, imagination's visions tend to be too much under the influence of desire for reason to accept them. Imagination tries to free itself from the seriousness caused by reason's concern with reality, and that brings it into conflict with Dickens's serious spiritual purpose. Dickens puts Flora to structural use, using her to show us that uncontrolled imagination lacks seriousness in order to teach us (and Arthur) the need to convert it into belief. Flora's failure to adapt imagination to a reality that is so unideal shows the need for a more serious belief. Dickens is criticizing the kind of playfulness he enjoyed in his earlier fiction.

Yet unreformed imagination also has a more positive function in the novel's structure. Dickens clearly also enjoys Flora's lack of seriousness; it makes the conflict between desire and reality bearable. Imagination's playfulness frees us from the need to try to believe seriously and lets us enjoy the imaginary without worrying about its unreality. By saying her imaginary Italy is beyond belief, Flora exempts it from reality-testing; thus she (and we) can enjoy it as a mere fiction, something playfully set aside from the sense of realistic limitations. The paradise she enjoys imagining here is admittedly fictional, existing only in works of art; if she is not clear on this point, at least we and Dickens know it. Dickens uses Flora to make an imperfect, playful belief possible by separating out realism, distancing it (for example, by transferring it to Mr. F.) so that imagination can be temporarily free of its doubts, rather as Dickens often locates doubt in characters whom he can distance. Characters like Flora give Dickens a partial way of dealing with the conflict between realism and belief by reducing that conflict, as Lewis Carroll does, to the absurd. Thus at the same time that serious, idealist imagination generates the central plot action, the forces in imagination that resist seriousness play a structural role also, counterbalancing the serious conflict.

Much of what Dickens does with his characters seems to result from this tendency imagination has to create conflicts. Like Flora, most of Dickens's comic characters are mock Romantics. They are like Romantic heroes, full of energy that seeks to burst all bonds, that cannot be expressed in mere words and is in conflict with their restrictive social selves; they long for some impossible ideal, and their excessive desire creates tensions that prevent it from being fulfilling. Yet (as in Lear) all of this has been divorced from seriousness by distorting the desire, making its expression self-defeating but also comic.

These conflicts generate the rich complexity of Dickens's novels. If imagination aroused no conflict, there would be no comic versions of idealism. *Little Dorrit* would simply be about Arthur's finding Dorrit, and Flora and all

her kin would never have been created. But imagination doesn't simply create a vision of the ideal. The wish for an ideal leads Dickens to create characters like Dorrit, but the conflict that wish arouses leads him to supplement
such idealized characters with alternative outlets for imagination, in which
idealization is strongly opposed. For example, Dorrit is accompanied by a
comic shadow, Maggie, who is like a deidealized version of her. Like Dorrit,
Maggie is a child victim who believes in an idealized parent figure, but that
childlike belief is here made ridiculous. One side of Dickens asserts his belief
in an ideal by creating Dorrit, but that attempt to believe in the ideal arouses
opposing, skeptical impulses that find expression in creating Maggie, a compromise formation that combines idealization with mockery of the ideal.

Similarly, in other novels we can see many of the comic (and villainous)
elements as reactions against Dickens's own idealization. For example, Little
Nell is surrounded by grotesques and villains (especially Quilp) whose very
existence seems to oppose Dickens's attempt to find an ideal through Nell.
He uses these negative characters to give expression to the side of himself
that doubts the ideal, hoping that he can overcome those doubts by enabling
the idealized character to overcome the characters that embody them. But
his attempt to locate the ideal in reality—to put Nell into a world that opposes her—intensifies the sense of how thoroughly reality and the ideal are
opposed, increasing conflict rather than resolving it. In the case of Nell, the
conflict becomes too great to resolve and she can only retreat from reality.

To make the conflict less stark, however, Dickens supplements Nell with
characters who occupy a middle ground between her and Quilp and who
represent imagination's attempt to deal with this conflict by combining desire and what opposes it in compromise formations. Dick Swiveller and the
Marchioness are thus a kind of parody of and antidote to the story of Little
Nell. The Marchioness is a girl victim like Nell, and Swiveller comes close to
death like Nell, but since their story is reduced to the comic, its idealization
largely undercut by skepticism, the desires expressed through them need not
be taken too seriously. Thus those desires need not overcome opposition as
serious as that Nell faces and need not be purified so much before they can be
accepted. Dickens can allow these characters more fulfillment than Nell,
whose desires are too serious to be fulfilled in this world. Here again Dickens
is allowing the wish for an ideal to coexist with reason's sense of the way
reality opposes that wish, giving Dick and the Marchioness a fairly idealized
happy ending but at the same time partly diminishing that ideal, not demanding serious belief in it.

We can see Dickens's comic characters, then, as the products of a tension
caused by his imagination. The tensions he implies within them—for ex-

ample, Flora's desire for romance and her opposing awareness of reality—are probably caused by a conflict in his own attitude. He partly sees Flora through the eyes of idealist imagination, wishing for a romantic heroine, as he partly sees Maggie as an idealized childlike woman. But at the same time the side of his mind that cannot believe in such idealizations sees these characters as unideal, so that he turns Flora into the negation of the ideal, the opposite of a romantic heroine. Flora's very existence mocks the belief in romantic heroines, and her attempts to be romantic render romantic desire ridiculous. It is the failure of imagination to create an ideal that makes his comic characters amusing and interesting. Reason's inability to believe in the ideal keeps interacting with and modifying imagination's attempt to envision an ideal. That interaction generates the complexities of characterization because these opposing forces find expression in his characters. Flora's desire to be romantic reflects Dickens's imaginative desire, and Flora's reaction against her desires reflects his skepticism.

This tension in characters is another version of the same conflict—idealism seeking to overcome reality—upon which Dickens's plots are based. Because he locates the same conflict in different elements of his work, he can interrelate those elements. His central plots are concerned with finding some sort of belief, and the minor characters surrounding those plots are related to that concern. They are usually either versions of the ideal that imagination seeks, whether in relatively pure or in mixed form, or else they are expressions of his sense that reality opposes the desire for an ideal. Micawber and Aunt Betsey, for example, are versions of the ideal parent Copperfield seeks (and ultimately finds in Agnes) combined (especially in Micawber's case) with a sense that the ideal cannot be found in reality after all, so that Dickens diminishes his idealization of them, making them less serious and less perfect. With Micawber it is as if Dickens has tried to create an ideal father (since Micawber does rescue David), but his inability to believe in that ideal has intervened and made Micawber ridiculous. Yet Micawber's very failings imply a desire for a good father, one who could be taken seriously.

Despite Micawber's imperfections, he (and characters like him) can be related to the main plot because he can serve as a partial object for the protagonist's desire and a lesson about the need to purify that desire in order to find a more fulfilling object. (The more Dickens idealizes a father figure, the more he tends to qualify that idealization by making the character less serious, like Captain Cuttle, expressing a feeling that the ideal father can only be imaginary.) Murdstone, on the other hand, is a complete negation of the ideal parent, another expression of the sense that reality actively opposes imagination's desires; the very wish for an ideal (a good father) intensifies the sense of how unideal reality actually is. The way Murdstone opposes the protagonist's desire is reflected in the way he also opposes his own imagination and desire; he tries to make David become repressed like himself. He too is related to the central plot—David's education—because he helps teach David how to deal with forces opposing desire.

In addition, Dickens sees many secondary characters as subjects of the same desire for an ideal that drives his central plots—imperfect outlets for that desire, like Flora, seeking something to believe in as the protagonist does, though in comically diminished forms. Miss Flite in *Bleak House*, for example, seeks some god to believe in but can find only the Lord Chancellor. While the serious characters struggle for belief, in comic characters the impulses that oppose belief find stronger expression, reducing belief to weak forms we do not take very seriously. Characters like Miss Flite, and like Mr. Toots and Captain Cuttle in *Dombey*, for example, share the tension in the main plot between the need for belief and the difficulty of believing, but they need to believe so strongly that they have sacrificed reason in order to do so. Given a choice between reason and belief (since the two are impossible to reconcile unless one can go through the difficulties of the serious plot), such characters choose belief; Dickens feels belief without reason is better than no belief at all. Thus Toots, like Florence, is struggling to find an ideal; inspired by Florence, he attempts to become like Paul and win Florence's love. Possessing her would be like possessing the ideal and thus attaining complete belief in it. But Dickens's sense of the forces opposing belief makes him show the efforts of a character like Toots as childish and deluded, seeking an impossible goal. In Toots's part of the novel, belief cannot be taken seriously (though clearly Dickens sympathizes with it).

Nevertheless, we can see Toots (like Flora) as a way of using imagination to partly protect belief from doubt; if belief is diminished so that reason need not take it seriously, it need not be strongly opposed. At the end of *Dombey*, for example, Toots is able to protect his belief in Florence because he does not try to make his ideal become too real; he does not try to possess her. Thus he can simultaneously believe in an ideal and yet accept its absence from his world. And (like Swiveller with Nell and the Marchioness) by giving up Florence, he can win Susan Nipper, which is like replacing belief with imagination, giving up the ideal and accepting the playful diminished version of it that is the best imagination can offer. This is like Captain Cuttle's belief in "a fiction . . . which is better than any reality" (972; ch. 62), accepting a fictional ideal because that is all he can find.

Similarly, Dickens creates the illusion of attaining the ideal by diminishing it to the merely fictional, though in his central plots he makes a more serious effort to overcome his sense that the ideal cannot exist in reality. Toots's attempt to have both Nipper and Florence is like Dickens's attempt to reconcile imagination and belief, to keep one from precluding the other. He seeks to believe the ideal is real but also feels it is only imaginary, something we cannot take too seriously (as we cannot take Nipper very seriously). Accepting one's inability to resolve this conflict is made possible by becoming childlike like Toots, allowing imagination to replace belief.

Dickens's minor characters thus often engage in imperfect versions of his central plots, versions that partly accept but partly qualify the idealism of those plots. By implicitly conceding in a comic subplot like Toots's story that the ideal is only imaginary after all, Dickens can quiet reason's doubts so it will be more likely to get us to believe in the ideal in his serious plot. His fiction thus does something rather like what Toots ends up doing: it gets us to accept a simulacrum of belief by simultaneously letting us think its ideal is only imaginary. Imagination both undercuts belief and helps it survive, though in a reduced, imaginary form. And it is through the comic details of characterization that imagination makes this compromise appealing.

Notes

Chapter 1

1. For a discussion of various theories of imagery, see Block; and see Pruyser 31, 38; Christopher Collins 91 ff., 119 ff., 130; Rollins 87 ff., and passim. Tye 33 ff., 90 ff., and passim; and Brann 18, 579 ff., and passim, argue that imagined images are much like perceptual ones.

2. Freud, *The Interpretation of Dreams* in *The Standard Edition* 5:565–67; and "Formulations on the Two Principles of Mental Functioning," *Standard Edition* 12:219; here he also discusses how this is related to art (222–24). Future citations to Freud will all be to *The Standard Edition* and will give the title of Freud's work followed by volume and page number in that edition. Elsewhere Freud discusses the way imagination gets the reality principle to serve unconscious desires (*Interpretation of Dreams* 4:102, 324), its use in art (*Civilization and Its Discontents* 21:75–81), and its relation to perception (*Introductory Lectures on Psychoanalysis* 15:172; *Dreams* 5:651). See also Isaacs 83 ff., 104 ff. I see no reason to sully the clarity of Freud's thought with the pretentious obscurantism of Lacan and his followers. However, several other theorists are of interest. Groos discusses the way imagination serves desire and uses reality (131–36); Piaget makes similar points (201–5, 213) (his terms *accommodation* and *assimilation* I think are merely restatements of Freud's reality and pleasure principles). Sartre says imagination involves intention (*Imagination* 133 ff.), which may be equivalent to saying it serves desire. Winnicott restates the interaction of reality and pleasure principles as a combination of adult and childlike attitudes ("Transitional Objects"). See also Warnock, *Imagination* 82; Casey 73; Pruyser 17–19, 37–38, 65–66; and Kearney, *Poetics* 51–55, 58, 100.

3. Quoted by Levi 79–80.

4. Sartre discusses this weakness; see Kearney, *Poetics* 51 ff.

5. Newman, *Essay in Aid of a Grammar of Assent*; see for example 80; ch. 5, sec. 1; James 53–73, 208–9, 495. On the relation of religion to imagination and desire, see also James 248–52, 460, 509–18; and Freud, *The Future of an Illusion* 21:30–31, and *Civilization and Its Discontents* 21:81. Other discussions of the relation of imagination to belief include Scruton, especially 95–99; Coulson v, 3–5, 12–16, and passim;

McKellar 108, 164, 201; Furlong 21, 33–34, 98–102; Warnock, "Religious Imagination" 142–57; Pruyser 152–53, 161–62, 166; and Bryant, e.g., 88 and 167.

6. William James discusses this kind of religious submission (47–51, 208–12, 243, 273–75, 289, 311). Freud relates religion to submission to paternal authority in order to deal with Oedipal guilt in *The Future of an Illusion* 21:30–31, 43; "A Religious Experience" 21:171; *New Introductory Lectures on Psycho-Analysis* 22:163; *Moses and Monotheism* 23:119; "Leonardo da Vinci" 2:123; and *Totem and Taboo* 13:151–56. See also Erikson 256–57, 264–66; and Winnicott, *Playing and Reality* 138–41, 180.

7. *Playing and Reality;* he calls art and religion transitional objects (3, 14). Meissner discusses Winnicott's ideas in relation to religion (164–82), as does Faber (165–66, 182). I would think that all mental activity is transitional in Winnicott's sense, involving some interaction between desire and the reality principle, though in areas like art this is more overt, consciously accepted.

8. Freud says in *Civilization and Its Discontents* that, unlike art, religion does not admit it is only an illusion and so tries to intimidate reason (21:81, 84). As Rudolf Kasmer puts it, religion unites "reason and imagination," whereas art exploits the "gulf between them" (quoted by Auden 459). See also Koelb 31 ff.; Price 307–11; and Newsom, *A Likely Story* 130–36, on the tension between belief and unbelief involved in literature.

9. I have discussed this in more detail in *Character and Structure* 24 ff.

10. Frye discusses realism as a displacement of this sort; see for example 34 ff. and 51–52.

Chapter 2

1. On the Romantic replacement of religion with imagination, see Abrams, *Natural Supernaturalism* 65–67, 118–19, 121, 212, 258–62, 296, 334–40, 347, 458, 466–67; Engell viii, 7–8, 244–75, 363–65 and passim; and McFarland 150–51, 187. The main theoretical source of the Romantic emphasis on imagination is probably Kant (see for example 88–89); his ideas are discussed by Levi (5, 17–22) and Kearney, *Wake of Imagination* (175–85).

2. *The Rise of the Novel* 60 ff.

3. Erikson discusses a related loss of belief that the ideal could be real (265).

4. Miller talks about this change in *The Disappearance of God* (6).

5. *Biographia Literaria* 2:6.

6. Ibid. 2:1–7. Abrams talks of this conflict between perception and imagination in *Natural Supernaturalism* (365), and Koelb discusses the difficulties in Coleridge's idea of belief (16–17).

7. Tuveson discusses the relation of Romanticism to empiricism; see especially 76 ff., 86, 94, 101, 133 ff., 157, and 164; and see Nuttall 127, 138–39.

8. This passage is discussed by Reardon (361).

9. Abrams's *The Mirror and the Lamp* is probably still the best statement of this idea; but see Spacks 5–8 and passim on similar theories before Romanticism (though I think the Romantics give imagination much more predominance than do these precursors).

10. *Lectures 1795* 338–39. On the way Coleridge associates religion and imagination, see Coulson 12–16; Engell 342; Scott 34–38; and Prickett, *Romanticism and
Religion* 195 and passim; and Barth, "Theological Implications."

11. Miller discusses this (*Disappearance of God* 13–14). On the Romantic concern
with symbols, see also Engell 349, 363; and Warnock, *Imagination* 99.

12. *Statesman's Manual* 29–30. On the relation of symbols to religion in
Coleridge's theory, see Baker (201–3) and Barth, *Symbolic Imagination* (11 ff., 134–35,
and passim).

13. I have discussed this development in *Character and Structure* (49).

14. *The Complete Works* 7:136.

15. Kearney discusses the way Romantic claims for imagination lead to disillusion
(*Wake of Imagination* 185–88).

Chapter 3

1. See also "Essay Supplementary to the Preface" (1815) in *Wordsworth's Literary
Criticism* 182, 195; and the preface to the Second Edition of the *Lyrical Ballads* (ibid.
71). For more on this aspect of Wordsworth's thought, see Engell 267–73; Heffernan
116, 193–94, 200–207, 236, 263, and passim; and Abrams, *Natural Supernaturalism*
145, 371, 458.

2. On the Victorian idealist reaction against realism, see Kaplan, *Sacred Tears* 6–7,
16, 72, and passim; Reed 452–73; Wheeler 75, 161–63; Buckley 46, 54, 195–201;
Stang 118, 146, 148, 153, 176–90; Graham 28 ff., 49 ff., 61–70; and Eigner and
Worth 3, 87, 150–51. Among discussions of Romantic influence on Victorian idealism, see Donald D. Stone, for example 2–8; and Prickett, *Victorian Fantasy* xiii–xvi, 2,
33.

3. On the Victorian search for an ideal in reality, see Houghton 392; and Reed 29.

4. On Ruskin's attitude toward realism and idealization, see Hough 7–8, 11, 31.

5. Miller, *The Disappearance of God* 96–100, 112, discusses the conflict in Browning
between seeing God as transcendent and as immanent.

6. On Arnold's religious attitudes, see also Miller, *Disappearance of God* 253; Scott
42, 47–50; Coulson 96–102; and Prickett, *Romanticism and Religion* 221–22.

7. Reprinted in *The Genius of John Ruskin* 394–96. Sprinker discusses Ruskin's view
that imagination transforms perception.

8. *Poems and Prose* 185. On imagination in Hopkins, see Downes 1 ff., 11–13, 22,
18–29, 36–41; and Fraser 67 ff., 76–78, 89–90. On Hopkins's use of imagination to
transform perception, see also Miller, *The Disappearance of God* 311–12, 320.

9. Fraser talks about Arnold's attempt to base belief on imagination (179–82); and
Moldstad discusses Arnold's ambivalence about imagination in "The Scholar Gypsy"
(159, 167 ff.).

10. Levine discusses Eliot's use of imagination and ways she goes against realism
(44–45, 268–70); and Knoepflmacher mentions the way she associates religion with
imagination like Feuerbach (*George Eliot's Early Novels* 111). Stang shows how Eliot
and Lewes, though distrusting imagination, did not simply reject it (161–66, 171–73).

11. Quoted by Buckley 164.

12. Kearney discusses this decline (*Wake of Imagination* 185–86).

13. See Hough on tensions in Rossetti and the Pre-Raphaelites (40, 48–49, 53–54, 59–61, 74–80).

14. *The Complete Works* 16:360.

15. *Collected Works* 3:1–2. Hough discusses the absence of reality in Morris's idealizations (122–23).

16. "The Aims of Art," ibid. 23:81–82.

17. Maison and Wolff describe many of these works.

18. Quoted by Graham 68; and see Wheeler 161. See Graham 64 ff. on the rise of romance; and Lester discusses the way late-nineteenth-century writers seek belief through imagination (101–9, 115–16, 120, 177–78).

19. On the development of fantasy and its nature, see Irwin 4 ff., 25, 59, 66–67, 155–56, and passim; Jackson 124, 130, and passim; Manlove, *The Impulse of Fantasy Literature* x, 14, and passim; and Siebers 35. Tolkien discusses the way fantasy produces something like belief (132, 155–56); and Sartre talks of how the loss of belief affects fantasy ("'Aminadab'" 58–60).

20. See Haggard on imagination in Graham 67; and on Haggard's concern with the supernatural, see Reed 466.

21. On Kipling's dreamlike fiction, see Prickett, *Victorian Fantasy* 204–14; and Julia Briggs 207.

22. On the religious use of imagination in MacDonald, see Carpenter 83–85; Prickett, *Romanticism and Religion* 241, and *Victorian Fantasy* 174–77, 184–86, 191–92; Maison 272; Manlove, *The Impulse of Fantasy Literature* 72, 77, 91, and *Modern Fantasy* 58 ff., 64–70, 91, 98, 196–97; Moss; and Riga.

23. Among discussions of nineteenth-century children's literature, see Green 13–14 and passim; Carpenter 1, 9, 11, and passim; and K. M. Briggs 171, 197, and passim.

24. On the way Grahame uses imaginative escape as a substitute for religion, see Carpenter 116–23, 158–62, 168.

25. On imagination in Nesbit, see Prickett, *Victorian Fantasy* 229, 233; Manlove, *The Impulse of Fantasy Literature* 53–64; and Moore 191–93. On Burnett, see Carpenter 188–90. On imagination trying to overcome reality in *Peter Pan* and other Barrie works, see Carpenter 179–86; and K. M. Briggs 199.

26. See Koelb on Wilde's rejection of a concern with reality (89–93).

27. On Lear's concern with a Romantic ideal, see Bowra 278–80; Carpenter 11–13; and Byrom 19–20, 42, 46, 57, 149–50, 152, 156, 172–75, 178, 193–94, 199–200, 208, 212–13, 218. On the nature of Lear's nonsense, see Irwin 22, 27; and Sewell 56 and passim. A good discussion of the way Victorian humorists avoid seriousness can be found in Gray 146 ff.

28. Stang quotes a review of 1862 which suggests that horror is a substitute for the sacred (181). Among critics who relate horror fantasy to Romanticism and to a loss of religious belief are McAndrew 3–8, 22, 151–54, and passim; Kiessling 41; Bloom, "The Internalization of Quest-Romance" 6; Jackson 9, 19, 24, 63, 66; and Hume 282 ff.

29. Todorov 24–25, 120, 156, 167–68. See also Sartre, "'Aminadab'" 58–60; Jackson 34, 36, 48; and Carter 2, 5–7, 14–18.

30. On Romantic idealism in *Frankenstein*, see Donald Stone 35; and Kiely 156–66. Baldick relates the monster to art (50), and Levine relates it to creativity (26). In *The Ringers in the Tower*, Bloom sees the monster as an aspect of the self (119–22). Carter discusses the book as a discovery of the supernatural (72).

31. Sullivan discusses the rise of stories about the supernatural in the late nineteenth century. Among critics who relate this to religious doubt are Julia Briggs 14–24, 52; Carter 83; and Hynes 147. On LeFanu's religious doubts, see Sullivan 17, 19, 22, 27, 30, 60–61, 68; Julia Briggs 22, 51; and Penzoldt 86. On Stoker's religious attitudes, see Jackson 119–20 and Reed 470–71.

32. Julia Briggs relates Hyde to imagination (66–67).

33. See Baldick 151 on imagination in *Dorian Gray*.

34. Among the critics who discuss Carroll's rationality are Empson 254, 262, 277; Lennon 258; Rackin 314 ff.; Blake 18, 26–27, 31–32, 44–46, 49–50, 109–13, 121–23; Greenacre 245; and Sewell 23, 27, 38, 44, 48, 65–66, 76, 97, 131–47. Auerbach points out that Alice is unlike the typical idealized child of Romantic ideology (32). Critics who have pointed out that Wonderland is unfulfilling include Empson 292; Sewell 47, 97; Rackin 313 ff.; Henkle 104; Blake 36, 105–6, 124–26, 139–40; Carpenter 60–61; and Jackson 141–43. Waugh describes Carroll's "religious skepticism" in a way I find convincing (511). For further discussion of Carroll's religion, see Lennon 6, 9, 84–85, 89–91, 95–100, 117, 260; Taylor 14, 24–25, 35; Hudson 117–20; Sewell 178–81; Henkle 114–15; Blake 66–69; Gattegno 64, 111, 119, 150, 161, 212, 215–17, 232–43, 312; Carpenter 62–68; and my article on Carroll.

35. On the tension between idealism and realism in Victorian literature, see Graham 36, 63–64; Stang 182–84; Kaplan, *Sacred Tears* 73; Qualls 9, 13; and Miller, *The Disappearance of God* 13–15.

36. On Carlyle's attempt to reconcile realism and idealism, see Qualls 13, 18, 29, 35, 64; and Prickett, *Victorian Fantasy* 8.

37. Miller, *The Disappearance of God* 158 ff., discusses Brontë's religious attitudes and their relation to imagination. On imagination and its relation to realism in Brontë, see Knoepflmacher, *Laughter and Despair* 94–98, 107–8; Kiely 234–36; and Gose 56.

38. Stang 17–19, 171–72, shows how Brontë shared the Romantic belief in imagination, but Qualls (43, 45, 48, 50, 56–57, 61–64, 73–74, 84) and Donald Stone (52, 100, 102, 108–9) discuss the way she also opposed imagination.

39. Among critics who discuss Tennyson's opposition to imagination are Buckler 51, 54, 58, 62; and Bloom, *The Ringers in the Tower* 148–49.

Chapter 4

1. On the conflict in Dickens between idealism and realism, see Donald D. Stone 261–63; Wilson, *The World of Charles Dickens* 150; Stewart xix, 17, 147, and passim; House 132; Stoehr 261–65; Larson 30–35 and passim. On the way Dickens tries to reconcile these, see Stang 155–58; Donald Stone 252–53; Eigner, *The Metaphysical*

Novel 178–79; Stewart xxii, 225–26; Harry Stone 65, 68–69; Kaplan, *Dickens* 240, 301, 308, 354; Stoehr 274–75, 252, 265, 269–70; Marlow; Hornback 1, 7; Newsom, *Dickens on the Romantic Side of Familiar Things* 3–9, 18, 86, 114, and passim; Newcomb 183–87; and Eigner, *Dickens Pantomime* 24.

2. On Dickens's idealist belief in imagination, see Stang 23, 157; Stewart xiii, xv, xix, 147; Harry Stone 13, 16, 57, 62; and Kaplan, *Dickens and Mesmerism* 236. On the relation of Dickens's spiritual concerns to imagination, see Kaplan, *Dickens* 175–76, 275, and *Sacred Tears* 44; Donald Stone 250, 271, 276–78; Qualls 118, 137; Eigner, *The Metaphysical Novel* 189; Stewart xiv, xxi, 227; Pope 36; and Harry Stone 3–4, 10, 48–49. On Dickens's transcendental and spiritual concerns, see Kaplan, *Dickens and Mesmerism* 137–39; Eigner, *The Dickens Pantomime* 60–63; Welsh 176–78, 197–98, 219, 222, and passim; and Walder.

3. Auden discusses the idealization of Dingley Dell (408–9), as does Marcus (51). On Dickens's attitude toward his parents, see Pratt 4 ff. and Hutter 32 ff. I have discussed this further in *Character and Structure* (161).

4. Stewart 43, 63, 68–69, 75–76, 83–85.

5. Stewart points out this separation (32–33).

6. Harry Stone discusses this conflict (84–85).

7. Harry Stone speaks of the way Dickens seeks to use a child's viewpoint (102–4); and Miller talks of the way *Twist* combines the real with the imaginary, as in creating heaven on earth (*Charles Dickens* 74, 78–79).

8. Kaplan, *Dickens* 174. On the way Mary's death affected Dickens's doubts, see Harry Stone 116. I have discussed Dickens's use of submissive, idealized characters like Nell more fully in *Character and Structure* (142–44, 159, 161).

9. On Swiveller, see Stewart 89, 97–106, 110–13. Donald Stone discusses the way characters like Swiveller use imagination to ward off reality (276).

10. I go into more detail on characters of this sort in *Character and Structure* 138–40, 148–49, 159–60.

11. See Kaplan, *Dickens* 140; and also 125, 137–38, 142.

12. There is a similar mistrust of the dark side of imagination in Dickens's previous novel, *Barnaby Rudge*, as is pointed out by Wilson, *The World of Charles Dickens* 150, and McMaster.

13. Hornback discusses the way Martin learns to give up his dreams (46).

14. Harry Stone discusses this combination of reality with the transcendent (95–97).

15. Walder 124 and Harry Stone 122–26, 141–43 discuss the role of imagination in this conversion.

Chapter 5

1. The combination of realism and antirealism in *Dombey* is discussed by Harry Stone 81, 99, 144–47, 150–57, 160–61, 177–78, 187, 190; and by Horton 54.

2. The religious aspect of *Dombey* is discussed by Vogel 66–69; Walder 113 ff., 124–38; Larson 76, 81, 85, 99–101, 105–13, 117, 119, 314–15; Welsh 184–85, 188–90; Miller, *Charles Dickens* 148–49; and Engel 113.

3. Forster 2:19.

4. Harry Stone 162 and Cockshut 111 are among those who discuss the sea symbol in *Dombey*.

5. See Lecker 21–30 on Dickens's ambivalence about imagination here.

6. Miller, *The Disappearance of God* 6 and passim discusses the conflict in Victorian thought between seeing the divine as transcendent and as immanent.

Chapter 6

1. On religious concerns in *Copperfield*, see Vogel 1–4, 9 (though I think she overstates); Friedman 128–50; Welsh 180–82; Donald D. Stone 266; and Eigner, *The Dickens Pantomime* 62–64, 84, 120. On the distrust of imagination in *Copperfield*, see Wilson, *The World of Charles Dickens* 214; and Hornback 64–82 (though I think he makes Dickens seem more realistic than Dickens actually is). On the relation between imagination and belief in *Copperfield*, see Walder 149; Harry Stone 194–97, 211, 215–19, 228–34, 241, 246–51, 261, 265–69; and Miller, *Charles Dickens* 151–52, 157.

2. I have discussed Micawber's characterization more fully in *Character and Structure* 139–40.

3. See Kaplan, *Dickens* 23–24.

Chapter 7

1. A portion of this chapter appeared in *Dickens Studies Annual* 17 (1989).

2. A spiritual interpretation of this division is offered by Walder 145; Miller, *Charles Dickens* 178–79, 211–13, 217–18, 222; Vogel 55, 58; Larson 31; and Eigner, *The Metaphysical Novel*, who sees this split not only in *Bleak House* but elsewhere in Dickens (172–73, 178, 205–6).

3. Stewart discusses the weakening of imagination in *Bleak House* (145–51).

4. Stewart discusses the way Skimpole perverts imagination (155), and Donald D. Stone discusses the criticism of Romanticism like Skimpole's in *Bleak House* (266–67).

5. The combination of realism with imagination here is discussed by Miller, *Charles Dickens* 159; and by Newsom, *Dickens on the Romantic Side of Familiar Things* 15–16, 66, and passim. See also Dickens's "Preliminary Word" to *Household Words*, in *Collected Papers* 1:223.

6. I give evidence for this interpretation in "*Hard Times* and Dickens' Concept of Imagination" 92–93; that paper also goes into more detail about other points I make here.

7. Among critics who find Dickens's treatment of the circus inadequate are Leavis 278–79; Dyson 198–99; Cockshut 140; Stoehr 262; Engel 175; Holloway 168–69, 172; Hornback 115; Stewart 148, 151–54; and Sonstroem 527. Sonstroem provides a good discussion of imagination in *Hard Times* (especially 521, 525–26, 528–29).

8. On the critique of imagination here, see Bracher 306–12; and Stewart 144–54.

9. Stewart xxi and Walder 124, 137, 149 talk about belief growing out of imagination; and see my paper on *Hard Times* for ways the circus and imagination are associated with religion (102).

10. *Collected Papers* 1:223; and "Frauds on the Fairies" in *Plays, Poems, and Miscellanies* 488, 495.

11. "Announcement in 'Household Words' of the Approaching Publication of 'All the Year Round,'" *Collected Papers* 1:225; *Letters* 5:569; Kaplan, *Dickens* 308; and *Speeches* 284.

12. See Bornstein 159 and Smith 117.

Chapter 8

1. On religious concerns and the prison in *Dorrit*, see Walder 171–72, 179–81, 190–92; Barickman 164–65, 173, 181, 184, and passim; Qualls 89, 137; Trilling 63–64; and Miller, *Charles Dickens* 228–30, 236–40, 332. Kelly says that Little Dorrit shows imagination's redemptive power.

2. Stewart discusses this conflict (185–86).

3. See Stewart on Flora (183 ff.).

Chapter 9

1. The way imagination misleads Pip is discussed by Stewart 187–89, 195–96; Ginsburg 116; and Wilson, "Dickens on Children" 225–26.

2. Stewart discusses this balance in Wemmick (159–60).

3. See Eigner, *The Dickens Pantomime*, on the pious frauds Dickens tricks characters with (52 ff.).

4. On imagination in *Mutual Friend* and its relation to Dickens's spiritual concerns, see Walder 206; Knoepflmacher, *Laughter and Despair* 144, 161, 164, 166–67; and Stewart, who relates this to Jenny Wren (155, 198–209, 216). Miller discusses transcendence in *Mutual Friend* (*Charles Dickens* 315–17, 325).

5. On Jenny's relation to imagination, see Donald D. Stone 279 and Stewart 148, 202–5, 218–19.

Chapter 10

1. See Clayborough 249 and Stewart 183–84.

2. "The Dickens World" 417–38.

3. *Charles Dickens* 151–52.

4. See Higbie, *Character and Structure*, for an explanation of subject and object characters (17–22) and a discussion of the way Dickens tends to turn object characters into subjects (122–23, 149 ff.).

Works Cited

Abrams, M. H. *The Mirror and the Lamp: Romantic Theory and the Critical Tradition.* New York: Norton, 1958.
———. *Natural Supernaturalism: Tradition and Revolution in Romantic Literature.* New York: Norton, 1971.
Arnold, Matthew. *God and the Bible. The Complete Prose Works of Matthew Arnold.* Ed. R. H. Super. 11 vols. Ann Arbor: U of Michigan P, 1960–77. 7:139–373.
Auden, W. H. *The Dyer's Hand and Other Essays.* New York: Vintage, 1968.
Auerbach, Nina. "Alice and Wonderland: A Curious Child." *Victorian Studies* 17 (1973): 31–47.
Baker, James Volant. *The Sacred River: Coleridge's Theory of Imagination.* New York: Greenwood, 1969.
Baldick, Chris. *In Frankenstein's Shadow: Myth, Monstrosity, and Nineteenth-Century Writing.* Oxford: Oxford, 1987.
Barickman, Richard. "The Spiritual Journey of Amy Dorrit and Arthur Clennam." *Dickens Studies Annual* 7 (1978): 163–89.
Barth, J. Robert. *The Symbolic Imagination: Coleridge and the Romantic Tradition.* Princeton: Princeton UP, 1977.
———. "Theological Implications of Coleridge's Theory of Imagination." *Coleridge's Theory of Imagination Today.* Ed. Christine Gallant. New York: AMS, 1989. 3–13.
Blake, Kathleen. *Play, Games and Sport: The Literary Work of Lewis Carroll.* Ithaca: Cornell, 1974.
Block, Ned. *Imagery.* Cambridge: M.I.T. Press, 1981.
Bloom, Harold. "The Internalization of Quest-romance." *Romanticism and Consciousness.* Ed. Harold Bloom. New York: Norton, 1970.
———. *The Ringers in the Tower: Studies in the Romantic Tradition.* Chicago: U of Chicago P, 1971.
Bornstein, George. "Miscultivated Field and Corrupted Garden: Imagery in *Hard Times.*" *Nineteenth-Century Fiction* 26 (1971): 158–70.
Bowra, C. M. *The Romantic Imagination.* Cambridge: Harvard, 1949.
Bracher, Peter. "Muddle and Wonderful No-Meaning: Verbal Irresponsibility and Verbal Failures in *Hard Times.*" *Studies in the Novel* 10 (1978): 305–19.

Brann, Eva T. H. *The World of Imagination: Sum and Substance*. Savage, Md.: Rowman and Littlefield, 1981.

Briggs, Julia. *Night Visitors: The Rise and Fall of the English Ghost Story*. London: Faber, 1977.

Briggs, K. M. *The Fairies in English Tradition and Literature*. Chicago: U of Chicago P, 1967.

Brontë, Charlotte. *Jane Eyre*. 2nd ed. New York: Norton, 1987.

———. *Villette*. Harmondsworth: Penguin, 1979.

Brontë, Emily. *Wuthering Heights*. New York: Norton, 1963.

Bryant, David J. *Faith and the Play of Imagination*. Macon: Mercer UP, 1989.

Buckler, William E. *The Victorian Imagination: Essays in Aesthetic Exploration*. New York: New York UP, 1980.

Buckley, Jerome Hamilton. *The Victorian Temper: A Study in Literary Culture*. New York: Vintage, 1951.

Byrom, Thomas. *Nonsense and Wonder: The Poems and Cartoons of Edward Lear*. New York: Brandywine, 1977.

Carpenter, Humphrey. *Secret Gardens: A Study of the Golden Age of Children's Literature*. Boston: Houghton Mifflin, 1985.

Carroll, Lewis (Charles Lutwidge Dodgson). *Alice in Wonderland: Authoritative Texts of Alice's Adventures in Wonderland, Through the Looking Glass, The Hunting of the Snark*. Ed. Donald J. Gray. New York: Norton, 1971.

Carter, Margaret L. *Spectre or Delusion? The Supernatural in Victorian Fiction*. Ann Arbor: UMI Research, 1987.

Casey, Edward S. *Imagining: A Phenomenological Study*. Bloomington: Indiana UP, 1976.

Clayborough, Arthur. *The Grotesque in English Literature*. Oxford: Oxford UP, 1965.

Cockshut, A. O. J. *The Imagination of Charles Dickens*. New York: New York UP, 1962.

Coleridge, Samuel Taylor. *Biographia Literaria*. 2 vols. Ed. J. Shawcross. London: Oxford UP, 1907.

———. *Lectures 1795 on Politics and Religion*. Ed. Lewis Patton and Peter Mann. *The Collected Works of Samuel Taylor Coleridge*. 14 vols. London: Routledge and Kegan Paul, 1971–90. Vol. 1.

———. *Statesman's Manual*. Ed. R. J. White. *Collected Works of Samuel Taylor Coleridge*, vol. 6.

Collins, Christopher. *The Poetics of the Mind's Eye: Literature and the Psychology of Imagination*. Philadelphia: U of Pennsylvania P, 1991.

Coulson, John. *Religion and Imagination: "in aid of a grammar of assent."* Oxford: Clarendon, 1981.

Dickens, Charles. *Bleak House*. New York: Norton, 1977.

———. *Christmas Books*. London: Oxford UP, 1954.

———. "A Christmas Tree." In *Christmas Stories*. Oxford: Oxford UP, 1956.

———. *Collected Papers*. Vols. 1, 5. *The Nonesuch Dickens*. Bloomsbury: Nonesuch Press, 1937.

———. *David Copperfield*. Harmondsworth: Penguin, 1966.

————. *Dombey and Son*. Harmondsworth: Penguin, 1970.

————. *Great Expectations*. London: Penguin, 1965.

————. *Hard Times*. New York: Norton, 1966.

————. "A Holiday Romance." In *The Uncommercial Traveller and Reprinted Pieces*. Oxford: Oxford UP, 1958.

————. *Letters of Charles Dickens*. Ed. Madeline House, et al. Oxford: Oxford UP, 1965- .

————. *Life and Adventures of Nicholas Nickleby*. London: Oxford UP, 1950.

————. *Little Dorrit*. Harmondsworth: Penguin, 1967.

————. *Martin Chuzzlewit*. Harmondsworth: Penguin, 1968.

————. *The Old Curiosity Shop*. London: Oxford UP, 1951.

————. *Oliver Twist*. Oxford: Oxford UP, 1982.

————. *Our Mutual Friend*. Harmondsworth: Penguin, 1971.

————. *Pickwick Papers*. New York: Penguin, 1972.

————. *Plays, Poems, and Miscellanies*. Boston: Houghton Mifflin, 1894.

————. *Speeches of Charles Dickens*. Ed. K. J. Fielding. Oxford: Oxford UP, 1960.

Downes, David Anthony. *Hopkins' Sanctifying Imagination*. Lanham, Md.: University Presses of America, 1985.

Dyson, A. E. *The Inimitable Dickens: A Reading of the Novels*. London: Macmillan, 1970.

Eigner, Edwin M. *The Dickens Pantomime*. Berkeley: U of California P, 1989.

————. *The Metaphysical Novel in England and America: Dickens, Bulwer, Melville, and Hawthorne*. Berkeley: U of California P, 1978.

Eigner, Edwin M., and George J. Worth, eds. *Victorian Criticism of the Novel*. Cambridge: Cambridge, 1985.

Eliot, George. *Mill on the Floss*. London: Oxford UP, 1903; 1950.

Empson, William. *Some Versions of Pastoral*. New York: New Directions, 1935.

Engel, Monroe. *The Maturity of Dickens*. Cambridge: Harvard, 1959.

Engell, James. *The Creative Imagination: Enlightenment to Romanticism*. Cambridge: Harvard, 1981.

Erikson, Erik. *Young Man Luther: A Study in Psychoanalysis and History*. New York: Norton, 1958.

Faber, Heije. *Psychology of Religion*. Trans. Margaret Kohl. Philadelphia: Westminster, 1973.

Fielding, K. J. *Charles Dickens: A Critical Introduction*. Boston: Houghton Mifflin, 1958.

Forster, John. *The Life of Charles Dickens*. 2 vols. New York: Everyman, 1966.

Fraser, Hilary. *Beauty and Belief: Aesthetics and Religion in Victorian Literature*. Cambridge: Cambridge UP, 1986.

Freud, Sigmund. *The Standard Edition of the Complete Psychological Works of Sigmund Freud*. 23 vols. Trans. James Strachey, et al. London: Hogarth, 1966–74.

Friedman, Stanley. "Dickens' Mid-Victorian Theodicy." *Dickens Studies Annual* 7 (1978): 128–50.

Frye, Northrop. *An Anatomy of Criticism: Four Essays*. Princeton: Princeton UP, 1957.

Furlong, E. J. *Imagination*. New York: Macmillan, 1961.

Gattegno, Jean. *Lewis Carroll: Fragments of a Looking-Glass.* Trans. Rosemary Sheed. New York: Crowell, 1976.

Ginsburg, Michael Peled. "Dickens and the Uncanny: Repression and Displacement in *Great Expectations.*" *Dickens Studies Annual* 13 (1984): 115–24.

Gose, Elliot B., Jr. *Imagination Indulged: The Irrational in the Nineteenth-Century Novel.* Montreal: McGill-Queen's, 1972.

Graham, Kenneth. *English Criticism of the Novel, 1865–1900.* London: Oxford UP, 1965.

Gray, Donald J. "The Uses of Victorian Laughter." *Victorian Studies* 10 (1966): 145–76.

Green, Roger Lancelyn. *Tellers of Tales.* London: Edmund Ward, 1956.

Greenacre, Phyllis. *Swift and Carroll: A Psychoanalytic Study of Two Lives.* New York: International Universities Press, 1955.

Groos, Karl. *The Play of Man.* Trans. Elizabeth L. Baldwin. 1901. New York: Arno, 1976.

Heffernan, James A. W. *Wordsworth's Theory of Poetry: The Transforming Imagination.* Ithaca: Cornell UP, 1969.

Henkle, Roger B. "The Mad Hatter's World." *Virginia Quarterly Review* 49 (1973): 99–117.

Higbie, Robert. *Character and Structure in the English Novel.* Gainesville: UP of Florida, 1984.

———. "*Hard Times* and Dickens' Concept of Imagination." *Dickens Studies Annual* 17 (1989): 91–110.

———. "Lewis Carroll and the Victorian Reaction against Doubt." *Thalia* 3 (Spring, 1980): 21–28.

Holloway, John. "*Hard Times:* A History and a Criticism." In *Dickens and the Twentieth Century.* Ed. John Gross and Gabriel Pearson. London: Routledge and Kegan Paul, 1962.

Hopkins, Gerard Manley. *Poems and Prose of Gerard Manley Hopkins.* Ed. W. H. Gardner. Baltimore: Penguin, 1953.

Hornback, Bert G. "*Noah's Arkitecture*": *A Study of Dickens's Mythology.* Athens: Ohio UP, 1972.

Horton, Susan R. *Interpreting Interpreting: Interpreting Dickens's Dombey.* Baltimore: Johns Hopkins, 1979.

Hough, Graham. *The Last Romantics.* New York: Barnes and Noble, 1961.

Houghton, Walter E. *The Victorian Frame of Mind: 1830–1870.* New Haven: Yale UP, 1957.

House, Humphrey. *The Dickens World.* London: Oxford UP, 1941.

Hudson, Derek. *Lewis Carroll.* London: Constable, 1954.

Hume, Robert D. "Gothic vs. Romantic: A Revaluation of the Gothic Novel." *PMLA* 84 (1969): 282–9O.

Hutter, Albert D. "Psycho-Analysis and Biography: Dickens' Experience at Warren's Blacking." *Hartford Studies in Literature* 8 (1976): 23–37.

Hynes, Samuel. *The Edwardian Turn of Mind.* Princeton: Princeton UP, 1968.

Irwin, W. R. *The Game of the Impossible: A Rhetoric of Fantasy.* Urbana: U of Illinois P, 1976.

Isaacs, Susan. "The Nature and Function of Phantasy." In *Developments in Psychoanalysis*, by Melanie Klein, Paula Heimann, Susan Isaacs, and Joan Riviere. London: Hogarth, 1952. 67–121.

Jackson, Rosemary. *Fantasy: The Literature of Subversion*. London: Methuen, 1981.

James, William. *The Varieties of Religious Experience: A Study in Human Nature*. New York: Longmans, Green, 1902.

Kant, Immanuel. *The Critique of Judgment*. Trans. J. H. Bernard. New York: Hafner, 1951.

Kaplan, Fred. *Dickens: A Biography*. New York: Morrow, 1988.

———. *Dickens and Mesmerism: The Hidden Springs of Fiction*. Princeton: Princeton UP, 1975.

———. *Sacred Tears: Sentimentalists in Victorian Literature*. Princeton: Princeton UP, 1987.

Kaufman, Gordon D. *The Theological Imagination: Constructing the Concept of God*. Philadelphia: Westminster Press, 1981.

Kearney, Richard. *Poetics of Imagining: From Husserl to Lyotard*. London: Harper Collins, 1991.

———. *The Wake of Imagination: Toward a Postmodern Culture*. Minneapolis: U of Minnesota P, 1988.

Kelly, Mary Ann. "Imagination, Fantasy, and Memory in *Little Dorrit*." *Dickens Studies Newsletter* 13:1 (March, 1982): 48–50.

Kiely, Robert. *The Romantic Novel in England*. Cambridge: Harvard UP, 1972.

Kiessling, Nicholas K. "Demonic Dread: The Incubus Figure in British Literature." In *The Gothic Imagination*. Ed. G. R. Thompson. Pullman: Washington State UP, 1974. 22–41.

Kincaid, James. *Dickens and the Rhetoric of Laughter*. London: Oxford UP, 1971.

Knoepflmacher, U. C. *George Eliot's Early Novels: The Limits of Realism*. Berkeley: U of California P, 1968.

———. *Laughter and Despair: Readings in Ten Novels of the Victorian Era*. Berkeley: U of California P, 1971.

Koelb, Clayton. *The Incredulous Reader: Literature and the Function of Disbelief*. Ithaca: Cornell UP, 1984.

Larson, Janet L. *Dickens and the Broken Scripture*. Athens: U of Georgia P, 1985.

Leavis, F. R. *The Great Tradition*. Garden City: Doubleday, 1954.

Lecker, Barbara. "Walter Gay and the Theme of Fancy in *Dombey and Son*." *The Dickensian* 67 (1971): 21–30.

Lennon, Florence Becker. *Victoria Through the Looking-Glass: The Life of Lewis Carroll*. New York: Simon and Schuster, 1945.

Lester, John A., Jr. *Journey Through Despair, 1880–1914: Transformations in British Literary Culture*. Princeton: Princeton UP, 1968.

Levi, Albert William. *Literature, Philosophy, and the Imagination*. Bloomington: Indiana UP, 1962.

Levine, George. *The Realistic Imagination: English Fiction from Frankenstein to Lady Chatterley*. Chicago: U of Chicago P, 1981.

McAndrew, Elizabeth. *The Gothic Tradition in Fiction*. New York: Columbia UP, 1979.

MacDonald, George. *A Dish of Orts: Chiefly Papers on the Imagination and on Shakespeare.* London: Sampson Low Marston, 1895.

McFarland, Thomas. *Originality and Imagination.* Baltimore: Johns Hopkins UP, 1985.

McKellar, Peter. *Imagination and Thinking: A Psychological Analysis.* New York: Basic, 1957.

McMaster, Juliet. "'Better to be Silly': From Vision to Reality in *Barnaby Rudge.*" *Dickens Studies Annual* 13 (1984): 1–17.

Maison, Margaret M. *The Victorian Vision: Studies in the Religious Novel.* New York: Sheed and Ward, 1961.

Manlove, C. N. *The Impulse of Fantasy Literature.* Kent, Ohio: Kent State UP, 1983.

———. *Modern Fantasy: Five Studies.* Cambridge: Cambridge UP, 1975.

Marcus, Steven. *Dickens from Pickwick to Dombey.* New York: Simon and Schuster, 1965.

Marlow, James E. "Memory, Romance, and the Expressive Symbol in Dickens." *Nineteenth-Century Fiction* 30 (1975): 20–32.

Meissner, W. W., S.J. *Psychoanalysis and Religious Experience.* New Haven: Yale UP, 1984.

Miller, J. Hillis. *Charles Dickens: The World of His Novels.* Cambridge: Harvard UP, 1958.

———. *The Disappearance of God: Five Nineteenth-Century Writers.* Cambridge: Harvard UP, 1963.

Moldstad, David. "The Imagination in *The Vanity of Dogmatizing* and 'The Scholar Gypsy': Arnold's Reversal of Glanvill." *Victorian Poetry* 25 (1987): 159–72.

Moore, Doris Langley. *E. Nesbit: A Biography.* London: Ernest Benn, 1967.

Morris, William. *Collected Works of William Morris.* 24 vols. London: Longmans, Green, 1910.

Moss, Anita. "Sacred and Secular Visions of Imagination and Reality in Nineteenth-Century British Fantasy for Children." In *Webs and Wardrobes: Humanist and Religious Views in Children's Literature.* Ed. Joseph O'Bierne Milner and Lucy Floyd Morcock Milner. Lanham, Md.: UP of America, 1987. 65–98.

Newcomb, Mildred. *The Imagined World of Charles Dickens.* Columbus: Ohio State UP, 1989.

Newman, John Henry. *Essay in Aid of a Grammar of Assent.* 1870. New York: Longmans, Green, 1947.

Newsom, Robert. *Dickens on the Romantic Side of Familiar Things:* Bleak House *and the Novel Tradition.* New York: Columbia UP, 1977.

———. *A Likely Story: Probability and Play in Fiction.* New Brunswick: Rutgers UP, 1988.

Nuttall, A. D. "Adam's Dream and Madeline's." In *Religious Imagination.* Ed. James P. Mackey. Edinburgh: Edinburgh UP, 1986. 125–41.

Penzoldt, Peter. *The Supernatural in Fiction.* New York: Humanities, 1965.

Piaget, Jean. *Play, Dreams and Imitation in Childhood.* Trans. C. Gattegno and F. M. Hodgson. New York: Norton, 1962.

Pope, Norris. *Dickens and Charity.* New York: Columbia UP, 1978.

Pratt, Branwen Bailey. "Dickens and Father: Notes on the Family Romance." *Hartford Studies in Literature* 8 (1976): 4–22.

Price, H. H. *Belief.* London: George Allen and Unwin, 1969.

Prickett, Stephen. *Romanticism and Religion: The Tradition of Coleridge and Wordsworth in the Victorian Church*. Cambridge: Cambridge UP, 1976.

———. *Victorian Fantasy*. Bloomington: Indiana UP, 1979.

Pruyser, Paul W. *The Play of Imagination: Towards a Psychoanalysis of Culture*. New York: International Universities Press, 1983.

Qualls, Barry V. *The Secular Pilgrims of Victorian Fiction: The Novel as Book of Life*. Cambridge: Cambridge UP, 1982.

Rackin, Donald. "Alice's Journey to the End of Night." *PMLA* 81 (1966): 313–26.

Reardon, Bernard M. G. *From Coleridge to Gore: A Century of Religious Thought in Britain*. London: Longmans, 1971.

Reed, John R. *Victorian Conventions*. Athens: Ohio UP, 1975.

Riga, Frank P. "From Time to Eternity: MacDonald's Doorway Between." In *Essays on C. S. Lewis and George MacDonald: Truth, Fiction, and the Power of the Imagination*. Ed. Cynthia Marshall. Lewiston, N.Y.: Edwin Mellen, 1991. 83–100.

Rollins, Mark. *Mental Imagery: On the Limits of Cognitive Science*. New Haven: Yale UP, 1989.

Ruskin, John. *The Genius of John Ruskin: Selections from His Writings*. Ed. John D. Rosenberg. Boston: Houghton Mifflin, 1963.

Sartre, Jean-Paul. "'Aminadab' or the Fantastic Considered as a Language." In *Situations* I. Paris: Gallimard, 1947.

———. *Imagination: A Psychological Critique*. Trans. Forrest Williams. Ann Arbor: U of Michigan P, 1962.

Scott, Nathan A., Jr. *The Poetics of Belief: Studies in Coleridge, Arnold, Pater, Santayana, Stevens, and Heidegger*. Chapel Hill: U of North Carolina P, 1985.

Scruton, Roger. *Art and Imagination: A Study in the Philosophy of Mind*. London: Methuen, 1974.

Sewell, Elizabeth. *The Field of Nonsense*. London: Chatto and Windus, 1952.

Shelley, Mary W. *Frankenstein*. London: Dent, 1912.

Shelley, Percy Bysshe. *The Complete Works of Percy Bysshe Shelley*. Ed. Roger Ingpen and Walter E. Peck. 10 vols. London: Ernest Benn, 1965.

Siebers, Tobin. *The Romantic Fantastic*. Ithaca: Cornell UP, 1984.

Smith, Frank Edmund. "Perverted Balance: Expressive Form in *Hard Times*." *Dickens Studies Annual* 6 (1977): 102–18.

Sonstroem, David. "Fettered Fancy in *Hard Times*." *PMLA* 84 (1967): 520–29.

Spacks, Patricia Meyer. *The Poetry of Vision: Five Eighteenth-Century Poets*. Cambridge: Harvard UP, 1967.

Sprinker, Michael. "Ruskin on the Imagination." *Studies in Romanticism* 18 (1979): 115–39.

Stang, Richard. *The Theory of the Novel in England, 1850–1870*. New York: Columbia UP, 1959.

Stevenson, Robert Louis. *Dr. Jekyll and Mr. Hyde. Minor Classics of Nineteenth-Century Fiction*. Ed. William E. Buckler. 2 vols. Boston: Houghton Mifflin, 1967. 2:61–109.

Stewart, Garrett. *Dickens and the Trials of Imagination.* Cambridge: Harvard UP, 1974.

Stoehr, Taylor. *Dickens: The Dreamer's Stance.* Ithaca: Cornell UP, 1965.

Stone, Donald D. *The Romantic Impulse in Victorian Fiction.* Cambridge: Harvard UP, 1980.

Stone, Harry. *Dickens and the Invisible World: Fairy Tales, Fantasy, and Novel-Making.* Bloomington: Indiana UP, 1979.

Sullivan, Jack. *Elegant Nightmares: The English Ghost Story from LeFanu to Blackwood.* Athens: Ohio UP, 1978.

Swinburne, Algernon Charles. *The Complete Works of Algernon Charles Swinburne.* 20 vols. Ed. Sir Edmund Gosse and Thomas James Wise. London: William Heinemann, 1925–27.

Taylor, Alexander L. *The White Knight: A Study of Charles Lutwidge Dodgson (Lewis Carroll).* Edinburgh: Oliver and Boyd, 1952.

Tennyson, Alfred. *Tennyson's Poetry.* Ed. Robert W. Hill, Jr. New York: Norton, 1971.

Thackeray, William Makepeace. *Vanity Fair.* Harmondsworth: Penguin, 1968.

Todorov, Tzvetan. *The Fantastic: A Structural Approach to a Literary Genre.* Trans. Richard Howard. Cleveland: Case Western Reserve UP, 1973.

Tolkien, J. R. R. "On Fairy Stories." In *The Monsters and the Critics and Other Essays.* Ed. Christopher Tolkien. Boston: Houghton Mifflin, 1984. 109–61.

Trilling, Lionel. *The Opposing Self: Nine Essays in Criticism.* New York: Viking, 1950.

Tuveson, Ernest Lee. *The Imagination as a Means of Grace: Locke and the Aesthetics of Romanticism.* Berkeley: U of California P, 1960.

Tye, Michael. *The Imagery Debate.* Cambridge: M.I.T. Press, 1991.

Van Ghent, Dorothy. "The Dickens World: A View from Todgers's." *Sewanee Review* 58 (1950): 417–38.

Vogel, Jane. *Allegory in Dickens.* University, Ala.: Alabama UP, 1977.

Walder, Dennis. *Dickens and Religion.* London: George Allen and Unwin, 1981.

Warnock, Mary. *Imagination.* Berkeley: U of California P, 1976.

———. "Religious Imagination." In *Religious Imagination.* Ed. James P. Mackey. Edinburgh: Edinburgh UP, 1986. 142–57.

Watt, Ian. *The Rise of the Novel.* Berkeley: U of California P, 1957.

Waugh, Evelyn. "Carroll and Dodgson." *The Spectator* 163 (1939): 511.

Welsh, Alexander. *The City of Dickens.* Oxford: Clarendon, 1971.

Wheeler, Michael. *English Fiction of the Victorian Period, 1830–1890.* New York: Longmans, 1985.

White, William Hale. *The Autobiography of Mark Rutherford. Mark Rutherford's Deliverance.* New York: Garland, 1976.

Wilde, Oscar. "The Decay of Lying." In *Literary Criticism of Oscar Wilde.* Ed. Stanley Weintraub. Lincoln: U of Nebraska P, 1968. 165–96.

———. *The Picture of Dorian Gray. Minor Classics of Nineteenth-Century Fiction.* Ed. William E. Buckler. 2 vols. Boston: Houghton Mifflin, 1967. 2:195–355.

Wilson, Angus. "Dickens on Children and Childhood." In *Dickens 1970.* Ed. Michael Slater. New York: Stein and Day, 1970. 195–227.

————. *The World of Charles Dickens*. New York: Viking, 1970.

Wimsatt, William K., Jr., and Cleanth Brooks. *Literary Criticism: A Short History*. New York: Knopf, 1957.

Winnicott, D. W. *Playing and Reality*. New York: Basic, 1971.

————. "Transitional Objects and Transitional Phenomena." In *Collected Papers*. New York: Basic, 1958.

Wolff, Robert Lee. *Gains and Losses: Novels of Faith and Doubt in the Victorian World*. New York: Garland, 1977.

Wordsworth, William. *The Poetical Works of William Wordsworth*. Ed. Ernest de Selincourt and Helen Darbishire. 5 vols. Oxford: Oxford UP, 1940–49.

————. *Wordsworth's Literary Criticism*. Ed. W. J. B. Owen. London: Routledge and Kegan Paul, 1974.

Index

Robert Higbie is professor of English at Appalachian State University in Boone, North Carolina. He is the author of *Character and Structure in the English Novel* (University Presses of Florida, 1984).